Selected Studies in Phenomenology
and Existential Philosophy   11

Board of Editors

052900

Descriptions

Descriptions

Edited by
Don Ihde
and
Hugh J. Silverman

State University of New York Press

Published by
State University of New York Press, Albany

Printed in the United States of America

For information, address State University of New York Press,
State University Plaza, Albany, N.Y., 12246

Library of Congress Cataloging in Publication Data
Main entry under title:

Descriptions.

    (Selected studies in phenomenology and
existential philosophy ; #11)
      1. Phenomenology–Addresses, essays, lectures.
I. Ihde, Don, 1934–   II. Silverman, Hugh J.
III. Series.
B829.5.D44 1985   142'.7   84-26748
ISBN 0-88706-075-7
ISBN 0-88706-076-5 (pbk.)

10 9 8 7 6 5 4 3 2 1

CONTENTS

Introduction

With this volume (and the previous one) the Society for Phenomenology and Existential Philosophy passes its twentieth year and is well on its way to its twenty-fifth anniversary. The essays selected here are from the 1981 to 1983 meetings. Because of thematic diversity, Hugh Silverman and I made the editorial decision that two volumes were appropriate. Thus *Hermeneutics and Deconstruction* (Volume 10) and *Descriptions* were organized. This thematic diversity reflects interests within the society as well, for in the more than twenty years of its existence a considerable diversification has occurred in the strains of philosophy presented at society meetings.

In his meditation on time and memory (chapter four), Edward Casey reminisces about the society's first twenty years, which first met as a small group at Northwestern University in 1962. Later, the society, taking its title from the then two strains of Euro-American thought at the core of its concern, phenomenology and existentialism, exhibited its first tensions in the arguments about which name would receive precedence in its title. Edward Casey also notes that since its beginning, SPEP, as it is now called, spun off other groups, such as the circles which now exist as specialized societies around Husserl, Heidegger, and Merleau-Ponty. In more recent years other groups – some not so small – have also proliferated, often in friendly conjunction with the society's meetings, such as the Nietzsche Society, The Society for Phenomenology and the Human Sciences, and the Center for the Advanced Study of Phenomenology.

But it terms of diversification, still in keeping with continental trends, interests within SPEP have included the family of structuralist and poststructuralist philosophies, including deconstruction, which originated primarily in France, and representation of the critical theory work associated with the Frankfurt School in Germany. Thus today SPEP represents a broad and multidimensioned set of philosophical styles, loosely connected with what is called "Continental" philosophy.

The same diversification can be noted within the dominant namesake of the society, phenomenology. In one sense, there are phenomenologies rather than one phenomenology. The essays collected here constitute about half of the 1981 to 1983 programs, but they, too, are diverse in that they represent the strains of transcendentally styled philosophy of Husserl, the existentially styled phenomenology of Merleau-Ponty and Sartre, although represented more in Volume 10, the hermeneutically styled thought of Heidegger.

Thus this volume concentrates on essays roughly grouped as phenomenology, although relationships to critical theory, poststructuralism, and deconstructionism are found here as well. What distinguishes these essays, to my mind, is the emergence of a certain maturity. While in no way forgetful of the past, there is a certain autonomy and freshness in the thinking of the contributors included here. The maturity shows itself by a lack of mere repetition and interpretation, and by the presence of a willingness to explore new areas of inquiry with confidence.

The volume opens with contributions by two of the best known American phenomenological philosophers, Maurice Natanson and Robert Sokolowski. Both present mature reflections on descriptive theory, distilling to its essence its role in philosophical thought. Then, as an example of original and fresh work, Iris Young presents a critical descriptive essay on pregnant subjectivity.

Time is not a new subject to philosophy or phenomenology, yet the large section on phenomena of time also displays a particular perspective. Edward Casey, relating time to memory, sketches a descriptive theory of memory. He is echoed critically by a British colleague, David Wood, who readdresses the problem from a different place. James Phillips and E. B. Daniels then take the topic into one of its components, nostalgia. The section concludes with an investigation into yet another temporal phenomenon, temporal sequence, through Peter McInerney.

Phenomenology in all its guises has long had a strong relationship to the arts or the artful. Exemplified here with both originality and critique, is to be found the outline of an aesthetics of the environment by Arnold Berleant. Karsten Harries, already distinguished by his work on architecture, continues the relationship between the experiential emphasis in phenomenology and the ethical function of architecture. Turning to literary artfulness, Peter Caws and William McBride focus their attention on Sartrean themes, especially those which have arisen around his long work on Flaubert.

The application of phenomenology to the human sciences has already had a long and successful history. But of late one may find more and more philosophers of this tradition turning to the natural sciences and their problems as well as to new areas within the human sciences. Elmar Holenstein, clearly a rising European eminence, addresses computer science and artificial intelligence. Next, three younger thinkers turn to Kuhn and phenomenology, first in a paper by Lenore Langsdorf and Harry Reader; then in an examination of Heidegger's implicit philosophy of science with particular reference to instrumentalities by Joseph Rouse; and finally, an exploration into the not often interrogated world of economics by Kenneth Stikkers.

Human social and political values are more often than not discussed by philosophers associated with critical theory. But here a substantial study of the political philosophy of Hannah Arendt vis-à-vis Heidegger is undertaken by Mildred Bakan. And Gary Overvold explores the role of ethics or ethical judgment in Husserl.

Spontaneously, we received a number of papers concerned with questioning the implications of the various Continental philosophies for the contemporary university. The selections here mark some of that spectrum of concern. Edward Ballard brings his careful thinking to bear on the liberal arts and phenomenology. A. Anthony Smith examines the technologically dominated society and university via Habermas. And David Thompson raises some rather difficult problems for the traditions of academic freedom in the light Foucault's impact.

What is clear from this collection is that in the twenty plus years of the society's existence, the impact of Euro-American philosophy has grown and diversified. This is reflected in part in the size and current structure of SPEP. No longer are the annual meetings uniformly plenary in form, but diverse interests divide into concurrent sessions. Whatever tensions existed between the existentialists and the phenomenologists of the sixties, have multiplied in the eighties – hopefully into a friendly set of arguments and comparisons. But at the same time this diversification has been accompanied by what I discern to be an increasing maturity, often with signs of originality and novelty.

There is, finally, a certain outward looking quality to the styles of philosophy represented within this grouping. Phenomenology has always been necessarily interdisciplinary. And at its best it has also been pluralistic. This stands in contrast to many tendencies in contemporary philosophies, which in a presumed purity find, instead, isolation.

What is to be hoped for is that the society's growth, diversification, and promise of maturity remains productive rather than stagnates and that the rivalries are stimulative rather than destructive.

Don Ihde
SUNY at Stony Brook

Contributors

MILDRED BAKAN is professor of Philosophy in the Department of Philosophy and Division of Social Science, York University, Downsview, Ontario. She is the author of "Hannah Arendt's Concepts of Labor and Work, in *Hannah Arendt: The Recovery of the Public World*, editor, Melvyn A. Hill

EDWARD G. BALLARD is Professor Emeritus of Tulane University and Professor of Philosophy at the University of the South. His many books include *Man and Technology* (Pittsburgh: Duquesne University Press, 1978).

ARNOLD BERLEANT is Professor of Philosophy at the C. W. Post Campus of Long Island University. He is the author of *The Aesthetic Field: A Phenomenology of Aesthetic Experience* (Springfield: C. C. Thomas, 1970).

EDWARD S. CASEY is Professor of Philosophy at the State University of New York at Stony Brook and the author of *Remembering* (Indiana University Press, forthcoming).

PETER CAWS is University Professor of Philosophy, The George Washington University and the author of *Sartre* (London: Routledge and Kegan Paul, 1984).

EUGENE B. DANIELS is a Psychiatrist in private practice. He is the author of the forthcoming article, "Nostalgia and Hidden Meaning," to be published in *American Imago*.

KARSTEN HARRIES is Professor of Philosophy at Yale University and author of *The Bavarian Rococo Church: Between Faith and Aestheticism* (New Haven: Yale University Press, 1983).

ELMAR HOLENSTEIN is Professor of Philosophy at the Institute of Philosophy, Ruhr-Universität, Bochum, Germany. He is author of *Roman Jakobson's Approach to Language: Phenomenological Structuralism* (Bloomington: Indiana University Press, 1976).

LENORE LANGSDORF is Associate Professor of Philosophy and Associate Dean for Graduate Humanities at the University of Texas at Arlington. She is author of "The Noema as Intentional Entity: A Critique of Follesdal," *The Review of Metaphysics*, Vol. 37 (June 1984).

WILLIAM LEON MCBRIDE is Professor of Philosophy at Purdue University and is author of *Social Theory at a Crossroads* (Pittsburgh: Duquesne University Press, 1980).

PETER K. MCINERNEY is Associate Professor of Philosophy at Oberlin College and among his articles he has published, "Self-Determination and the Project," *Journal of Philosophy*, LXXVI, (November 1979).

MAURICE NATANSON is Professor of Philosophy at Yale University and among his many books is the National Book Award winning, *Husserl: Philosopher of Infinite Tasks* (Evanston: Northwestern University Press, 1973).

GARY E. OVERVOLD is Associate Professor of Philosophy and Adjunct Professor of Education at Clark University. He has authored, "The Humanities and the Human Sciences," *Interpreting the Humanities* edited by Tamar March and Gary E. Overvold, forthcoming from the Woodrow Wilson National Fellowship Foundation.

JAMES PHILLIPS is Assistant Clinical Professor of Psychiatry at the Yale School of Medicine and is the author of, "Transference and Encounter: The Therapeutic Relationship in Psychoanalytic and Existential Psychotherapy," *Review of Existential Psychology and Psychiatry*, Vol. 17 (1980–81).

HARRY REEDER is Assistant Professor of Philosophy at the University of Texas at Arlington. He is the author of *Language and Experience: Descriptions of Living Language in Husserl and Wittgenstein*, Current Continental Research, No. 301 (Washington: University Press of America, 1984).

JOSEPH ROUSE is Assistant Professor of Philosophy at Wesleyan University in Connecticut and author of "Kuhn, Heidegger and Scientific Realism," which appeared in the October 1981, *Man and World*.

A. ANTHONY SMITH is Assistant Professor of Philosophy at Iowa State University and the author of "Two Theories of Historical Materialism: G. A. Cohen and Jurgen Habermas," Theory and Society, Vol. 13 (1984).

ROBERT SOKOLOWSKI is Professor of Philosophy in the School of Philosophy at Catholic University. He is author of *Presence and Absence* (Bloomington: Indiana University Press, 1978).

KENNETH STIKKERS is Assistant Professor of Philosophy and Lecturer in Economics at Seattle University. He authored the introduction and is the editor of Max Scheler's *Problems in the Sociology of Knowledge* (London: Routledge and Kegan Paul, 1980).

DAVID L. THOMPSON is Associate Professor of Philosophy at the Memorial University of Newfoundland. His article, "Intentionality and Causation in John Searle" is forthcoming in the *Canadian Journal of Philosophy*.

DAVID C. WOOD is Lecturer in Philosophy at the University of Warwick, England. His *The Structures of Time* is forthcoming from Humanities Press.

IRIS MARION YOUNG is Associate Professor of Philosophy at the Worcester Polytechnic Institute and publishes on theories of justice and feminism. "Humanism, Gynocentrism, and Feminist Politics," in *Hypatia*, special issue No. 3 of the *Women's Studies International Forum*, 1985, is her most recent article.

Acknowledgments

The following chapters have been previously published or copublished, with the publications noted, and are here published by permission:

Chapter 4, "Keeping the Past in Mind," was published in a revised form in the *Review of Metaphysics*, Vol. 37 September 1983.

Chapter 10, "The Ethical Function of Architecture," appeared in revised form under the same title in the *Journal of Architectural Education* 29; 1 (1975).

Chapter 13, "Natural and Artificial Intelligence," appeared in *Philosophy of Science* (Tokyo) 16 (1983).

Chapters 1, 2, and 19, were copublished in *Essays in Memory of Aron Gurwitsch*, edited by Lester Embree (Washington: Center for Advanced Research in Phenomenology & University Press of America, 1983).

Acknowledgment should also be given to the Department of Philosophy at the State University of New York and its staff for the help given in typing and preparing this volume.

Part I.
Theory of
Phenomenological
Description

1. Descriptive Phenomenology

Maurice Natanson

It is commonplace to refer to Husserlian phenomenology as a descriptive discipline and to treat the phenomenologist's findings as descriptive in character. In these terms descriptive phenomenology is understood – broadly, to be sure – as a neutral, close and thorough account of phenomena. At least three considerations are involved in such a placement of phenomenology: first, that descriptive phenomenology is not limited to Husserl's methods, that such philosophers as Sir William Hamilton and Charles Peirce were concerned with the same problems; second, that the early and persistent meaning of the term "descriptive" in Husserl's thought is allied with descriptive psychology; and third, that within what may be called "pure" phenomenology, it is necessary to distinguish between a larger and narrower sense of "description" – between reports which do not and which do presuppose phenomenological reduction. To this account a further caution needs to be introduced at the outset: despite the widespread use of the term "descriptive" in conjunction with phenomenology, it is not clear what "descriptive" means. In fact, there is a two-fold unclarity: it is not evident – to this author, at least – what place "description" holds in phenomenology and it is not evident what precisely Husserl meant by the word "descriptive," if it is conjoined with phenomenology. If the double uncertainty is warranted, it stems from a philosophical puzzle or set of puzzles rather than from methodological inexactitude on Husserl's part. What is of interest here is the philosophical puzzle; it is not intention of this author to chew on methodological hardtack.

Of the three considerations cited here, the first will be dispensed with. Although it is especially instructive to look into the broader history of phenomenology as well as the alternative uses philosophers other than Husserl have made of the phrase "descriptive phenomenology," it is important to turn instead to the more pressing matter of Husserl's view of "descriptive psychology." In the first edition of the *Logical Investigations*, published in 1901, Husserl wrote:

> Phenomenology is descriptive psychology. Epistemological criticism is therefore in essence psychology, or at least only capable of being built on a psychological basis. Pure logic therefore also rests on psychology – what then is the point of the whole battle against psychologism?
>
> The necessity of *this* sort of psychological foundation of pure logic, i.e., a strictly descriptive one, cannot lead us into error regarding the mutual independence of the two sciences, logic and psychology. For pure description is merely a preparatory step towards theory, not theory itself. One and the same sphere of pure description can accordingly serve to prepare for very different theoretical sciences. It is *not the full science of psychology that serves as a foundation for pure logic*, but certain classes of descriptions which are the step preparatory to the theoretical researches of psychology. These in so far as they describe the empirical objects whose genetic connections the science wishes to pursue, also form the substrate for those fundamental abstractions in which logic seizes the essence of its ideal objects and connections with inward evidence. Since it is epistemologically of unique importance that we should separate the purely descriptive examination of the knowledge-experience, disembarrassed of all theoretical psychological interests, from the truly psychological researches directed to empirical explanation and origins, it will be good if we rather speak of 'phenomenology' than of descriptive psychology.[1]

In the second edition of the *Logical Investigations*, published in 1913, Husserl wrote:

> If *our* sense of phenomenology has been grasped, and if it has not been given the current interpretation of an ordinary 'descriptive psychology,' a part of natural science, then an objection, otherwise justifiable, will fall to the ground, an objection to the effect that all theory of knowledge, conceived as a systematic phenomenological clarification of knowledge, is built upon psychology. On this interpretation pure logic, treated by us as an epistemologically clarified, *philosophical* discipline, must in the end likewise rest upon psychology, if only upon its preliminary descriptive researches into intentional experiences. Why then so much heated resistance to psychologism?
>
> We naturally reply that if psychology is given its old meaning, phenomenology is not descriptive psychology: its peculiar 'pure' description, its contemplation of pure essences on a basis of exemplary individual intuitions of experiences (often freely *imagined* ones), and its descriptive fixation of the contemplated essences into pure concepts, is no empirical, scientific description. It rather excludes the natural performance of all empirical (naturalistic) apperceptions and positings. Statements of descrip-

tive psychology regarding 'perceptions,' 'judgements,' 'feelings,' 'volitions' etc., use such names to refer to the real states of animal organisms in a real natural order, just as descriptive statements concerning physical states deal with happenings in a nature not imagined but real. All general statements have here a character of empirical generality: they hold for *this* nature. Phenomenology, however, does not discuss states of animal organisms (not even as belonging to a possible nature as such), but perceptions, judgements, feelings *as such*, and what pertains to them *a priori* with unlimited generality, as *pure* instances of *pure* species, of what may be seen through a purely intuitive apprehension of essence, whether generic or specific.[2]

If there is a shift in meaning between the two editions, it is more a matter of understanding – or misunderstanding – the station of psychology than of Husserl having changed his mind about the relationship between psychology and logic. There is a perfectly good sense of psychology which, in its nonreductive meaning, yields a preliminary accounting of the "same" phenomena which phenomenology in *its* preliminary fashion reports. The "same" phenomena signifies the central fact that what is naively presented in the natural attitude is no different than what is presented from the standpoint of what, for the present, may be called the "phenomenological standpoint." What the phenomenologist chooses to attend to in respect to those givens is guided by philosophical demands. Thus, it is satisfactory from a theoretical vantage point to speak of phenomenology as descriptive psychology, provided that psychology is not taken in its empirical setting, as an empirical science. But that provision is worrisome, despite all of Husserl's efforts to repudiate psychologism. To insure a correct delimitation of psychology, Husserl prefers to use the language of phenomenology. The "old" psychology has not been forsaken, nor has the "new" psychology replaced it. Husserl has not taken up the chant of the old clothes man; neither has he abandoned him.

A third consideration – that which has to do with description and phenomenological reduction – presents the most urgent philosophical (rather than methodological) problem. But before turning to that problem, let us examine the nature of description more generally. Within the domain of the natural sciences, purified (if not pure) description is to be found in quite disciplined ways. What is sometimes called "descriptive anatomy," for example, offers a strong instance of sharp description which, at its most exacting, would appear to be independent of judgement. Consider a standard kind of anatomical description, that of "bounding" some feature of the human anatomy. The antrum of Highmore (or maxillary sinus), one anatomy book informs us, "follows in the main the shape of the body of the maxilla and may be described as having a roof, a floor, and three walls."[3] There follows a naming of the anatomical parts that comprise the roof, floor, and walls. Properly bounded, the sinus leaps to its descriptive ephiphany. But surely, there is no phenomenology here. Let us proceed to a more difficult case. "With upright posture," we are told,

> the vertebral column takes on, for the first time, the architectural function of a column. The skull rests on the articular surfaces of the atlas (which here, indeed, deserves its name) like an architrave on the capitals of columns. This arrangement makes it possible and necessary for the atlanto-occipital joint to be moved forward toward the center of the base of the skull, resulting in the typical configuration of the human skull, the extension of the base, and the closing vault, which in turn provides wider space for the orbitae. The skulls of the other primates still show the shape characteristic of other quadrupeds, in which the head does not rest on the vertibral column but hangs down from it. The foramen magnum accordingly is in a more caudal position; the clivus cuts the vertical at a more obtuse angle. The other primates – as has been said – are built to stand upright but not for upright posture.[4]

This quotation from Erwin Straus' essay "The Upright Posture" goes beyond the method of descriptive anatomy. Analogy is utilized, comparative anatomy is introduced, and a distinction is drawn between standing upright and the upright posture. Apart from what we may know about Dr. Straus and his work, it is clear that this passage from his essay, taken on its own, sounds a rather different note than that struck when we followed the bounding of the antrum of Highmore. The anatomy of that antrum was an exercise in locations; the anatomy of the upright posture is a portrait of human emergence. Not a word has been said about the complexity of the two descriptions. Indeed, on purely anatomical grounds, it is much harder to bound the antrum of Highmore than it is to describe the way in which the skull sits on the top of the vertebral column. But the two descriptions move in different directions: the one on a "horizontal" in which each additional piece of information is on par with its predecessor; the other on a "vertical" in which anatomy leads to an expression of human dignity. Has Straus given us a sample of descriptive phenomenology? Not in the passage which is quoted. The question of whether the full essay "The Upright Posture" qualifies as phenomenology will be left aside. All that may be said for the quotation, for the moment, is that whatever marks its difference from the bounding of the antrum of Highmore does not qualify Straus's statement as an example of descriptive phenomenology.

The opposite might be suggested, in fact. Straus's turn to analogy, comparative anatomy, and the ambiguity of being "upright" introduces extra-descriptive elements of analysis and evaluation into what is otherwise fairly straightforward anatomical description.

Our excursus into anatomy yields a larger conclusion: that a method which restricts itself to a kind of "reading off" does not qualify as phenomenology. A direct turn toward experience, however subtle that experience may be, does not guarantee phenomenological results. Subtlety, of course, is what excites direct observation. The danger is that the "reading off" of an elusive piece of the spectrum of human experience will be confused with genuine phenomenological reportage. I am in agreement with Herbert Spiegelberg when he writes:

> Phenomenology begins in silence. Only he who has experienced genuine perplexity and frustration in the face of the phenomena when trying to find the proper description for them knows what phenomenological seeing really means. Rushing into descriptions before having made sure of the thing to be described may even be called one of the main pitfalls of phenomenology.[5]

At the same time, I wonder whether one can make sure of the thing to be described without already having made descriptions of it. This is not a matter of agreement or disagreement here but a problem of emphasis. The most painstaking phenomenological description is *of* something which must be located through descriptions. If the last statement demands revision – philosophical revision – qualification must come through the meaning and implications of phenomenological reduction. We arrive in this way at the larger and narrower sense of "description" mentioned earlier, at reports which do not and which do presuppose phenomenological reduction.

In the first volume of *Ideas*, Husserl distinguishes between generic and ideal concepts, between what might be termed descriptive and constructive essentiality. He writes:

> The geometer is not interested in actual forms intuitable through sense, as is the descriptive student of nature. He does not, like the latter, construct *morphological concepts* of vague types of configuration, which on the basis of sensory intuition are directly apprehended, and vague as they are, conceptually or terminologically fixed. The *vagueness* of the concepts, the circumstances that they have mobile spheres of application, is no defect attaching to them; for they are flatly indispensable to the sphere of knowledge they serve, or, as we may also say, they are within this sphere the only concepts justified. If it behoves us to bring to suitable

conceptual expression the intuitable corporeal data in their intuitively given essential characters, we must indeed take them as we find them. And we do not find them otherwise than in flux, and typical essences can in such case be apprehended only in that essential intuition which can be immediately analysed. The most perfect geometry and its most perfect practical control cannot help the descriptive student of nature to express precisely (in exact geometrical concepts) that which is so plain, so understanding, and so entirely suitable a way he expresses in the words: notched, indented, lens-shaped, umbelliform, and the like — simple concepts which are *essentially and not accidentally inexact*, and are *therefore* also unmathematical.[6]

Husserl contrasts the "ideal essences" of geometry with the *morphological essences*, as correlates of descriptive concepts.[7] The moral of the contrast is that ideal and morphological essences have their proper stations, their particular excellences, and their distinctive limits. As I would put it, construction and description are related but essentially different enterprises. Husserl sums up the distinction in this way:

The *constancy and clear-cut distinguishability* of generic concepts or generic essences, which have their scope within the flux of things, *should not be confused with the exactness of the ideal concepts*, and the general whose scope includes an ideal element throughout. We must further realize that *exact* and *purely descriptive sciences* can indeed unite their efforts, but can never take each other's place; that however far the development of exact science, the science, that is, that operates with an ideal ground-work, is pushed, it cannot discharge the original and authentic tasks of pure description.[8]

In this context, Husserl leaves undecided the question of whether "within the eidetic domain of reduced phenomena an idealizing procedure may be adopted *side by side with* the descriptive, substituting for the intuitable data pure and rigorously conceived ideals, which might then indeed serve as the fundamental nexus for a mathesis of experiences and as a counterpart to *descriptive* phenomenology.[9] I would take it that by such a "counterpart" Husserl meant a phenomenological grounding of formal properties of logical systems which would undercut the purely deductive aspect of such systems by setting forth their eidetic structure from the standpoint of phenomenological reduction. If geometry is a stock example of an eidetic science, it must swiftly be added that it is an example only at a surface level of phenomenological inquiry. At the transcendental level, matters are quite different. Qualifications regarding the eidetic character of geometry hold true for a much broader domain. Indeed, Husserl maintains that "transcendental phenomenology as descriptive science of Essential Being belongs in fact to *a main class of eidetic science wholly other than that to which the mathematical sciences belong.*[10]

In the passages that have been quoted from Husserl's *Ideas* (and the contexts from which those passages have been taken), the tenor of his remarks is basically one of hesitancy in the presence of major disclossures. In particular, Husserl is aware of the tentative characterization of such terms as "description" and the unexplored connection between "description" and "explanation." He makes reference to further studies of these issues in the sequel to the first volume of *Ideas*. His own words are worth hearing:

> The problem we have just been glancing at is inwardly bound up with the fundamental and still unsolved problems of setting out clearly on grounds of principle the relation of *"description"* with its *"descriptive concepts," "unambiguous," "exact determination,"* with its *"ideal concepts;"* and running parallel to this, of clearly setting out the relation so little understood between "descriptive" and "explanatory" sciences.[11]

However uncertain the status of description may be, Husserl is certain about the goal of his procedure. He writes:

> As concerns Phenomenology, it aims at being a *descriptive* theory of the essence of pure transcendental experiences from the phenomenological standpoint, and like every descriptive discipline, neither idealizing nor working at the substructure of things, it has its own justification. Whatever there may be in "reduced" experiences to grasp eidetically in pure intuition, whether as a real portion of such experience or as intentional correlate, that is its province, and is a fast source of absolute knowledge for it.[12]

We are left with two points: first, that despite the common and informed reference to phenomenology as a "descriptive" science, the meaning of "description" in phenomenology is ambiguous; second, that the ambiguity is not dispersed or resolved by referring description to the phenomenologically reduced sphere. Nevertheless, it is of critical importance to understand that what is distinctive about phenomenological description is that it presupposes, in its transcendental or deepest aspect, the stance made possible by phenomenological reduction. I spoke to a "larger" and "narrower" sense of "description," at reports which do not and which do involve reduction. Now it may be seen that the geometer presents descriptions which, different as they are in eidetic standing from those given by the anatomist, are qualitatively at distance from the realm of the transcendental phenomenologist. In a general way, it is certainly not misleading to say that phenomenological description has a level or stratum of relatively easy access at which careful and penetrating statements concerning phenomena may be presented – especially phenomena which are fugitive to mundane expression. Still further, there is a loose but intuitively interesting flitting across some experiential theme which, in the hands of a shrewd investigator, may yield results which – so some would say – are illustrations of phenomenological description. For example, Sartre's monograph, *Anti-Semite and Jew,* may not only be read in this way but has, in fact, been attacked (despite high, but also highly qualified praise) for, among other things, its method. Sidney Hook wrote:

> Sartre's 'antisemite' and 'Jew', authentic and inauthentic, are ideal psychological types based not on what most Jews and antisemites are but on the kind of Jews and antisemites literary people are interested in. In virtue of his phenomenological approach, all Sartre needs is just a few specimens to construct a timeless *essence* of Jewishness and antisemitism.[13]

I am not concerned at present with the accuracy of saying that *Anti-Semite and Jew* is an example of Sartre's "phenomenological method" applied or with the at least tacit assumption that a few specimens suffice to construct timeless essences (or even that Sartre's notion of phenomenological method is put into effect in this way). What is clear is that phenomenology is being accused of utilizing instant psychology and elevating the results to absolute truths. Since the genius of medicine has hovered over this discussion, let us call this kind of criticism "Hook's complaint." Surely it reminds us of an earlier warning about "rushing into descriptions before having made sure of the thing to be described." But there the similarlity ends. Hook's criticism may be justified but it does not suggest that utilizing a more rigorous phenomenological method is the answer; Spiegelberg's warning is not about phenomenological method but rather about the dangers of its facile appropriation. With such criticism and warning in mind, we come now to the "narrower" sense of description, that which presupposes phenomenological reduction.

If, strictly speaking, the phenomenologist restricts himself to the examination of the phenomena – the intended objects insofar as they are intended – and records only the presentations *as meant,* then the casual, historical, axiological, and taken for granted aspects of experience are purposely set aside for purposes of phenomenological reportage – no use is made of them; phenomenological abstention is practiced. The observations which the phenomenologist does make under these circumstances are neutral with respect to the reality-status of the phenomena. Not presumption or explanation but description thus becomes the operative mode. "Obviously," Aron Gurwitsch writes, "phenomenological investigations must be carried out in a *strictly descriptive* orientation, since after the performance of the phenomenological reduction we find only things and objects meant and intended which, accordingly, have to be *taken as they are meant and intended*, that is *exactly as they present themselves in* actual or potential *experience*."[14] It is noteworthy that Gurwitsch speaks of a "descriptive orientation" rather than of "descriptive phenomenology." What the reduction provides is a radically new orientation which is "descriptive" because the phenomenologist chooses not to attend to the implicit claims made by the natural attitude and instead investigates only that which presents itself in intentional terms. The "descriptive" of Gurwitsch's phrase "descriptive orientation" is a rather negative term, a term of exclusion. The "descriptive" of what has been called "descriptive phenomenology" has a more positive overtone, that of a kind or level of phenomenological work. The refinement of the term "descriptive" in Gurwitsch's account assures the clear and disciplined understanding of the "narrower" sense description. In fine, phenomenological reports are reliable if, as a necessary condition, they are the result of a properly carried out reduction. The phrase "phenomenological reports" covers, of course, more than descriptions. For present purposes, I am restricting myself to descriptive matters. Here, then, we have a firm and unambiguous methodological determination: "A strictly descriptive orientation," Gurwitsch tells us, "purports disengagement and explicitation of all constituents included in a certain perception, for that perception to be what it is experienced as and for its noematic correlate to be the intended 'object' taken exactly as it appears to the perceiving subject's consciousness."[15] It would seem as if we have reached our goal or that, after a few preliminary distinctions and qualifications, we have followed the trail Gurwitsch cleared. I think that such an exercise would be good in itself but its goal is not the one I have been pursuing. It is time to turn to the philosophical puzzle which underlies our discussion.

The ambiguity about description arises in phenomenology because reduction, which is first a tool, becomes a means of enlarging and deepening the phenomenologist's range of experience. What started as an instrument becomes a way of seeing. The different motives at work in the reduction are best described by Merleau-Ponty. We are all familiar with his statement: "The most important lesson which the reduction teaches us is the impossibility of a complete reduction."[16] The passage immediately preceding that sentence is of more immediate importance to us. "The best formulation of the reduction," Merleau-Ponty writes,

> is probably that given by Eugen Fink, Husserl's assistant, when he spoke of "wonder" in the face of the world. Reflection does not withdraw from the world towards the unity of consciousness as the world's basis; it steps back to watch the forms of transcendence fly up like sparks from a fire; it slackens the intentional threads which attach us to the world and thus brings them to our notice; it alone is consciousness of the world because it reveals that world as strange and paradoxical."[17]

And now, at last, we come to the center of our problem. The ambiguity of the "descriptive" in phenomenology arises out of the difference between an essentially methodological interpretation of the reduction and a more nearly "existential" reading. The last formulation is provocative: to speak of an "existential" interpretation of the reduction made some of the phenomenologists I most respected wince; and I respected that wince immensely. It is well to proceed slowly here. In a continuation of the passage I cited from *Phenomenology of Perception*, Merleau-Ponty says: "All the misunderstandings with his interpreters, with the existentialist 'dissidents' and finally with himself, have arisen from the fact that in order to see the world and grasp it as paradoxical, we must break with our familiar acceptance of it and, also, from the fact that from this break we can learn nothing but the unmotivated upsurge of the world."[18]

Perhaps it would be prudent to take a step back. I said that the ambiguity of the "descriptive" in phenomenology arises out of the difference between an essentially methodological interpretation of the reduction and a more nearly "existential" reading. It would be both fairer and more productive to say that "a more nearly 'existential' reading" might be replaced by "a more nearly 'philosophical' reading." The issue is less whether existential thought has provided the most urgent alternative to methodology than whether the reduction, to begin with, delivers the inquirer into a philosophical morass. From the standpoint of the reduced sphere, the investigator is able to restrict himself to a rigorous description of intentional presentations, but that which is *not* being taken into descriptive account (and self-consciously so, of course) is also "present" within the brackets which set it off. It would be problematic to say that, *at the descriptive moment at which the phenomenologist focuses his gaze,* the bracketed world, treading water as it were, ceases to haunt the description made. In a non-temporal sense, the phenomenon has "already" been described; interpretations if not explanations of it have been tacitly if not overtly given. What Fink and

Merleau-Ponty refer to as "wonder" – or we might say "astonishment" – in the face of the world is the "first-given" sense of the effulgence of subjectivity as its "already-given" objects are newly displayed in the theater of consciousness. The consequence of that display is the propogation of meaning, the enlargement of experience. The world is, in Merleau-Ponty's formulation, "strange and paradoxical" because, I suggest, phenomenological reduction reveals the creative ambiguity which description conceals: philosophy as the redemption of method.

Notes

1. Edmund Husserl, *Logical Investigations*, Vol. I, trans. J.N. Findlay, London: Routledge and Kegan Paul, 1970, 262–63.

2. *Ibid.*, 261–62.

3. J. Parsons Schaeffer, ed., *Morris' Human Anatomy: A Complete Systematic Treatise*, 11th ed., (New York: The Blakiston Co., 1953), 1436.

4. Erwin W. Straus, *Phenomenological Psychology: Selected Papers*, trans., in part, Erling Eng, (New York: Basic Books, 1966), 138–39.

5. Herbert Spiegelberg, *The Phenomenological Movement: A Historical Introduction*, 3rd rev. and enlarged ed. (with the collaboration of Karl Schuhmann) (The Hague: Martinus Nijhoff, 1982), 693.

6. Edmund Husserl, *Ideas: General Introduction to Pure Phenomenology*, trans. W.R. Boyce Gibson (London: George Allen and Unwin Ltd., 1931), 207–8 (section 74).

7. Ibid., 208.

8. Ibid.

9. Ibid., 210–11.

10. Ibid., 211.

11. Ibid., 207.

12. Ibid., 209.

13. Sidney Hook, "Reflections of the Jewish Question," *Partisan Review*, XVI (1949); 463.

14. Aron Gurwitsch, *The Field of Consciousness (Pittsburgh, Pa: Duquesne University Press, 1964), 167–68.

15. Ibid., 233.

16. Maurice Merleau-Ponty, *Phenomenology of Perception*, trans. Colin Smith (London: Routledge and Kegan Paul, 1962), xiv.

17. Ibid., xiii.

18. Ibid., xiv.

2. The Theory of Phenomenological Description

Robert Sokolowski

The first issue to be decided is why a theory of phenomenological description is needed. Is it not possible to simply carry on our descriptions? Three reasons come to mind why a theory is needed. First, without a theory the descriptions might seem rather pointless. If it is observed, for example, that all perceived material objects have an other side that is not being perceived while one side is being perceived, or if it is said that any statement can be repeated by someone else, sometimes with belief and sometimes without belief, the point of making such comments about things may not be easy to see. This may appear to be belaboring the obvious. Thus a theory of transcendental description is needed in order to justify the descriptions actually carried out.

Secondly, a theory of transcendental descriptions is helpful for us to be able to understand the status and the stance of ourselves as transcendental describers. This is a more positive reason than the first one, which is somewhat exculpatory. If we are able to describe our own being in the world, and if we are able to describe our most fundamental attitude in the world (the world-belief that underies all our particular convictions), then we are able to take a distance to all the forms of appearing through which things manifest themselves to us. This means that we are quite extraordinary while we are carrying on such descriptions. What are we like when we do this, and what are things and being like in order to allow us such an analysis of them and of us to take place? A theory of transcendental description thus tells us about ourselves, about being, and about the world.

The third reason why we need a theory of phenomenological description is to overcome a systematic bias that has been implanted in our philosophy and our culture during the past five or six hundred years. We have been led to think that when we describe the way things appear, we are describing something in a merely subjective way and saying nothing about the way things are. We are told that we are engaged in a merely psychological venture, that we are examining just our ideas and our impressions but not examining things. A theory of phenomenological description must set this issue straight and bring out the proper relationship between things and appearances; it must allow us to recognize our place in the world and the world's power of manifestation. Thus there are three reasons for a theory of transcendental descriptions: one is exculpatory, a second is contemplative, and a third is polemical.

It might be supposed that only those who have carried out transcendental descriptions have anything that looks like a theory of transcendental descriptions. But this is not the case. Since what we describe in such descriptions is our own being in the world and the activity of being truthful, we think about activities that every human being is engaged in, both singular and in communities. Everyone is involved in the world and asserts positions within it. And everyone has some sort of opinion about what it is to be part of the world and to be involved in truthfulness. Such opinions about the whole are expressed in religious beliefs, in world views, and in the general attitudes we pick up in education, common opinions, science, and the like. But the opinions people have about the whole are, in general, not well sorted out and they may be subject to serious distortion. For example, the opinion that there is a screen of consciousness, a wall of ideas, between ourselves and the "outside" world is a very common opinion in our culture. Very many people who have been through some years of higher education are subject to this conviction. So when we get involved in a systematic theory of phenomenological description, we are not entering something that has no anticipations in prephilosophical life. What we try to do is to formulate clearly and distinctly what everyone possesses vaguely and indistinctly. We do not begin something absolutely new, and there really is little problem in entering the transcendental attitude, the stance from which we can carry out phenomenological descriptions and have a theory about them. We always have entered it more or less clearly; the problem is to clarify what we are in already. Thus the theory of phenomenological description is not a theory constructed to deal with something entirely new, nor is it an unanticipated theory.

One of the things that the theory of phenomenological description has to accomplish is to show us how this kind of description is different from the descriptions we carry out in ordinary life. Suppose I describe a building to someone: it is the large red brick building standing next to the Sears Roebuck store on Wisconsin Avenue. When I carry out such a description, I have mentioned a few features of an object. These features will appear to anyone who experiences the object in question. I can describe illnesses, people, trees, types of animals, and human practices, such as rituals or games, in this way. But when I carry out a transcendental, phenomenological description, I describe an object not in terms of special features that it has, but in terms of the ways in which it can be experienced. I describe the modes of experience and the modes of presentation, not the contents of what is presented. I can describe noematically, in which case I describe the presentational forms of the object experienced; or I can describe noetically, in which case I describe what I and anyone else must do in order to let the object appear.

In carrying out such a description, it is important to note that what is essentially done is to list the forms of presence and absence that are possible for the object in question. For example, to describe the acoustic presentation of a sentence I must note that the sentence can never be given instantaneously; it must extend over time, with one part coming into being when another part lapses out of action. I must anticipate the end of the sentence as soon as I start the first parts of it. And although there is a continuum of sound and silence that extends through the utterance of the sentence, each word comes forward as a distinct, not a continuous, part of the whole. Each of these words is such that it needs to hook on to other words and that it could have been replaced by another word. These and other dimensions are the sentence noema. They are aspects of how a sentence can and must present itself. Moreover these aspects are not some sort of screen behind which the sentence really exists; they are the sentence in its presentational form. They make up the eidos, the look of the sentence. We could, of course, also provide a description of the manifestation of a material object, and it would involve the play of presence and absence among the sides, aspects, and profiles in which the object is recognized as one. If we were to describe the experience of other minds, we would get into the special kinds of presence and absence that work when we recognize another organism as another human being and a person. Here the very complex arrangements of emotions, initiatives, disclosures and deceptions, statements, position takings, and the like, would be analogous to the sides, aspects, and profiles in which a material object is presented to us.

Now when we are in our ordinary, prephilosophical, natural attitude, we have one part of an object present and other parts absent. All our filled intentions are accompanied by empty intentions. Presences are involved with absences. But what if we turn our minds to these presences and absences themselves? If we focus on the present and the absent as such, a new dimension becomes thematic for us. It is not the case that this side is present and the other sides are absent, but rather

[the presence of this side and the absence of those sides]

are what becomes "present." Now whatever problems we might have in understanding this new theme, one thing is obvious: what is inside those brackets does not suffer from the kind of absences that "those sides" suffer from when we are in the natural attitude. We do catch a kind of sheer presence in this new attitude. "Perception of a material object" and "the material object as perceived" have been presented to us in a way different from the way the material object is presented to us. Or to take one of our earlier examples, the "perception of a sentence" and "the sentence as perceived" are presented to us in a way different from the way a sentence is presented. Let us move to a more complex example: "the perception of a deceiver" and "a deceiver as perceived" are presented to us in a way different from the way a deceiver is presented in our ordinary life. For one thing, we cannot be cheated in the reflective, philosophical description, but we could indeed be cheated by the deceiver. This is all that Husserl meant when he said that the tree could burn down, but the noema tree could not. He does not mean to imply that the noema tree is a mental concept that is not subject to fires.

I want to emphasize that the sequence of presences and absences is not merely a screen of ideas that comes between us and the object as it really exists. The object is the identity that is achieved and recognized and presented in the mixture of presences and absences. The "way of ideas" that we have assumed in modern philosophy, since the medieval nominalists, Hobbes, Descartes, Locke, Hume, and others, has given us the inclination to think that appearances are only a matter of our sensibilities and our mental states, and that the object itself is quite distinct from what appears. We are also inclined to think that science gives us the true object, which is reached as an object of reference through the impressions and ideas that affect our sensibility. But the novelty of phenomenological analysis is the claim that the object itself is given in the mixture of presence and absence, that the presences and absences are forms belonging to the object in its presentational possibility, in its being, and that the mind is with the object and not only with representations of it. This is the meaning of intentionality. A theory of phenomenological description must remember that all such descriptions are descriptions of the various forms of intentionality, so that what we have been talking about throughout this paper have not simply been forms of presentation, but the forms of intentionality as well. Intentionality is simply another name for presentation. In both cases we name the correlation between a thing and its dative of manifestation; when we say "intentionality" we emphasize the side of the dative, when we say "presentation" we emphasize the side of the object being given.

Thus when we carry on a phenomenological description we are with the objects and not merely with our own sensibilities or our own ideas. Moreover in these phenomenological descriptions we are more concretely with the objects than we are when we are involved with the objects from the natural attitude. It might seem to us that the turn into the phenomenological stance is a move toward abstraction, a move away from things and into a concern only with the appearances of things. But in fact it is the natural attitude that is abstractive. The natural attitude is focused on objects and overlooks, systematically, the appearances, the presentational possibilities, through which things are given to us. It overlooks the forms of "being a picture," "being a verified object," "being an imagined object," "being proposed," and the like. It also overlooks the temporal forms of presentation such as "being now" and "being anticipated" and "being forgotten." The natural attitude is so obsessed with objects that it looks through and does not look at the forms through which the object is given. But in the phenomenological stance we look at all these forms of presentation and thus we recover the concreteness of an object manifesting itself. It is with the phenomenological attitude that we are able to fill in the gaps. It is in that attitude that we stop overlooking and pay attention to all the dimensions that let there be objects. We do not therefore let go of the world and the things in it when we enter this descriptive stance; we become aware of more of the world. And furthermore, since we are essentially constituted as human by being a center of understanding and awareness, and since we are essentially a dative of manifestation, when we unravel the forms of presentation in which objects are given to us, we also unravel the forms that let us be human, the forms that allow us to have a personal self-identity.

Husserl has discussed the nature of phenomenological description and has said that the statements uttered when descriptions are done in this way are apodictic. By this he meant that the what is described is not described simply as a matter of fact, but as not capable of being otherwise. When we make these analyses, we realize that what we are disclosing has to be the way that it is. We have given to ourselves not only the structure we describe, but also the inability of the structure to be other than it is. The necessity of the structure is presented to us along with the structure itself. This claim to apodicticity scandalizes many of Husserl's readers. It is said to be a vestige of the old metaphysics of presence, the desire to have a clear, fixed, unquestionable basis for life. But such a dismissal of Husserl's claim to apodicticity does not do justice to the claim. There is more to the claim than this criticism acknowledges. In order to bring out the positive features of Husserl's claim, let us look at the author Jacques Derrida, who has been one of the major critics of the metaphysics of presence. In his well-known exchange with John Searle, Derrida describes what is to be a written sign, and stresses that writing involves the possibility of a written survival in the absence of the one who did the writing. In making this point, Derrida says some rather strong things: he says that the absence of the author "is possible . . . and that this possibility must therefore be taken into account: it pertains, qua possibility, to the structure of the mark as such, i.e., to the structure precisely of its iterability."[1]

Further on he says, "If one admits that writing (and the mark in general) must be able to function in the absence of the sender, the receiver, the context of production, etc., that implies that this power, this being able, this possibility is always inscribed, hence necessarily inscribed as possibility in the functioning or the functional structure of the mark."[2] He goes on to say that, "This re-mark constitutes part of the mark itself. And this remark is inseparable from the structure of iterability."[3] He says that in such descriptions we are dealing with "the value of a law, here of an eidetic law."[4] And finally he says, "Once again, to be precise: what is at stake here is an analysis that can account for structural possibilities."[5]

Derrida here uses terms such as "structure," "always," "necessarily inscribed," "eidetic law," and "the analysis of structural possibilities." How can all this really differ from Husserl's claim to be carrying out eidetic and apodictic analyses? Derrida, of course, is insisting on a structural necessity of absence as pervading any element of presence that we might pretend to have; he is working out what he calls "the supplement, mark, or trace of presence-absence."[6] But isn't this what Husserl is doing when he examines the blends of empty and filled intentions, or the mixtures of presence and absence, that constitute the givenness of any kind of object with which we an be involved? And Derrida is claiming to be describing how these forms necessarily have to be, how certain forms of absence *have* to be implicated with certain forms of presence and in the constitution of particular kinds of things, such as signatures, texts, words, pictures, promises, decisions, and the like. These necessities surface for us only when we adopt the stance of phenomenological description, when we begin to look at presences and absences and not through them. They are necessities in the presentation of things, or necessities in intentional structures. And even according to what Derrida has written, an object such as a signature, a text, or a word is precisely the identity that is constituted in the interplay of presence and absence.

My appeal to Derrida is primarily rhetorical. If he, as critical as he is of the metaphysics of presence, must acknowledge structural necessities, and also the possibility of the analysis of structural necessities, then Husserl's claim to be able to carry out apodictic descriptions or analyses may seem less scandalous to those who are philosophically faint of heart. But having reassured the reader, perhaps I can move beyond the rhetorical and address the problem of what apodicticity means in such analysis. It means that even though the things we experience in the world — the types of animals, the types of gases and metals, and so on — might have been very different from the way they are, the presentational forms through which they are given could not have been different from the way they are. For example, the form of picturing could not be different from itself in the way that snakes might have been different from themselves. The form of "being distinguished" could not be different in the way that gold or iron might have been different. There is a kind of necessity in the presentational forms that is different from the kind of empirical necessity we find in things. The presentational forms are what they are by being mixtures of presence and absence, and sameness and otherness. In thinking about these mixtures we come upon a kind of necessity that is, so to speak, more iron-bound than the necessities that rule in the structures of birds' wings and the digestive systems of worms. Instead of professing shock at Husserl's claim to apodicticity, we would do much better, philosophically, to see what is going on in these strange dimensions of presence, absence, and identity, of sameness and otherness, and rest and motion; and to see what we are doing when we try to talk about the uncanny relationships that go on there. There is more in these areas than what meets the eye, and we really are not doing very much serious philosophical reflection if we don't try to come to terms with whatever it is that occurs there.

There are two ways in which we can talk, philosophically, about the forms of presence and absence, sameness and otherness. One is to talk directly about these forms and to contrast them with one another; to speak about presence just as presence, absence just as absence, and so on. This is an extreme form of analysis and very little can be said in it. It is better not to approach it directly, but to touch it simply by coming at it from a less extreme level. And the second, less extreme way of talking about presence and absence, sameness and otherness is to talk about the way these forms occur in the various forms of presentation. For example, we might discuss how pictures are the same and not the same as the things depicted in them; how the pictorial presences and absences can be compared with those of a perceived material object or with those of a written text. Such instantiations of presence and absence, sameness and otherness are less extremely formal than the sheer forms of presence as such and absence as such, but of course they are still formal in contrast to the things that are given in pictures or in perception.

A good example of how we can study presence and absence, sameness and otherness as they occur in one of the forms of presentation is the case of categorial articulation. A whole array of distinctions must be made if we are to describe correctly how an object becomes articulated and then how it becomes the content of a judgement or proposition. Let us sketch several of these levels of analysis. To begin with, on the basic level we have the direct perception of the object, or the object as given in perception. One profile after another is presented, and so the presentation or the perception is continuous, but the object keeps being identified as the same object as we keep perceiving. On a second level, as Husserl described it, it is possible for us to highlight one of these profiles or features, to make this feature thematic. Let us say that we focus on this feature. This focus alone is not enough to constitute an articulation. What happens is that the feature we focus on becomes identified with one of the aspects that we had gone through in the object while we were in the mode of continuous perception. This identification allows us to register the articulation, "S is p." The "is" is an expression of the identification between the object (which is now appreciated as a whole) and the feature which is now highlighted. At this point the continuity of perception or perceptual disclosure gives way to discrete parts; the whole is recognized as whole, a part is recognized as part. Instead of the continuous experience or presentation, we have, what I would like to call, an "arrest." The articulated is fixed and discrete as articulated. However, the entire articulation has taken place in the object; it is the object that has undergone a change in the way it is presented. New presentational forms, new dimensions of presence and absence, sameness and otherness, rest and motion (as the word "arrest" suggests) have been at work in the object. I wish to emphasize that this object-focused articulation can take place in either the perceptual presence of the object, in which case we should say that the articulation is being registered; or it can take place in the perceptual absence of the object, in which case we can conveniently say that the articulation is being reported.

But we move to a third, to a new dimension, when we interpret the articulated as merely being proposed by someone. We are not caught naively in the object being articulated, but we consider this articulation only as being proposed by someone. This can be called a "propositional reflection." In it we taken some cognitive distance from what we have been told and we can approach the object again with some critical anticipation. If we then find we can register the object in the way the proposition anticipates, we cancel or disquote the propositional mode and go on back to a kind of naive belief, but we do so after a critical detour, and our belief can now be considered confirmed in a way it was not confirmed before. There is a kind of identification at work in the propositional reflection and the return to registration because we identify the state of affairs as proposed with the state of affairs as registered, if indeed we are successful in our confirmation. Now in elaborating these differences of presentation, we can account for the elements of truth that operate when we talk to one another and try to see if what others say, or if what we ourselves say, is true. We have carried out a phenomenological description. We have illustrated how presence and absence, sameness and otherness work in the activity of articulation and propositional truth.

If we expand our analysis, we could also show how these dimensions also allow us to come forward as persons who can hold opinions, who can follow what others say, who can question and confirm or disconfirm what others say, and who are the same selves as the perceivers who provide the experiential substratum for all these categorial achievements. We come to realize that in speech we are engaged in a presentational articulation: we do not merely articulate for the sheer sake of articulation, but as presenting things to ourselves and to others. And we do not present bluntly, simply placing one thing after another in front of ourselves and others; we presented articulatedly, with all sorts of nuances and shadows in what we say. Out language, with its grammar, gives us the articulational resources to accomplish all this, but we never merely apply the language mindlessly. If we think while we use the language, we will present things in ways that will sometimes require adjusting our language, with metaphor and other tropes, in order to bring out what we want to express. Thus we become prominent in our description as agents of the language and as disclosers of what is, as datives of manifestation. It should also be clear that in providing such descriptions, we are circumventing the need for Cartesian or Lockeian ideas, and avoiding the need for internal concepts as the way of explaining how we can make judgements and carry out the process of verification.

Most of the remarks we have made about phenomenological description have dealt with what Husserl calls the transcendental reduction. We have tried to show how the stance we adopt in carrying out these descriptions is different from the stance we adopt when we simply talk about things in the world. But we should say something about the eidetic reduction, the second reduction required for phenomenological analysis. We intend any descriptions we make to be valid for more cases than simply the one we are involved with at the moment. The way we get to such a general validity is through the eidetic reduction. Husserl has given us a rather prosaic description of the eidetic reduction. He said that we may begin with a particular real instance, but that we move from the perceived into the imaginary. We begin to process our case imaginatively and try to vary the case in different ways. When we run up against projections that we realize cannot be made without breaking up the nature of the thing we are dealing with, we find we have touched on an element that is part of the eidos of the thing. Now this somewhat plodding procedure is not the way imagination really functions in philosophical analysis. In fact what usually happens is that the writer or the speaker will project a single imaginative variant, but one that is strategic, crucial, and usually colorful, one that brings out a certain necessity in the thing we wish to examine. It is not easy to capture the right imaginative variant, to pick out the dramatic, vivid example that shows a necessity. We need fantasy to do so. We thus need imagination to be good at philosophical analysis. We have to be able to think of things being very different from the way they are, and it is by no means in everyone's power to do so. We have to be able to imagine the impossible and to see it as impossible. But no experience could have given us the impossible, so we can move into this domain only by fantasy. Fantasy is the element for philosophical insight.

Try for example to imagine an animal, a dog or a cat, that could be quoted by us. What could it mean to be able to quote an animal? We can imagine ourselves finding out through an animal that something is happening; from the dog's particular way of barking, I can realize that the mailman is at the front door. But such a way of being informed by a dog is not the same as being able to quote the dog; why can I not say, "Fido tells me that the dog food is not as good as it used to be? " What is it in the human registration of facts that makes it specifically human activity? Thus if we try to imagine an animal with the ability to be quoted, and a human being without the ability to be quoted, we seem to violate eidetic necessities. We appreciate this necessity not through empirical generalizations, not by simple experience, but by experience penetrated by imagination and the negativity that imagination tries to impose on what we know. A felt resistance to the negating force of imagination amount to the disclosure of an eidetic necessary. Now all philosophers do carry out such eidetic analyses and convey them through the use of imaginative examples. But Husserl was able to see the structure that such institutions have; he was able to show the place of imagination in them. In doing this he achieved an extraordinary insight into what goes on all the time when we analyze things, and into what goes on when we carry on phenomenological descriptions.

The theory of phenomenological descriptions that we have received from Husserl allows us to recover the ancient Greek philosophical sense of being and form, of eidos, while at the same time coming to terms with the issue of appearances or ideas as they have been developed in the philosophy of the last five centuries.

Notes

1. Jacques Derrida, "Limited Inc abc . . . " *Glyph* 2 (1977) 183.

2. Ibid., 184.

3. Ibid., 186.

4. Ibid., 194.

5. Ibid., 194.

6. Ibid., 186.

3. Pregnant Subjectivity and the Limits of Existential Phenomenology

Iris M. Young

A recent business magazine recently ran an article on pregnant managers. It described how women, now in their thirties with established positions on corporate ladders, have chosen to become pregnant and continue to work nearly to term. This has caused changes in corporate policies and attitudes toward the presence of pregnant women at meetings. Restaurants catering to the business crowd, moreover, no longer whisk the pregnant woman into a hidden corner. The article did its best to treat the topic nonchalantly, displaying a photograph of a pregnant manager leaning casually against her desk. Public pregnancy, however, is subversive stuff. The big bureaucracies struggle to constrain the expolsive potential of this social change, and they will probably win, but their hulking spirits will likely be rendered a bit more fluid.

Existential phenomenology also is transformed by bringing pregnancy into view. Its male bias becomes apparent. Existential phenomenology made a revolutionary move in philosophy by turning to the body as the locus of reflection on experience. This entails climbing down from the Platonic heaven of universals to mire in the concrete, the relative, to attend to differences without solidifying them into universal categories. Existential phenomenology, however, did not live up to its promise, and conceived the lived body as a sexless freak, itself as a universal. With very few exceptions, phenomenologists of the body have failed in their descriptions to articulate the differences in experience that arise from different kinds of bodies, most obvious of which are male and female bodies.

Even when phenomenologists have reflected on the lived experience of the sexed body (Lingis 1977), they have failed to take note of the fact that there are (at least) two sexes, whose sexual experiences are necessarily and probably irreducibly different, though some day perhaps they will not be experienced as opposed. When examples appear of lived-body experience, they are usually male examples, as in Merleau-Ponty's reflection on Schneider. (Merleau-Ponty 1962, 153–57). Implicit or explicit assumptions of the male experience of the lived body haunts existential phenomenology, even while it submerges differences in an account that claims to describe the lived body in general. More than any other body experience, perhaps, pregnancy can jolt philosophical reflection on the body from such humanistic slumbers. Experience of the pregnant body is limited, unsharable, and untransferable. Disclosure on the pregnant body is subversive to philosophy precisely because it cannot be universalized.

I

In its latent humanism, existential phenomenology harbors an attachment to the idealism it purports to overturn. The move to locate consciousness in the body jeopardizes dualistic metaphysics, but the mind-body, subject-object dichotomy often appears in the form of a distinction between the transcending body and the body as merely physical (Sarano 1966, 62–63). Existential phenomenologists of the body usually assume a distinction between transcendence and immanence as two modes of bodily being. They often assume that insofar as one adopts an active relationship to the world, one is not aware of one's body for its own sake. In the successful enactment of one's aims and projects, one's body is a transparent medium (Merleau-Ponty 1962, 138–39). And should one be thrown back onto an awareness of one's body, this counts as a disruption and estrangement. Thus Herbert Plugge, for example, writes:

> The bodily as physical and objectal appears as a sort of *thickening* in the sense of a change in an aggregate state of the otherwise unnoticed live bodiness – much as if I were suddenly to notice the air, which I usually do not feel during respiration, as something thinglike, having consistency. The bodily as physical intrudes as something strange. The *res extensa* emerges phenomenologically at the heart of the otherwise unnoticed pre-reflective lived body (1970, 305).

Thus the dichotomy of subject and object appears anew in the conceptualization of the body itself. These thinkers tend to assume that awareness of one's body in its materiality is an alienated objectification of one's body, in which one is not one's own body and that body is imprisoning. To the degree that existential phenomenology retains such a dichotomization of body experience, it fails to follow through on its rejection of mind-body dualism. This author's earlier work on feminine-body subjectivity (Young 1980), manifests this same tendency. As will now be shown, reflection on the experience of pregnancy reveals most directly the inappropriateness of a distinction between body as transcending and the body as immanent.

To the extent that existential phenomenology harbors a distinction between subject and object, it does so at least partly because it assumes the subject as a unity. In *The Phenomenology of Perception*, for example, Merleau-Ponty locates the "intentional arc" that unifies experience in the body rather than in an abstract constituting consciousness. He does not abandon, however, the ideal of a unified self as the source and condition of experience (see, for example, Descombes 1981, 69).

> There must be, then corresponding to this open unity of the world, an open and indefinite unity of subjectivity. Like the world's unity, that of the I is invoked rather than experienced each time I perform an act of perception, each time I reach a self-evident truth, and the universal I is the background against which these efulgent forms stand out: it is through one present thought that I achieve the unity of all my thoughts (Merleau-Ponty 1962, 406).

Richard Zaner (1981) has sought to eliminate the transcendental ego lurking in this passage by describing the embodied self as a "contexture." The embodying organism is a "gestural display" of concrete feelings, desires, efforts, reactions, existing within a structured context or patterning. He describes that structure of embodiment as a part/whole relation, a structure of identity-in-difference, unity-in-diversity. Despite his organicism, however, the Cartesian ego does not entirely disappear. Zaner seeks to describe the unity to this diversity of motion and effort, and he finds it in the reflexivity of existence: that I am present to myself.

Recent French philosophy has exploded the unity of the transcendental ego, the illusion of the self as an origin, and the unity of a coherent identity. The writings of Lacan, Derrida, and Kristeva show subjectivity as multiple and shifting, and always already outrun by the sociolinguistic world. For Kristeva, the unity of the self, its self-referring consciousness and identity as the self-same origin of meaning, rests precisely on its cleavage, on the splitting of the process of subjectivity that enacts language into two moments: the logical, assertive consciousness and the slippery, desiring, playful, violent unconscious. The unitary subject, which Cartesian philosophy, and all subsequent transcendental egos, wills as comprehending the whole, existing as universal humanity, is thus exceeded by the subject in process which spills over into the contradictions, ruptures, and encounters of sensuous experience.

In pregnancy, Kristeva suggests, the multiple character of all subjectivity enters experience itself.

Pregnancy seems to be experienced as the radical ordeal of the splitting of the subject: redoubling up of the body, separation and coexistence of the self and an other, of nature and consciousness, of physiology and speech (Kristeva 1981, 31; see also Kristeva 1980, 238).

Pregnancy is a kind of "institutionalized psychosis," Kristeva asserts, in which the woman renews a connection with the preconscious, presymbolic experience. Through the experiences of pregnancy and childbirth, the woman renews the primordial connection to her own mother's body, before speech has formed the infant into an ego, a unitary "I." Instead of that unified "I" which is the subject of the eternal symbolic order, the order of coherence and clarity "where legislators, grammarians, and even psychoanalysts have their seat" (1980, 242), the pregnant subject straddles the spheres of language and instinctual drive, felt as a process of connectedness to nature becoming social. In this splitting of the subject, the pregnant and birthing woman taps into the "jouissance" of the experience of the maternal body, which must be censored in her in order for her to enter the unity "where everybody is made homologous to a male speaking body" (1980, 242).

Kristeva's remarks about the experience of pregnancy are immensely suggestive and truthful. Yet the psychoanalytic discourse she speaks within is somewhat too *a priori*, and removes me from reflection on the lived experience of pregnancy. In the spirit of phenomenology I shall engage here in a description of the lived experience of pregnancy. Through reference to diaries and literature, I seek to let women speak in their own voices. This reflection confirms Kristeva's notion of pregnancy as split subjectivity. The lived pregnant body is decentered, disintegrated, where "alterity becomes nuance, contradiction becomes a variant, tension becomes passage, and discharge becomes peace" (Kristeva 1980, 240). It reveals a mode of body existence in which the borders between self and other, subject and object, transcending action and attention to self, come into question and dissolve.

II

As my pregnancy begins, I experience it as a change in my body, that I am becoming different from what I have been. My nipples become reddened and tender, my belly swells into a pear. I feel this elastic around my waist, itching, this round, hard middle replacing the doughy belly with which I still identify. Then I feel a little tickle, a little gurgle in my belly, it is my feeling, my insides, and it feels somewhat like a gas bubble, but it is not, it is different, in another place, belonging to another, another that is nevertheless my body.

The first movements of the fetus produce this sense of the splitting subject; the fetus's movements are wholly mine, completely within me, conditioning my experience and space, they are mine, subjective, because only I have access to these movements, a privileged knowlege. For months only I can witness this life in my belly, and even after another can feel the movements it is only under my direction of where to put her or his hand. Adrienne Rich reports this sense of the movements within me as mine even though they are another's.

> In early pregnancy, the stirring of the fetus felt like ghostly tremors of my own body, later like the movements of a being imprisoned within me; but both sensations were *my* sensations, contributing to my own sense of physical and psychic space. (Rich 1976, 47).

The experience of pregnancy and motherhood challenges the way Western philosophy has typically described the relationship of self and other as opposition and confrontation. In pregnancy the relationship of self and other is experienced not as negation, but as continuity in difference. The diary of a woman quoted by Rich expresses this sense of I-other continuity.

> I was one and the other at once. It stirred inside of me. Could I control its movements with my will? Sometimes I thought I could, at other times I realized it was beyond my control. (Rich 1976, 161)

The splitting of subjectivity occurs in the fantasies of pregnancy too, as I fantasize a relationship with another really myself in the mode of not being myself. I experience a deep ambivalence toward the fantazied other, sliding between narcissistic identification and paranoia. On the one hand, I fantasize this potential subject growing in my body in a relationship of perfect communication with me, another of myself, my daughter, my mother, my sister as I would have them be.

On the other hand, as my belly swells and the fetus moves aside my ribs, my stomach, my bladder, I can feel myself overtaken by this other life. I imagine myself gnawed at, drained away, possessed by another existence that has taken over my body. Fear and resentment characterize my feelings toward this unceasingly demanding, ever-present, parasitic other. Yet the only existent is my myself in a splitting disintegration.

Pregnancy also challenges the integration of my body experience by rendering fluid the boundary between what is within, myself, and what is outside, separate. I experience my insides as the space of another, yet my own body.

> Nor in pregnancy did I experience the embryo as decisively internal in Freud's terms, but rather, as something inside and of me, yet becoming hourly and daily more separate, on its way to becoming separate from me and of itself . . .
> Far from existing in the mode of "inner space," women are powerfully and vulnerably attune both to "inner" and "outer" because for us the two are continuous, not polar (Rich 1976, 47–48).

The birthing process entails the most extreme suspension of the bodily distinction between inner and outer. As the months and weeks progress, increasingly I feel my insides, strained and pressed, and increasingly I feel the movement of a body inside me. Through pain and blood and water this inside thing emerges between my legs, for a short while both inside and outside of me. Later I look with wonder at my mushy middle, and at my child, amazed that this yowling, flailing thing, so completely different from me, was there inside, a part of me.

The integrity of my body is undermined in pregnancy not only by this externality of the inside, but by the fact that the boundaries of my body are themselves in flux. In pregnancy I lose the sense of where my body ends and the world begins. The style of bodily existence, such as gait, stance, sense of room I inhabit, which have formed in me as bodily habits, continue to define my body subjectivity. My body itself changes its shape and balance, however, coming into tension with those habits. The continuity between my customary body and my body at this moment, as Merleau-Ponty puts it (1962, 62), is broken.

I move as though I can squeeze around chairs and through crowds as I could have seven months before, only to find my way blocked by my own body sticking out in front of me, in a way not me, since I did not expect it to block my passage. As I lean over in my chair to tie my shoe, I am surprised by the graze of this hard belly on my thigh. I do not anticipate this touching of my body on itself, for my habits retain the old sense of my boundaries. In the ambiguity of bodily touch (Merleau-Ponty 1962, 93; Straus 1969, 46), I feel myself being touched and touching simultaneously both on my knee and my belly. The belly is other, since I did not expect it there, but since I feel the touch upon it, it is me (cf. Straus 1963, 370).

As already noted, existential phenomenologists often assume that free action entails that one is not aware of one's body. For several of these thinkers, moreover, awareness of the physicality of the body occurs only or primarily when this instrumental relationship to the world breaks down, in fatigue or illness. Being brought to awareness of the physical processes of one's body, they often suggest, entails a self-estrangement (Straus 1963, 245; Plugge 1970, 298; Zaner 1981, 54–57.).

Certainly there are occasions when one experiences one's body only as a resistance, only as a painful otherness preventing one from accomplishing one's goals. It is inappropriate, however, to tie such a negative meaning to all experience of being brought to awareness of the body in its weight and materiality. Sally Gadow (1980) has argued that in addition to experiencing the body as a transparent mediator for our projects or an objectified and alienated resistance or pain, we also at times experience our bodily being in an aesthetic mode. While Gadow suggests that both illness and aging can be experiences of the body in such an aesthetic mode, pregnancy is most paradigmatic of such experience of being thrown on to awareness of one's body. Contrary to the mutually exclusive categorization between transcendence and immanence that underlies some theories, the awareness of one's body in its bulk and weight does not impede the accomplishing of one's aims.

This belly touching my knee, this extra part of me that gives me a joyful surprise when I move through a tight place, calls me back to the matter of my body even as I move about accomplishing my aims. Pregnancy consciousness is animated by a double intentionality: my subjectivity splits between awareness of myself as body and awareness of my aims and projects. To be sure, even in pregnancy there are times when I am so absorbed in my activity that I do not feel myself as body; but when I move to feel the look of another I am likely to be recalled to the thickness of my body.

Pregnancy roots me to the earth, makes me conscious of the physicality of my body not as an object, but as the material weight that I am in movement. The notion of the body as a pure medium of my projects is the illusion of a philosophy which has not quite shed the Western philosophical legacy of humanity as spirit (Spelman 1982). Movements always entails awareness of effort and the feeling of resistance. In pregnancy this fact of existence never leaves me. I am an actor transcending through each moment to further projects, but the solid inertia and demands of my body call me to my limits, not as an obstacle to action, but only as a fleshy relation to the earth (Griffith 1970; see also Spicker 1976). As the months proceed the most ordinary efforts of human existence, like sitting, bending, and walking, which I formerly took for granted, becomes apparent as the projects they themselves are. Getting up, for example, increasingly become a task which requires my attention (Straus 1966, 137–165; 1969, 35–37).

In the experience of the pregnant woman, this weight and materiality often produce a sense of power, solidity, and validity. Thus whereas our society often devalues and trivializes women, regards women as weak and dainty, the pregnant woman can gain a certain sense of self-respect.

This bulk slows my walking and makes my gestures and my mind more stately. I suppose if I schooled myself to walk massively the rest of my life, I might always have massive thoughts (Lewis 1950, 83).

The pregnant woman's relationship to her body can be an innocent narcissism. As I undress in the morning and evening, I gaze in the mirror for long minutes, without stealth or vanity. I do not appraise myself, ask if I look good enough for others, but like a child take pleasure in discovering new things in my body. I turn to the side and stroke the taut flesh that protrudes under my breasts.

The dominant culture projects pregnancy as a time of quiet waiting. It refers to the woman as "expecting," as though this new life were flying in from another planet, and she sat in her rocking chair by the window, occasionally moving the curtain aside to see if the ship is coming. This image of uneventful waiting associated with pregnancy reveals how the discourse of pregnancy leaves out the subjectivity of the woman. From the point of view of others, pregnancy is primarily a time of waiting and watching, when nothing happens.

For the pregnancy subject, on the other hand, pregnancy has a temporality of movement, growth, and change. The pregnant subject is not simply a splitting in which the two halves lie open and still, but a dialectic. The pregnant woman experiences herself as a source and participant in a creative process. Though she does not plan and direct it, neither does it merely wash over her; rather, she *is* this process, this change. Time stretches out, moments and days take on a depth because she experiences more changes in herself, her body. Each day, each week, she looks at herself for signs of transformation.

> Were I to lose consciousness for a month, I could still tell that an appreciable time has passed by the increased size of the fetus within me. There is a constant sense of growth, of progress, of time, which, while it may be wasted for you personally, is still being used, so that even if you were to do nothing at all during those nine months, something would nevertheless be accomplished and a climax reached (Lewis 1950, 78).

For others the birth of an infant may be only a beginning, but for the birthing woman it is a conclusion as well. It signals the close of a process she has been part of for nine months, the leaving of this unique body she has moved through, always surprising her a bit in its boundary changes and inner kicks. She welcomes the birth, but not without a certain sense that her own mode of being is ending.

The lived experience of the pregnant body, I have argued, entails a positive disintegration of subjectivity, in a splitting of the self into process. The pregnant subject, moreover, attends to the body's materiality and physicality for its own sake at the same time as she carries on an active relationship with the world. Description of the pregnant body in these ways challenges the generalizations often made by phenomenologists of the body.

Description of pregnant subjectivity is subversive to the social structure as well. For our culture does not understand pregnancy as the experience of a subject, but as a "condition," or in instrumental terms, as the means of life of a fetus. The insertion of the pregnant subject into male-dominated medicine greatly exacerbates this instrumental orientation toward pregnancy in ways that deny and devalue a woman's own experience (Young 1983). To speak from the point of view of the pregnant subject means for women to make a gesture of appropriating and celebrating this irreducibly specific body experience.

Notes

Descombes, V. 1981. *Modern French Philosophy*. Oxford: Oxford University Press.

Gadow, S. 1980. "Body and Self: A Dialectic." *Journal of Medicine and Philosophy* 6: 172–85.

Griffith, R.M. "Anthropology Man-a-Foot," *The Philosophy of the Body: Rejections of Cartesian Dualism*, ed. Stuart Spicker (Chicago: Quadrangle Books, 1970).

Hirsch, M. 1981. "Mothers and Daughters." *Signs* 7: 200–222.

Kristeva, J. 1980. "Motherhood According to Giovanni Bellini." In *Desire in Language*, translated by Gora, Jardine, and Roudiez, 237–70. New York: Columbia University Press.

_____. 1981. "Women's Time." translated by Jardine and Blake. *Signs* 7: 13–35.

Lingis, A. 1977. "Sense and Non-sense in the Sexed Body." *Cultural Hermeneutics* 4: 345–65.

Lewis, A. 1950. *An Interesting Condition*. Garden City, N.Y.: Doubleday.

Merleau-Ponty, M. 1962. *The Phenomenology of Perception*. translated by Colin Smith. New York: Humanities Press.

Plugge, H. 1970. "Man and his Body." In *The Philosophy of the Body: Reflections of Cartesian Dualism*, edited by Spicker. Chicago: Quadrangle Books.

Rich, A. 1976. *Of Woman Born*. New York: W.W. Norton; page references are to the Bantam Paperback edition.

Sarano, J. 1966. *The Meaning of the Body*, translated by James H. Farley. Philadelphia: Westminster Press.

Spelman, E. V. 1982. "Woman as Body: Ancient and Contemporary Views." *Feminist Studies* 8, no. 1: 109–23.

Spicker, S. "*Terra Firma* and Infirma Species: From Medical Philosophical Anthropology to Philosophy of Medicine," *The Journal of Medicine and Philosophy*, vol. 1, 1976, 104–35.

Straus, E. 1963. *The Primary World of the Senses*. London: The Free Press.

_____. 1966. *Phenomenological Psychology*. New York: Basic Books.

_____. 1969. *Psychiatry and Philosophy*. New York: Springer-Verlag.

Young, I. M. 1980. "Throwing Like a Girl: A Phenomenology of Feminine Body Comportment, Motility and Spatiality." *Human Studies* 3: 137–56.

_____. 1984. "Pregnant Embodiment: Subjectivity and Alienation." *The Journal of Medicine and Philosophy* 9: 45–62.

Zaner, R. M. 1981. *The Context of Self: A Phenomenological Inquiry Using Medicine as a Clue*. Athens, Ohio: Ohio University Press.

Part II.
Phenomena of Time

4. Keeping the Past in Mind

Edward S. Casey

It was lost to sight but kept in memory.
— Augustine, *Confessions*

Memory, therefore, is certainly not the mental process
which, at first sight, one would imagine . . .
— Wittgenstein, *Philosophical Grammar*

I

Keeping the past in mind: where *else* is it going to be kept? We could perhaps try to keep it in the past itself; but then we would have the past containing itself; but then we would have the past containing itself, swallowing its own tail. An event would die out the moment it was born: it would have no continuing protentional halo – fulfilled or unfulfilled – nor would it be rememberable. Yet an event shorn of all these attributes would no longer be an event at all. To keep a past event entirely past, with no possible repercussions in the present, would be to deprive it of its very eventfulness. "Remembrance is now," says George Steiner in *After Babel*;[1] but this is so only because the past itself is now: is now being reenacted, relived.

A timely instance of this very principle is with us tonight. Here we are, in *this* present, the second evening of yet another SPEP conference, but with an awareness that this conference marks the twentieth such meeting since the founding of the Society for Phenomenology and Existential Philosophy in 1962. (Not 1961: anniversaries, like the birthdays we have come increasingly to dread, are always one in advance of our expectations; when I became forty, it was pointed out to me by a sadistic friend that I was in fact entering the *fifth* decade of living on this earth; the arrow of calendrical and clock time is indeed ever-advancing, always being one-up on us. Lived time, in contrast and especially as our body declines, seems always one-down: to lag behind the calendar and clock, until we reach a point in old age when we may be living more in the past of childhood than in the present. But notice that even then we are not living in the past as past but in a past that has become, that has taken over, the present.) In any case, we are here, strategically poised in a twenty-year shadow of a past which I am fortunate enough to have known in the first person. How then do I keep it in mind?

Of course mainly by remembering it. It is curious, though, how little detail we can often recall, even of a "founding event" as Eliade might call the first meeting of SPEP. Indeed, it could be argued that the less detailed the better with regard to commemoration of origins, not because they were ignominious or confused but because they encourage repetition of just the sort that Eliade considers essential to celebrations of cosmogonic *Urzeiten*. There is Washington crossing the Delaware, a group of gentlemen meeting in Philadelphia, a Tea Party earlier on, a few other such happenings, and little else. And yet this suffices to enable us to commemorate our origins as a nation. It is as if something inexorably schematic is at work in matters like this – as if the gaps in memory are so functional that they are not even missed.

So perhaps it is fine that I cannot remember more than the following fragments from the past that was the founding event of the society under whose auspices we are meeting tonight:

- brilliant October weather on the shores of Lake Michigan.

- the meetings (attended by about twenty people, among them eight or ten graduate students like myself) were held in a single classroom in Kresge Hall, a classroom that I think I could relocate to this day (*to this day*: here is the long arm of the past extending itself into the present).

- some rheoscopic films shown by Erwin Straus, who was then working on the nature of facial expression (Straus later, at a SPEP meeting in Boston, rose dramatically from the floor and pleaded for recognition of the permanent dimension of the past: yet another testimony to its inreach into the present).

- an interminable wrangle one evening over the proper title for the fledgling society: should "existentialism" or "phenomenology" come first in order, with all the weighty implications of literal precedence? (Actually, this *was* a genuine philosophical issue, since John Wild's more or less Heideggerian wish to merge the two currents wherever possible was not the wish of certain Husserlian purists: an issue that was finally defused by the subsequent founding of Husserl, Heidegger, and Merleau-Ponty Circles).

– an early Saturday morning meeting that was much too early for the likes of a nightowl like myself to attend: here there is nothing to report except a not-going; the event is a nonevent.

Now there you have it: my way of keeping this past in mind. Just four or five items survive. Disappointing, is it not? Positively paltry, you might say. Is not the role of an appointed memnon, the official reminder of heroes, to conserve the past in toto, or as nearly so as possible? Have I not failed miserably in this mission?

But let us reflect for a moment on the very disappointment. Or rather more exactly, the lack of it in the circumstance. You do not really expect of me, nor I of myself, that total recall be practiced on this or any comparable occasion of recollecting. The mystery is why we do not expect more of ourselves in these matters – why we are willing to put up with partial recall only, with schematic representations of the past rather than the past returning in full regalia. If recollection is really reproduction – as both Kant and Husserl insist on calling it – then why do we not more often keep the *whole* past in mind down to its last detail? Why not, when (a) there are occasions when this would be extremely useful (for example, in court trials; in examinations; in historical-mindedness generally); and (b) we know that it is in fact a human possibility: as witnessed by Sheresheveski, the Russian mnemonist studied by Luria who could recall fifteen years later, and word-for-word, several stanzas of *The Divine Comedy* read to him just once in Italian, a language he did not know? Nevertheless, the occasions in adult life when full recollection is called for are relatively rare, and many of them can be aided by mechanical devices (for instance, the always-operative camera that records all transactions at banks); and the possession of eidetic memory can be more a curse than a blessing: Sheresheveski was so overburdened and even incapacitated by his "gift" that he had to develop techniques to forget much of what he would otherwise have perfectly retained!

But the question will not go away quite so quickly. Apart from reasons of utility or psychic tranquility, why do we not remember more than we usually do remember? Thinkers as contraposed as Bergson and Freud have both posited that we do in fact hold the entire past in mind – only in a form whose reactivation is impeded (for example, by the distraction of current concerns or by repression). This view dies hard; even after the belief in discrete engrams of memory has been given up, elaborate electrochemical models of the brain continue to imply that somehow, somewhere (if not in engrammatic traces then in reticular circuitry pervading the brain as a whole), the past continues to exist intact, coiled up cozily. Contemporary cognitive psychologists distinguish between "availability" and "accessibility" in memory storage: "available" means what is presently on tap and "accessible" what could become on tap, the unmistakable implication being that in principle everything experienced or learned is ultimately accessible given the right means of access. Indeed, all of mnemotechnics from Simonides to Lorayne and Lucas rely on precisely the same premise: it can all be recovered if only we go about it in the right way. But this premise is otiose even if it turns out to be true. Surely not even most of the past has to be retained for it to be effectively and successfully kept in mind.

II

What is bound to mislead us is the dichotomist assumption that keeping in mind must be either an entirely active or an utterly passive affair. This assumption has plagued theories of memory as well as other mental activities. On the activist model, keeping in mind would be a creating or recreating in mind of what is either a mere mirage to begin with or a set of stultified sensations. Much as God in the seventeenth century was sometimes thought to operate by continual creation, so the mind was given the same lofty powers in the Romantic thought that represented a reaction to much of what the seventeenth century stood for. But the activist model is by no means limited to the Romantic idealists or *Naturphilosophen*; it reappears in more than one phase of phenomenology; and it informs the sober theorizing of Bartlett and Piaget on the nature of remembering.[2] On the passivist model, on the other hand, the mind is mute and unconfigurating; it takes in but does not give back other than what it takes in; it is a recording mechanism only. Something like this view is at work in empiricist theories of memory, considered as restricted to the contents of Humean "impressions," and arranged according to their order and position in time; it continues in Kant's notion of "reproductive imagination" as operating by association alone; and it is found flourishing today in psychological accounts of what is revealingly called "human associative memory."[3]

It is all too evident, I think, that where the activist model gives too little credit to the incomings of experience, the passivist model gives too much. To begin with, there is too much *there* in experience, too much density in it, to claim that we are continually creating or constructing it.[4] And yet it is equally mistaken to believe that it is *all* there, graven in preestablished tablets of truth. Mere "registration," as Sokolowski has recently shown, is only one epistemic stage among others; it is not an adequate analogue for such diverse activities as evocation or reporting. And if it is not all there to begin with, then we have to do with what we end with, including what we remember of what was there.

III

The extremes of activism and passivism join curiously in their exaggerated monisms, leading us to look elsewhere for a suitable model of keeping the past in mind. Let us begin by asking ourselves what *keeping in mind* amounts to and how it bears on remembering the past. "Keeping" is, to begin with, more than retaining – where "retaining" may mean such diverse things as the mere retention of facts and formulas, the fringe-like retentions that cling to each successive now-point in Husserl's version of James's idea of primary memory, or that "retaining-in-grasp" in Husserl's later conception of a memorial capacity that lies between primary and secondary memory and is considered essential to the method of free variation in imagination. In fact, keeping in mind is more even than secondary memory, "recollection" in the ordinary sense of a depictive representation of past events. The tendency to reduce keeping in mind to recollection is a powerful one, despite early warnings from Bergson (who found "habit memory" an at least equally significant form of keeping) and more recent caveats by Heidegger, who inveighs against confining memory to the recovery of the past in the form of "remembrance" (*Wiedergedächtnis*).[6] The "wieder" of *Wiedergedächtnis* or *Wiedererinnerung* (both of which signify secondary memory) is especially telling, as is the semantically equivalent "re-" of "recollection." Secondary memory is secondary precisely because it is somehow a *re*-enactment of the past, its return in representational guise. No wonder so many theories of recollection have emphasized its reproductive aspect – without paying sufficient attention to the fact that reproduction normally includes a simulacrum of the scene recaptured. But the past can be recaptured in nonisomorphic modes of representation, just as it can be kept in mind in a more fundamental way than that of explicit recollection or secondary memory.

Memor, the root of *memoria* or "memory," means "mindful." Being mindful of something differs from retaining it in any of the senses just discussed as well as from recollecting it or even being reminded of it.[7] Being-mindful-of is being *full of mind* about something: being or becoming *in mind* of it, heeding it in a way that exceeds the simple apprehension which lies at the core of retention, recollection, and being reminded. It exceeds all of these precisely by virtue of keeping something in mind. What then is such keeping? Its main action is one of *remaining* or *staying with* what we come to be mindful of. Instead of just grasping, or noting, or pigeonholing, or stockpiling, we remain with what we have become mindful of. "Remaining with" is a form of abiding by, and it is compatible with not representing the minded item of it in any express form. It is staying alongside the item, letting it linger longer than if one were to classify it, shunt it into a convenient position in secondary memory, or act on it in some immediately effective way. Such staying has staying power; it stays on beside what is minded.

If remaining or staying with is the essential action of keeping in mind, conservation or preservation is the essential result: hence the "keep," "the innermost and strongest structure . . . of a medieval castle, serving as a last defense" (O.E.D.) as well as the "keepsake," which I give to you so that you will keep me in mind. But conserving often involves concealing, *keeping hidden*, keeping out of the daylight of open perception by remaining within the dark cellars of the mind's keep. Far from this being a cause for regret – something to be overcome with an efficient mnemotechnique – it tells us something important about remembering: namely, that it is as much a withholding of the past as a holding of it in mind. We preserve the past as truly in not exhibiting it to ourselves or others in so many words or images as in representing it in these ways. Consider only the way the body keeps the past in a veiled and yet entirely efficacious form in its continuing ability to perform certain skilled actions: I may not remember just how, or even when, I first learned the breaststroke, but I can keep on doing it successfully – remembering how to do it – without any representational activity on my part whatsoever. In such a case, the nonexhibition of a particular past is clearly an advantage, since its sudden recollection might impede my spontaneous bodily movements. Many instances of habitual or skilled remembering how to do (or say, or think) things are exemplary of a keeping that, withholding its own historical origin, nevertheless reenacts it in our conduct in the present.

When we play the game of memory we play it for keeps. Remembering consists in a keeping action that combines elements of remaining and preserving, holding and withholding – all held within the keepful reach of mind. Even the breaststroke is kept in mind as it is displayed bodily; for the mind is itself a vast keep that guards the past in more forms of reappearance than the apprehension-based notions of retention, recollection, or reminding can sustain.

IV

Here we must ask: how do things now stand with regard to the vexing issue of whether remembering is an active or passive affair?

Let us go back to the language of "keep" for a moment. It is a striking fact that both as a noun and as a verb this word has both active and passive meanings. As a noun, "keep" can mean either "the act of keeping or maintaining" *or* "the fact of being kept." As a verb, it means either "take in, receive, contain, hold" (and more specifically to "take in with the eyes, ears, or mind") *or* to "guard, defend, protect, preserve, save." These bivalent meanings, differing as they do, are not at all incompatible. Indeed, precisely by means of the component actions of keeping, traced out just above, they are complementary to each other and (more crucially) *simultaneously realizable*. Thus "the act of keeping," by virtue of its remaining with what is kept, helps to constitute "the fact of being kept." And the taking in or holding is a guarding or saving thanks to the element of withholding that conceals the keeping and thus the kept itself.

Consider how this occurs in a concrete case of remembering. I remember attending a SPEP conference in New York at the New School for Social Research and having to change lecture halls at the last moment to accommodate Hannah Arendt's talk, for which a large crowd had showed up. Since I had helped to plan this conference, I felt responsible for things going smoothly. After the new hall had been arranged, I walked over with Arendt, who had been quite upset about the change. But she cooled down in the course of the walk and went on to deliver a marvelous lecture on the Socratic conception of virtue. As with so many memories, this is very schematic in character: I remember little more of the occasion than I have here reported. Yet I would certainly want to say that I have kept it in mind all these years, and in precisely the bivalent senses just discussed. The memory has been actively maintained by being revived from time to time (for example, when ever I think of Hannah Arendt for whatever reason), and by this very revival it has attained a state of "being kept" in mind throughout. At the same time, it was received, taken in, at a most impressionable point (both in my life and during the meeting itself) and preserved or saved thanks to this very receptive sensitivity.

What we can observe in any such example is a delicate dialectic of the active and the passive, the receptive and the spontaneous. There is, at the very least, a constant going back and forth between these dimensions. Heidegger was attuned to much the same thing when he wrote that "what keeps us in our essential nature holds us only so long, however, as we for our part *keep holding on to what holds us.*[8] "The hold is held"[9] in remembering, and this is accomplished by its keeping. The hold, what holds me, is constituted by the particulars of a memory (Ms. Arendt's ire, her piercing dark eyes, the mollifying walk) as they are assembled by the setting in which they in-here (here the New School meeting itself). These are givens of the past of which I can be no more than a more or less receptive witness; they bear down upon me and may even burden me if I become obsessed by them. But I bear up on them in turn by holding, keeping hold on the memory itself. I bear it in mind actively, keeping it on the agenda there. It is not that I simply store this experience and regain access to it as if it had been packaged or pickled on some psychical or neuroanatomical shelf. Having taken in the experience, being kept by it initially ("impressed," "struck," we say inadequately), *I* keep it subsequently by bringing it back to mind again, thereby restoring it. And *myself* as well: for not only Hannah Arendt but my-being-in-her presence is kept on, recollected from the shards of the scene so imperfectly recalled in terms of detail. No matter: the experience has been kept in mind. It has been remembered, and in a way that is at once active and passive – so much so that we are no longer constrained to choose between these traditional alternatives.

V

Now that we know something about how the past is kept in mind, its basic holding action, we must pursue a quite different line of thought by asking: is the past kept within the mind alone? Can we confine it to this tenure, critical as it is, and important as it is to stress, in the fact of efforts to locate remembering elsewhere? Such efforts currently tend to seek the essence, or at least the formal structure, of memory either in the functioning of the brain or in information-processing mechanisms. Neither is adequate to the task of providing a truly comprehensive account of remembering. Neurophysiologists are still bitterly divided over determining the minimal unit of memory – whether it be celluar, molecular, synaptic, or holographic – and cannot begin to explain its higher-order operations (except to say that these somehow involve the rhinencephalon, the mamillary bodies, and various parts of the cerebral cortex). In fact, the most significant work to emerge from this perspective concerns the *pathology* of memory as this is occasioned by the brain's malfunctionings; and in this respect, the contribution of neuroanatomy to the understanding of human memory curiously rejoins the findings of psychoanalysis, also adept at telling us about the misfortunes of remembering but inept at explaining how memory functions in the normal case. As for information-processing models, they are elegant but only pseudoexplanatory. Their stage-wise approach to memory breaks it down into such plausible units as iconic, short-term, and long-term stores; but they fail to explain how coherent experiences of remembering emerge from the concatenation of these phases, and must resort to such stop-gap notions as "encoding," "rehearsal," and "transfer" to fill in the gaps. Concerning these two dominant modes of construing memory, we can say that each possesses what the other lacks: brain physiology is persuasive as to flow and transmission of memories (given a view of the brain as a dynamic field of electrochemical forces) but disappointing as to ultimate units, while information processing is lucid on the modular level but opaque when it comes to circulation and development.

It has been characteristic of phenomenologists to underline how much mind matters in a fundamental experience like remembering. This is imperative when confronting expressions of the "natural attitude" such as are found in neurophysiology and information processing: for them, only matter matters in memory (whether the matter be that of the brain or bits of information mechanically conveyed). Husserl's 1905 lectures on inner time-consciousness, which did so much to inaugurate phenomenology as we now know it, can be read as an extended pleas to consider remembering from an exclusively mental perspective. The "exclusion of objective time" with which the lectures begin is tantamount to a suspension of naturalistic models of memory; and it is telling that this first use of the pheomenological reduction bears directly on remembering – rather than on, say, perceiving or imagining. For indeed urgency surrounds memory, which is unusally tempting to grasp in naturalistic terms. The temptation is due to the fact that recollection rescues experiences from "death's dateless night," the oblivion to which every human experience is subject and against which mechanical and physiological models seem to promise hope of fixity, of stable storage of the past.

Against *this*, phenomenology offers the counter-defensive of an understanding of memory in strictly psychical terms. Thus Husserl denies that we recover the past in any pristine format, a format that continues to be a working assumption in trace and storage theories of memory: "I can re-live the present, but it [the present] can never be given again."[10] One thing Husserl does not provide, oddly enough, is an explicit intentional analysis of memory in terms of its various noetic and noematic phases. In work in progress, I have tried to make up for this lacuna by discerning not just two main act-forms of remembering (that is, primary and secondary) but a plethora of such forms, including remembering-to (do X or Y), remembering-on-the-occasion-of, and several species of remembering-that and remembering-how. On the noematic side, I have found meaningful distinctions to be made between the mnemonic presentation, the specific content remembered, the world-frame of remembered space and time, and an encircling "aura" (as I call the fading fringe of what we remember). Yet an intentional approach to memory is still not sufficient to capture the full phenomenon of keeping the past in mind.

We can no longer assume, in polemical opposition to naturalistic models, that memory is played out on the surface of the psyche – that mind qua "consciousness of X" is the only, or even the main, arena in which the past abides and is recovered. Where then are we to turn? We already have on hand one instance of extramental memory: habitual memory, wherein the past is sedimented into the body, becoming amassed there. Not only in the case of skilled actions of the breaststroke sort, but in many other ways as well, memory moves massively into the body – as we can see in the case of certain ritualistic actions, in dancing (which can be densely memorious without being highly skilled), and even in plain walking (where our body "knows the way" along a familiar route without requiring any recollecltion).

Habitual remembering of various sorts thus leads us out of mind. Into what? Into the *world*, which is where the body takes us in any case. And this is just where we must now take memory itself. Remembering has been esconced too long in the cells of the brain, the vaults of computerized memory banks, and the machinations of mentation. Let us try putting it back into the lived world, where it has always been in any event, though barely recognized as such at the level of either description of theory.

Think of it: *the past kept in things*, those very "things themselves" that the phenomenological method was designed to bring to us. It does not matter that it did not always do so in its haste to reabsorb the world into the sphere of immanence known as "pure consciousness." For the things will bring themselves forward to us, and in fact are never not doing so in some fashion. They come to us bearing the past manifestly in monuments, relics, and mementoes; less obviously, but just as forcefully, in the dwellings we inhabit (buildings bear memories as much as our bodies do); and still less obviously, but still crucially, in the collective memories we share with each other as coexperiencers of certain situations. This is not even to mention such evident keepers of the past as archival documents, the casually and yet tellingly leftover marks of human and nonhuman activities, or, for that matter, the automobiles in which so much of our lives have come to be encapsulated.

VI

I shall, however, restrict consideration here to one basic dimension of the world in which the past is kept. This is *place*. Despite its primordiality in human experience, place has been conspicuously neglected by philosophers. As for memory of place, this is hardly considered a topic worth pausing over, even though an ancient (and still quite effective) method of memorizing, called the "place method," used an ordered grid of places as its main device. Frances Yates has written so eloquently about it in *The Art of Memory*.[11] Moreover, many memories are, if not expressly about places, richly rooted in them and inseparable from them. Even the idea of "keeping the past in mind" carries with it distinct echoes of location in place, albeit a nonworldly mental 'place.'

Notice, to begin with, that it is the body itself that establishes the felt directionality, the sense of level, and the experienced distance and depth that together constitute the main structural features of any given place in which we find ourselves and which we remember. But granting that it is by our mobile bodies that we become oriented in place, what is place itself? Aristotle's definition in the *Physics* remains apposite: "the innermost motionless boundary of what contains."[12] The operative notion here is that of the snug fit of the container, and Aristotle's own favorite analogy to place is the vessel, whose inner boundary coincides exactly with the outer boundary of what it contains: "just as the vessel is transportable place, so place is a non-portable vessel" (212a 13–15).

Although Aristotle does not discuss memory of place as such, his basic conception of place is highly suggestive in this regard: a given place may derive its haunting power (a "haunt" is certainly a memorable place) from its "distinct potencies" as a container which exerts an "active influence" on us, whether by way of attraction or repulsion. (See *Physics* 208b 10–25). A place is not a setting of indifferent space, homogeneous and isotropic (I prefer to call this characteristically seventeenth century view of space a "site"). Place works on us, and on our memories, by its very peculiarities and tropisms, its inhomogeneity.

If we begin pressing in this direction, we very soon reach the notion of "landscape," which is where the Aristotelian idea of place naturally leads us when we extend the idea of a particular place with its irregular protruberances and nonmetrically determinable enclosure to a simultaneously given collocation of places as these form part of our ongoing experience. What holds the collocation together is the landscape's horizon – within which I am situated by means of a distinguishable here vs. there that form the epicenters of the place where I am at. Moreover, within a given landscape, I am always moving from place to place.

I am never not in place, not placed, even if I do not know precisely where I am in geographic space, the space of sites.[13]

Place as it effloresces in landscape is, therefore, one of the main ways in which my being-in-the-world manifests itself. If landscape can be said to constitute the world's felt texture, place is the congealing of this texture into discrete here/there arenas of possible action. In and through places, what Husserl called the "rays of the world" illuminate the landscape as their horizontal setting. And, through the movements of my "customary body,"[14] I come to find something abidingly familiar in the landscape I inhabit, now or formerly; I feel attuned to its sympathetic space – or out of tune when I have been away too long or when painful memories disorient me.

I do not want to suggest that place only draws us outward into the landscape. There is a counter movement as well. Not only do I inhibit a given landscape but it can be said to inhabit me: the "in" of "inhabitation" is bidirectional. And thanks to this doubly pervasive action, we can begin to grasp one basis of the power of place as remembered. For when I recall myself in a particular place set within a landscape, I am not only recollecting how it was *for me*, but how it, the whole visible spectacle, came *to me* and took up dwelling *in me*, as henceforth part of me. It is no longer a matter, as in the experience of site, of parts merely alongside other parts. Place in its landscape being imparts itself to me, permeates me. And, as the "spirit of place," the *genius loci*, enters me, the visible becomes increasingly invisible. As Rilke has put it in the ninth *Duino Elegy*:

> Earth, isn't this what you want: an invisible
> re-arising in us? Is not your dream
> to be one day invisible? Earth? Invisible?

Indeed, this can occur to such an extent that I may need geography (a map), a painting or photograph, just a fresh look at my surrounding, or (most pertinently) a remembering to make visible again what has become so thoroughly embedded within. By speaking of "embedded within" or "incorporation," I do not mean to suggest that the landscape has been internalized by a voracious *res cognitans*. The invisibility in question can just as well be described as my getting lost in the landscape: as my becoming one with it.[15]

If this is beginning to sound increasingly implausible (have we not merely moved from one kind of invisible, that inherent in mind, to another, that found in the empathic experience of landscape?) consider a concrete case: your own circumstance as you read these lines. You too are in a particular place, wherever this may be; and you are also situated within a landscape, whether this be part of unfettered nature, a university campus, or a set of city blocks. Unless you are deeply alienated from them, such a place and landscape offer a snug fit indeed − so much so that it would be difficult to establish the exact boundaries of either. As you inhabit your place so it inhabits you, while landscape provides an abiding setting for habitations of many kinds (cognitive and social as well as corporeal). If and when you come to remember this present experience, place and landscape will together hold and preserve its explicitly recalled content. This latter need not concern place per se. Indeed, place and landscape may be more effectively operative in memories when they are not the focus of what we remember but are merely adumbrated: their most forceful position is often a marginal one. Yet however indistinctly a given place − *cum* − landscape may have been experienced at first and will be subsequently remembered, it offers enclosure for whatever we do recall in detail. It is the circumambience of our ongoing remembering, that which *gives place* to the focally remembered. It is the scene for the proscenium brought back to mind.

VII

Back to *what*? Have we not just been trying to transcend mind by resolutely moving out into place? Is any mediation possible between anything as diaphanous and lambent as mind and something so dense and obdurate as place? If mind is still to matter to us in an account of memory − if we are still to be able to speak of keeping the past genuinely *in mentis* − it becomes evident that mind itself must be reconceived. And it is precisely mind as an internal theater of representations that is at once too confining and incompatible with something as blatantly worldly as place. Before we can get out of mind, however, we must get mind out of itself: out of its own self-encapsulation, its epistemological primary narcissism. It is, in short, a matter of mind expansion, and one key to it is to be found precisely in memory of place. If we are not to keep the past in a mind from which there are no meaningful exits, we must come to appreciate how it is kept in place.

How then is this possible? Primarily by place's "active power" of holding memories for us. The hold is held − in place. This is not mysterious; it does not require invoking a World Soul. It is a given particular place that holds significant memories of ours, acting as a veritable gathering place for them. When I remember certain experiences that took place there, my mind and my past coalesce in, and around, such a place. Each is drawn out of the isolation, the undifferentiation, of forgetful nonremembering and drawn into the redifferentiation which remembering realizes.[16] Place furnishes a matrix for mergings of many kinds – most obviously of past with present, a process which could be called "presentment" and which itself has many forms. (Indeed, the remembered past does not merely terminate in the present of remembering but can be said to begin there, and to do so everytime we recall it. Keeping in memory is a continual rekeeping: hence the many variant versions of the "same" past with which we regale ourselves in remembering and which lead us naturally to connect remembering to storytelling.)

Yet a remembered place can also present us with not just a fusion of past and present but with a merging of itself and the remembering mind that wanders freely into its midst – much as happens with the body in its moving insertion into the perceived world. Such a place, a genuine memory-place, gathers in to keep; it not only keeps my past and my memories alive by furnishing them with a "local habitation and a name"; it moves my mind there for the duration of the remembrance: *out there*, outside of its own self-imposed strictures.

Notice that I am saying more than that mind is itself some kind of place – which it also is, whether we conceive it (with Aristotle) as "the place of forms" or merely as a passing place for imaginations, recollections, and thoughts. Being mindful, as mentioned earlier, is allowing the mind to fill, to distend, with memories. It is only when we take mind-as-place too literally, getting carried away with its own containing capacities, that the slippery slope to idealisms and representationalisms of many sorts starts in earnest. In fact, the mind is only a "quasi-locality." Merleau-Ponty, who employs this last term, also says that "the mind is neither here, nor here nor here [which it would have to be if it were a genuine place]. . . . And yet it is 'attached,' 'bound,' it is *not without bonds*.[17] The bonds are not just to body, itself a "place of passage" as Bergson called it,[18] but to place. And the mind is attached, and continually reattached, to place precisely through memory, which is the main means by which we keep the past in mind.

Mind in place: which is to say, out beyond its own internally generated indices and icons of a world outside. If the self is mainly what we remember it to be,[19] and if its remembering is inexorably place-bound, bound to be implaced in some locale (for not to be so located is not only to be profoundly disoriented; it is not be be at all),[20] then the mind will always already be out there in place, clinging to it as to its own self-definition. Narcissus, after all, gazed at himself not in a mental image but in a reflection given back by a pool – that is, in a

place that exceeded his own self-infatuation even as it supported it. Mind
and place lose their antithetical relationship to one another once they
are brought together in remembering, which binds itself to place even
as it constitutes the self who remembers. One might say, therefore, that
mind and place are both modulations of our being-in-the-world, along
with body, language, and history. Or perhaps even that place is "the
body of the mind,"[21] its extraorganic organ. More than a simple *Spielraum*
for mind's effusions, more than a mere scene for its actings-out, it is
that "other scene" (in Freud's descriptive phrase for dreams), in whose
very alterity mind comes to know itself as it is and to keep itself as
it has been: two activities not inseparable from each other in the end
– or even in the beginning.

Memory recalls mind to place – takes it decisively there and not
to its mere representation. We revisit places in remembering (just as
we do in dreams); and in so doing our minds reach out to touch the
things themselves, which are to be found in the very places they inhabit.
Mind coadunates with world in memory of place.[22]

VIII

Place, then, plain old place, proves to be a liberating factor in matters of memory and mind. An appreciation of the place of place in our
experience helps to free us from the naturalistic and mentalistic strait-
jackets within which both mind and memory have for too long been
confined. Memory of place offers a way out of this confinement and
back into the lived world – while encouraging us to rethink the mind
itself as continuous with this world, conterminous with it, and actively
passive (or passively active) there. This is not to say that when we begin
to reconceive memory and mind in terms of place we are without problem or paradox. For instance, why is it that place, itself best understood
on a container model, aids us in overcoming the persistent temptation
to regard mind and memory as themselves forms of strict containment?
Meditation on place leads paradoxically to the opening out from within
that which it encloses from without.

Nonetheless, I have persevered in underscoring the primordiality
of place; and I have done so not just because it is a generally neglected
topic in philosophy (Norman Malcolm's recently published *Memory and
Mind* does not deign to mention it), but because most discussions of
memory in Western thought (including Aristotle's own seminal discussion in his short treatise on the subject) have emphasized the primacy
of *time*, particularly *past* time, in remembering. Almost all such con-

siderations, from Plato to Husserl, Heidegger, and Minkowski, has sub-
sumed memory under a temporal problematic – as if remembering
were just one more way of being in time. It matters little in this regard
whether we place memory (as *anamnesis*) under the sign of eternity or
reduce it to the reproduction of expired durations; either way, it is
assumed that remembering, since it has to do with the past, is exclusively a temporal affair. But is it? Does not place, which is at least
equiprimordial with time, require us to reconsider this assumption?
Thus when Heidegger claims that "what is past, present, [or] to come
appears in the oneness of its own *present* being,"[23] we cannot help but
notice that "present being" (*An-wesen*: literally, "being *at*") always occurs
in place, the arena wherein both temporal and spatial determinations
are at once rooted and specified.

The poet puts it best:

> I can only say, *there* we have been: but I cannot say [just] where.
> And I cannot say, how long, for that is to place it in time.
> > T.S. Eliot: "Burnt Norton," Four Quartets

I would suggest that "where have we been?" is often a more appropriate
heuristic device in matters of memory than "what have we been?" –
providing that we do not restrict interpretaion of the "where" to the
shrunken sense of site. Site is levelled-down place, and is functionally
and metrically defined (as in a "building site"). To reduce place to site
is comparable to reducing lived time to date: the "*just* where" is
homologous to the "*just* how long." The where that counts in remembering is, as Eliot indicates, a *there* and thus a matter of place, which we
have seen to be structured by a here/there opposition played out within
the horizoning spread of landscape. To remember is in effect, and often
in fact, to claim that "*there I was* doing X or Y in the presence of A and
B." Place is the operator of memory, that which puts it to work in presenting past experience to us in an inclusive and environing format.

IX

The most insistent direction, the main drift, of this essay has been
from the inside out – from the innards of memory to its exoskeletal
outreaches. Most accounts of memory try to keep all the significant
action contained within – within the inner acrobatics of representation or within the microstructures of neuroanatomy or of information
flow. In this internalization of memory phenomenology has played its

part by conceiving of remembering as a "'positing' presentification" of
the past, its re-presentaiton to mind by mind.[24] And mind, being thought
of almost entirely in terms of consciousness and intentionality, has
served as a physical container for the remembered. In questioning this
deeply interiorizing tendency I have had recourse primarily to place,
still another form of containment but one considerably more diffuse,
elastic, and porous. Mind and memory exfoliate in place, even though
place's own activity is that of closing in or down (not pinning down:
that is site's task). Time's basic action is one of breaking out (out of the
fixed boundaries of calendar and clock) and breaking up (of all that
wastes away in time). Time "disperses subsistence,"[25] and it is not at
all surprising that our distressful thoughts concerning the oblivion to
which the past is prone are tied to time – to its dispersing movement.
The same movement is evident in the more hopeful, but still threatening, thought (implicit in Nietzsche as in Freud) that "the past begins
now and is always becoming."[26]

Place offers protection against this very dispersal – against time's
diasporadic or "ecstatic" proclivity which Heidegger made so much of
in *Being and Time*. By its encircling embrace, place shields, holds within
(and withholds) rather than scattering subsistence in dissemination.[27]

In contrast with time, therefore, place is eminently suited for the
keeping operation which we found earlier to lie at the core of remembering: as remaining with and conserving, holding and concealing, taking
in and protecting. In fact, it becomes clear that the past itself can be
kept in place, *right in place* – especially when place is taken in its full
landscape being. This happens saliently in the simultaneously given,
vertically arranged strata of geological formations, which compress their
own amassed past within them. Places, even ordinary places, often do
much the same: presenting to us their unreduced verticality over against
the already reduced horizontality of temporal dissolution.

Place, then, not only offers aegis before time's ravages but may take
time into itself, encasing its disarray in its own structure. Something
like this happens in all remembering even when it is not explicitly of
place. In keeping the past in mind, it is safekeeping it from an inherent
temporal dispersiveness. But we keep the past most effectively in mind
when we also keep it expressly *in place* – when mind embraces place
and not just its own representations. This is one more reason why
memory of place is liberating, since it frees us from time's dissevering
action, its disbanding of human experience into the antagonistic
segments of "past" and "future," the "no longer" and the "not yet."

That leaves us, as remembering always does leave us, *in the present*, a present massively enriched through the coeval actions of present-

ment and implacement (as we may call the "placing" action of memories).
Remembrance is indeed now. It is also *here*, reminding us that
remembering begins and ends in place even as it traverses the most
distantly located personal past: a past it brings incisively into present
place, into the now-and-here of remembrance.

X

And here we are together, still in this place, where I was along with
several others among you (*there* we *were*) some twenty years ago when
the Society for Phenomenology and Existential Philosophy made its
straggling start. Straggling is defined as "wandering from the direct
course or way . . . trailing off from others." And so this society did: it
took a risk, a decided gamble, and wandered off from the main course
of Anglo-American philosophy of the time. Historians will have to judge
whether the risk was worth it, though I for one have no doubt it was,
since it has led to a remarkable revitalization of the doing, and the
reading and teaching, of non-main current philosophy in the United
States.

Looking back from this vantage point, what strikes me most is not
only the sketchy and schematical character of my remembering of this
inaugural event, but a more powerful phenomenon altogether: what
might be dubbed "the future perfection of the memory mantle." By this
I mean the capability of any event, however seemingly trivial it may
be at the outset, to assume a considerable and unexpected importance
upon eventual remembrance of it at some future point.

The idea of the future perfection of the memory mantle requires
us, however, not to look back to an event now *perfected* in the present
but to regard the very present itself as a future past, as a past-to-be.
It is a matter of viewing the present not *sub specie aeternitatis*, nor as
a subject for possible nostalgia, nor even as an occasion for anticipatory
resoluteness, but as having an unsuspected significance as it *shall have
come to be remembered* as not-yet-determinable future moments. This
takes imagination, indeed a special form of it that colludes deeply with
memory. The "shall have come to be remembered" cannot be read off
or predicted from the present itself − for that would be prophesy, a
fully intuitive protentive power which few of us can claim to possess.

I do not know how many threw this kind of memory mantle on
the founding event of this society; I know that I did not. This was short-
sighted, for the effect of future perfecting is to valorize the present, to
show it as more than we take it to be. It also helps to discourage our

chronic tendency to cast back to a regretted or glorified past or to leap forward to a merely projected future. In short, it keeps us in the present and allows us to savor it more fully.

And what of this present? Can we valorize it similarly? We can if in celebrating the past now, here, we do not neglect to regard our commemoration as itself bearing the mantle of its own future perfect being. Where? There, in that time-to-come when the present will be what it is at least partly because the past, our present, will have become what it is capable of being remembered as. In allowing this to happen, we shall have kept the past in mind – as well as mind in place.

Notes

1. George Steiner, *After Babel* (Oxford: Oxford University Press, 1977), 3.

2. For Bartlett, the "schema" is a strictly constructivist notion; for Piaget, the "scheme" serves to "assimilate" experience in keeping with the exact stage of one's cognitive development. Both views are decidedly Kantian in their stress on the mind's actively shaping role. See F. C. Bartlett, *Remembering: A Study in Experimental and Social Psychology* (Cambridge: Cambridge University Press, 1932), 199ff., 300ff.; and Jean Piaget and Bärbel Inhelder, *Memory and Intelligence*, trans. A. J. Pomerans (New York: Basic Books, 1973).

3. See John R. Anderson and Gordon Bower, *Human Associative Memory* (Washington, D.C.: Winston, 1973).

4. A phenomenon like nostalgia, with its almost irrestible pull to the past, testifies to the already informed ingression of events we undergo rather than bring forth.

5. Robert Sokolowski, *Presence and Absence* (Bloomington, Ind.: Indiana University Press, 1978), 7–9, 100–102.

6. "Retention is mostly occupied with what is past, because the past has got away and in a way no longer affords a lasting hold. Therefore, the meaning of retention is subsequently limited to what is past, what memory draws up, recovers again and again. But since this limited reference originally *does not* constitute the sole nature of memory, the need to give a name to the specific retention and recovery of what is past gives rise to the coinage: re-calling memory – remembrance (*Wiedergedächtnis*)." (Martin Heidegger, *What is Called Thinking?*, trans. J. Glenn Gray [New York: Harper, 1968], 140–1; his italics.)

7. Plato's use of *anamimnéskesthai* is normally in the passive form of "to be reminded of," as when some particularly equal things remind me of equality. Reminding is a matter of being put in mind of X or Y (not themselves

necessarily belonging to the past) by a presently perceived particular; and it can be so associative or automatic as not to include being-mindful-of at all. On reminding in Plato, see Richard Sorabji, *Aristotle on Memory* (London: Duckworth, 1972), 35ff.

8. Heidegger, *What is Called Thinking?* op. cit., 3 (my italics).

9. Maurice Merleau-Ponty, *The Visible and the Invisible*, trans. A. Lingis (Evanston, Ill.: Northwestern University Press, 1968), 266.

10. Edmund Husserl, *The Phenomenology of Internal Time-Consciousness*, trans. James S. Churchill (Bloomington, Ind.: Indiana University Press, 1964), 66.

11. Frances Yates, *The Art of Memory* (London: R. Bentley and Son, 1884).

12. Aristotle, *Physics*, ed. Richard McKeon, trans. R. P. Hardie and R. K. Gage (New York: Random House, 1941) 212a 20–21 (hereafter *Physics*).

13. "In a landscape we always get to one place from another place, each location is determined only by its relation to the neighboring place within the circle of visibility." (Erwin Straus, *The Primary World of Senses*, trans. J. Needleman [Glencoe, Ill.: Free Press, 1963], 319.)

14. Maurice Merleau-Ponty, *Phenomenology of Perception*, trans. C. Smith (New York: Humanities Press, 1962), 82.

15. On this point, see Straus, *The Primary World of Senses*, p. 322.

16. For further comment on this conception of forgetting, see Merleau-Ponty, *The Visible and the Invisible*, 196–97.

17. *Ibid.*, 222; his italics.

18. The body is "a place of passage [for] movements, received and thrown back" (Henri Bergson, *Matter and Memory*, trans. N. M. Paul and W. S. Palmer [New York: Doubleday, 1959], 145).

19. "The self can only be remembered" (Louis Dupré, *Transcendent Selfhood* [New York: Seabury, 1976], 72).

20. On this point, see Aristotle, *Physics* 208a 30: "the non-existent is nowhere."

21. Merleau-Ponty, *The Visible and the Invisible*, 253.

22. It ensues that in this situation the mind's modes of operation do not merely correspond to the structures of the world: they *are* the latter, or at least become profoundly akin to them in remembering. Plato, precisely when discussing recollection, remarks that "all of nature is akin" (*Meno* 81d). Merleau-Ponty, who speaks of "the 'Memory of the World'," says that "Being is the 'place' where the 'modes of consciousness' are inscribed as structurations of Being . . . " (*The Visible and the Invisible*, 253; preceding phrase from *ibid.*, 194).

23. Heidegger, *What is Called Thinking?* op. cit. 140 (his italics).

24. See Husserl, *Ideas*, trans. Boyce Gibson (New York: Macmillan, 1931), sects. 99, 111.

25. Aristotle, *Physics* 221b 2. I owe this felicitous translation to Peter Manchester.

26. Stanley A. Leavy, *The Psychoanalytic Dialogue* (New Haven: Yale University Press, 1980), 94, see also, 97, 110–111.

27. I take this last word in Derrida's sense, and would like to remark that place as I have described it does not fall prey to his critique of the metaphysics of presence. The outgoing "there" of place prevents its collapse into that proximity of the "here" which is the essence of presence as Derrida interprets this latter term.

5. From Another Past

David Wood

I hope I may be forgiven if I too begin with a reminiscence. Ten years ago at a British Society for Phenomenology meeting in Oxford I listened to a paper by a young American philosopher who was at the time working on the phenomenology of imagination. It was extremely well received. Afterward he and I met, and although the meeting was over very shortly, I was enormously impressed with the breadth of his philosophical concern and with his originality. At that time I had not thought about the future perfection of the memory mantle, nor did I imagine that the later interweaving of our paths would confer a founding significance on that original meeting. And yet here I am, and here he is, almost as young, still not wearing the bottoms of his trousers rolled, this time giving us a glimpse of what I am sure will one day be seen to have been a turning point in our understanding of memory.

Edward Casey's rethinking of memory is a product of a lively and imaginative "dialogue among thinkers" – in particular I suppose, Aristotle, Husserl, Heidegger, and Merleau-Ponty. Their questions and suggestions are kept in mind in a masterly way, in a thinking that, as Heidegger would say, is also a thanking.

Keeping the past in mind, is our mutual topic. Historically, "mind" has had two distinct senses, one relating to memory, and the other the attention to intention, to thought. There is no better way of loosening our deficient hold on the concept of mind than by considering the way it is implicated in a range of idiomatic expressions. And of these, none is better at unifying those senses of mind – mind as memory, and mind as attention – than the expression "keeping in mind." And it is from this dual sense that it derives its power to direct the path of our thought.

When Casey talks about keeping the past in mind, what is essential is not accuracy of recall, but a preservation of its power to speak to us, a preservation brought about by a reactivation which is, prop-

erly speaking, neither active nor passive. Accuracy is not fundamental. Might I perhaps add my Dylan Thomas to Casey's Eliot:

> One Christmas was so much like another . . . that I can never remember
> whether it snowed for six days and six nights when I was twelve or
> whether it snowed for twelve days and twelve nights when I was six
> Dylan Thomas, A Child's Christmas in Wales

And as for *keeping*, well, anyone who as a child possessed a horseshoe
magnet will remember that the bar across the poles, which preserved
its magnetic power, was called a "keeper."

How are we to understand this sense of the "neither active nor passive"? Let us listen to Heidegger;s words again: "what keeps us in our
essential nature holds us only as long as we for our part keep holding
on to what holds us."[1] And he says much the same thing when talking
about meditative thinking. Now the force of Casey's reference to Heidegger seems to me to be to give memory, as *keeping in mind,* an ontological
sense. Memory is here understood as a return to and a releasing of an
energized source, a source with a power to sustain and direct our being.

But in saying this I begin to ask myself whether I am just making
explicit what Casey intends, or whether I am running off in another
direction. In the first half of Casey's paper, he offers a phenomenological
exploration of various sorts of keeping in mind, one which listens to
and responds to language as well as to memory experiences. In consequence, he establishes the power and validity of a phenomenological
approach to memory over a naturalistic account (such as a physiological
one). In the second half, using a dialectical method he attempts to transcend the limitations of even a psychical account of memory, by an exemplary account of memory at work in the world – a phenomenology
of place.

Casey describes his first approach as an "intentional account." And
yet there is already so much more. First of all he puts to one side all
representational forms of memory and only then does he have the space
to talk about memory as a keeping and a keeping in mind. And this,
as I have indicated, leads him, still in the first half, to a grasp of memory
as something like self-appropriation, an understanding which I call
"ontological." By "ontological" I mean a *concern* for the being of the
thinker, for his or her self-understanding, and self-enactment. And to
the extent that such an ontological understanding of memory already
transcends mind understood purely intentionally and psychically, the
first half of the paper exhibits something like an autodeconstruction
of the intentional. It is not by chance that this should be brought about

by a thinking guided by a reflection on language, as well as on experience.

The ontological dimension returns, I would suggest, at the end of the paper. It returns, I believe, at a point at which Nietzsche's Sils Maria experience of the Eternal Recurrence is being reworked, and to great profit. It returns in the form of a recommended ideal of experience, one which gives this whole account of memory an application to both the present and to the future. Let me quote:

> It is a matter of viewing the present not *sub specie aeternitatis,* nor as a subject for possible nostalgia, nor even as an occasion for anticipatory resoluteness, but as having an unsuspected significance as it *shall have come to be remembered* at not-yet-determinable future moments.

This he goes on to say does not involve prophecy, but imagination, and its effect is to "valorize the present," "to show it as more than we take it to be."

I am very sympathetic to ideas on how we can reflexively intensify the present. But I wonder if this way of valorizing the present does not involve a restricting of the very imagination it employs. It is important that we talk about the significance that the present shall come to have at different future moments (with an *s*) because that emphasizes that the work of interpretation is never done, that the significance of the present is infinitely deffered, at least in principle. But what of all the unfulfilled significances of the present, what of those meanings destined to fall by the wayside, what of the infinite wealth of its weave, of things seen and half seen, wondered or imagined, what of the insane desire, say, to send one's audience into undreamed of intellectual raptures, hopes, possibilities which, when judged in any realistic way, are fantastic, but give depth and texture to the present? Is there not a danger that in giving future retrospections the last word that we subject the present to the limitations of likely or possible future judgements? Is therenot, in short, a conflict between two different values associated with the present: (1) the joyful play of possibilities *not* subject to the rule of judgement and; (2) the reflective intensity born of the awareness of the possible future significances of the present?

Yet this is a fascinating account both for its descriptive subtletier and the theoretical shift it inaugurates and encourages. Casey mentions the role of the body in constituting *place* on a number of occasions. But perhaps because Merleau-Ponty has already trodden this ground, it is not the body and its memory structure that Casey traces, but that of place, which is incontrovertibly "out there." As he says at one point:

> It is this building itself which holds certain significant memories of mine
> . . . acting as a veritable gathering place for them.

And who has not had this experience? Think of one's study and its memories of deadlines only just met, books whose slow accumulation seems to defy the active/passive distinction, the filing cabinets with their memories, and those coffee-stained traces of the past. Think of returning to the Latin Quarter and the smell of North African pastries. Think of where you grew up and all the sights and sounds still clinging to that place, or those places. Is one's memory not in some vital respect *kept* quite outside oneself, coded in those places where so much has happened?

Rather than pick my way carefully through Casey's admirable account, I would like to delineate three reservations that occurred to me while reading his paper. First, the reality status of "place," second, the basis of place's "primordiality," and particularly the relationship between place and repeated event, or repetition, and thirdly, the priority of place with respect to time.

The first point is quite simple, I am not sure from Casey's account whether places have to continue to exist to function the way he suggests, and whether, even if they do exist, one has to have continued acquaintance with them. Are there not important differences between the role of memory in (1) places we inhabit, (2) places we return to having previously inhabited or frequented them, and (3) places in which some of our strong memories have their setting, but which may not even exist any more? Casey picks out for special note the second case, which is close to what he calls "presentment." But I am not sure whether it matters to him which we choose. Two years ago, on an ordinary evening in New Haven, while visiting Yale, I set off to revisit the house in which I had lived for a year as a boy. With difficulty I found the street. I could not remember the name, but I recognized the street when I saw it. I had a vivid memory of the house and the street, and yet all that I remembered had vanished. Yes, the houses were there, the street was there, but I could find nothing corresponding to my detailed memory of the place. The whole street had fallen on hard times. Even the cherry tree in the backyard was gone. In contrast, my subsequent memory of that place grew even more vivid as my failure to find it as it had impressed itself on me. In this experience, the memory of place is preserved despite the radical failure of presentment. And the experience is made sense of only by my understanding each place as occupying a different epoch, a different temporal stratum. In any town in which urban renewal has taken place, an even more radical version of this experience, that of the physical destruction of the places in which one grew up, must be commonplace. In these circumstances, is not the possibility of temporal ordering, such that one can say *once that,* and *now this,* is a great reassurance? Now if places that no longer exist (or perhaps even fictional places one has read about, or seen in the movies) can function as memory banks, is it not memory that preserves the place rather than the place memory? If one restricts *place* to continuing existing places that one inhabits or frequents, as I suspect Casey would do, is not the memory preserving function dependent on the temporal persistence of the place, and on the temporal structure of one's eventful frequenting of the place? This is my first reservation.

My second concern is with the status of "place." When first introduced it is as "one basic dimension of the world" and yet later Casey refers to its "primordiality." And I get the feeling that equiprimordiality would not do. Now some of the natural candidates for the title of primordiality are those features of the world that Casey mentions: things (monuments, relics, mementos), and tools, dwellings, collective memories shared with others, archives, those strange ontic hybrids, automobiles, and much of our technoskeletal existence.

Now given the choice between things and places, I would agree that places, offering as they do the possiblity of total body hook-up, an absorption that surrounds and permeates, have a more powerful role to play in memory. But I am not convinced that place is more primordial than the repeated event. Think of birthdays, festivals, the recurrence of the seasons, of meetings (like SPEP), sporting events, the daily arrival of the paper and the mail, the regularly scheduled departures of airplanes, the flowering of the lilac tree by the back door, doing the income tax returns, the succession of days and nights, and so on. Are not such events just as public and part of the external world as places? Cannot the repeated event equally lead us out into the world from the fictional sanctuary of the mind?

And do not many places derive the memory power they do have from the repeated events associated with them, or which have occurred there? Does not the structure of repetition bring about something like a scaffolding of time that may be quite independent of place? SPEP is such an event, an annual event, a moveable feast. By participation in this event, we can commemorate the event that began the series, the founding event. We say quite generally of events that take place. Do not repeated events take over place? Do they not appropirate the places they take over? It it not the structure of repetition of events that makes many a place into a place in which to accumulate memories? On this view, places would often be preserved via event repetition, rather than vice versa.

I am a little hesitant about opposing repeated events, cyclical events, events that contain within themselves the traces of their repetition structure, to places in this way, because Casey has shown us, in the first half of his paper, how seriously he himself takes events. Perhaps I could put my question in this way: would we really want to try to relegate the repeated event to the psychical level of memory? And if not, do not repeated events have as strong a claim to worldliness as place? Lastly, is not the structure of event repetition – which Casey himself seems to acknowledge when he talks about the need for memories to be revived from time to time – the basis for much of the significance for memory that places have?

The last point is the priority of place to time. I think Casey is absolutely right to say that time should not have a monopoly of our understanding of memory. Place, primordial or not, clearly makes a considerable contribution to our keeping the past alive and allowing ourselves to be directed by it. But I am not wholly convinced by the account he gives to time, such that place becomes *such an important* corrective to a temporal understanding of memory. If his account of time fairly reflects the way it is thought of in treatments of memory, we ought not just correct the privilege of time in memory, but transform our understanding of time itself.

Place is needed, it is suggested, to protect us against "the ravages of time"; time is inherently dispersive. Place holds on to what time scatters, and allows us to hold on to it. But are things really quite like that? Places can be destroyed, and all they have gathered in can be scattered to the winds. And time exhibits structures of repetition, of rhythm, of ordering, of sequential intelligibility of many sorts that are essential to the preservation that memory requires. In Conrad Aitken's words

> All's here, all's kept, for now
> Spring brings back the self same apple bough
> that braved the sea three hundred years ago.
>
> from the *Mayflower*

Time does not just destroy, it sets up transtemporal identities by repetition, and it also heals. Moreover it establishes that distance which is essential for memory in the first place. My temptation is to point the finger at the concept of time as dispersiveness, rather than just a historical blindness to place. Arguably, in the structure of the repeated event, we have a paradigm of a temporal gathering on which place memory often, but not always, depends.

In my view the real importance of Casey's thesis lies firstly, in the opening up of the whole field of nonrepresentational memory by a potent mixture of theoretical justification and phenomenological description, and secondly, in his rediscovery, or reminding us, of place and its place in memory, and lastly, his account of the founding event and the future perfection of the memory mantle.

I conclude with a comment from C. S. Lewis, *Out of the Silent Planet*, which illustrates the principle well:

> A pleasure is full grown only when it is remembered. You are speaking . . . as if the pleasure were one thing and the memory another. It is all one thing. . . . What you call remembering is the last part of pleasure. . . . When you and I met the meeting was over. Very shortly, it was nothing. Now it is growing something as we remember it. But still we know very little about it. What it will be when I remember it as I lie down to die, what it makes me in all my days till then that is the real meeting. The other is only the beginning of it.
>
> C. S. Lewis *Out of the Silent Plant*

Note

1. Martin Heidegger, *What is Called Thinking?* trans. J. Glenn Gray (New York: Harper and Row, 1968), 3.

6. Distance, Absence, and Nostalgia

James Phillips

Nostalgia was a term first used in 1678. It was coined in order to elevate to the status of a formal medical entity the pathologic homesickness frequently observed at the time, and over the next three hundred years nostalgia's use as a medical equivalent to pathologic homesickness slowly receded and evolved into the phenomenon we now recognize by the term.[1] In pursuing nostalgia in this paper, I will approach the experience from two different perspectives, phenomenologic and psychoanalytic, hoping through this double approach to shed light both on nostalgia and the differences between these two perspectives.

II

Beginning first with a phenomenologic consideration of the nostalgic experience, I will suggest approaching nostalgia through a reflection on the transformation of homesickness into nostalgia. If there is any doubt that there is a significant difference between the two experiences, merely reflect on the attitude of the subject toward each. Consider first the sufferer of homesickness, whether an exile or a child at summer camp. Which of these would welcome his condition, would see it as anything but a deprivation, as something to be overcome? Now consider the nostalgic, who not only would not deplore his condition but would even revel in it, feel enhanced by it, and wish to linger in it. This marked difference in attitude alerts us to how extensive has been the change which homesickness has undergone in its transmutation into nostalgia.

The terms of homesickness are home, exile, distance, longing, and return. We readily grasp the sense of these terms, whether they be used to describe the young conscripts posted on foreign soil who were the occasion of the first description of nostalgia,[2] or whether the exile in question is Odysseus, twenty years trying to return to Ithaca. The issue is always that of someone who has been wrenched from his home, who misses it, and longs for return. What then is the fate of these terms as homesickness becomes nostalgia?

In order to address this question we must trace the process of interiorization, which homesickness has undergone in becoming nostalgia.[3] Nostalgia is more subjective, less literal than homesickness. In nostalgia, concrete experiences of separation from one's homeland become merely symbolic of internal states of mind. Terms such as home, exile, and return assume metaphoric meaning. Since time and not space the the more internal modality, the emphasis in modern nostalgia shifts from space to time.[4] Odysseus longs for home; Proust is in search of lost time. Further, since space is retraversable but time is not, the return is possible for the homesick exile in a way that it is not for the nostalgic.

This contrast of homesickness and nostalgia may be summarized around the notion of distance, to which both are related. Homesickness and nostalgia each represents a longing to bring the distant near. For each, exile is the distant and home the near. Now distance is, as Straus indicates, "the overarching, spatio-temporal form of sensing."[5] We cannot understand distance except as a spatio-temporal unity. However, while it is in the distance of homesickness that the spatial dimension prevails over the temporal, it is in the distance of nostalgia that the reverse occurs, the temporal dimension prevailing over the spatial. Thus we may even reread the *Odyssey* by the canons of nostalgia and remark that Odysseus does not fully return, for he recovers his home but not his youth. And even his home has been altered by time. The temporal loss is thus more profound, always encroaching on the spatial sphere.

It is to the time-laden distant world of nostalgia to which we now turn for closer analysis. In trying to describe the distinctive way in which the past is posited in nostalgia, we may first question just how past the nostalgic's world must be. I will suggest a nostalgic threshold, on the side of which events are too recent to evoke nostalgia. The time of nostalgia stretches out vaguely from the more than recent to the indefinitely distant past. I might feel nostalgic over a song from the sixties, a scene from my childhood, a story of American settlers, a tableau of prehistoric paintings, or a sense of a lost Eden.

The past of nostalgia is not just experience; it is memorialized as past. The nostalgic's world is always stamped, made in the past. But for events to be experienced *as past*, they must be experienced in relation to what follows them. The "I was" of recall is always accompanied by an "and I was to become." When I recall events from my childhood, they are experienced in retrospect, with a view to what followed, and are labeled, "my childhood." Further, when I long nostalgically for my childhood, that childhood is in a sense created now, in nostalgia; back then I merely lived and was not a spectator of my childhood.

Understanding how the past is memoralized in this manner, we can also appreciate how the present may be experienced nostalgically. For this it must be experienced as past — that is, in the future perfect. In experiencing myself from the point of view of a projected future, I accomplish the same nostalgic distancing which I carry out with regard to the past. This is very far from Minkowski's vital present, always creating the future before it.[6] It is closer to Rilke's vision of man in the eighth elegy as "someone who's departing . . . for ever taking leave."[7]

Related to this sense of nostalgic time as memorialized is its tendency to crystallize into precious moments. Indeed, any moment may seem precious just because past, because inscribed "once only." But, in fact, I select out certain moments, assign them more nostalgic valency. Events are fashioned into a kind of imaginary product in which memory, distortion, forgetting, and reorganization all play a role.

Related to the preciousness of the nostalgic past is its peacefulness. In the present, life as lived, is stretched out, divisive, confused, conflicted, or anxious, while nostalgia imposes a unity and simplicity — and thus a peacefulness — on the past of which the present is not capable.

A final quality of the nostalgic past is its irrecoverability. There is no nostalgic memory, no nostalgic image, which is not accompanied by an awareness of the event as past and irrecoverable. It is this awareness which imparts to nostalgia its peculiar pain. And it is this awareness of irrecoverability combined with the other, more satisfying, qualities described above which makes for the bittersweet feeling distinctive of nostalgia. The past as experienced in nostalgia is both pleasurable and painful. The precious moments are at once bitter and sweet — bitter because lost, all the more sweet for being lost.

These features of the nostalgic past are aptly illustrated in a familiar piece of literature, Thornton Wilder's *Our Town*, a drama which produces a powerful nostalgic response through the evocation of the passage of time. From the beginning of the play spatial factors give way to temporal ones. The voice of time is that of the narrator, who speaks from the present and follows the action of the play with a knowledge of what will come later. The drama culminates in the final act when, from the perspective of the graveyard, one of the characters, Emily, looks back and relives a day of her childhood, thus sharing in death the prescience of the narrator. He tells her, "you not only live it; but you watch yourself living it. . . . And as you watch it, you see the things that they – down there – never know. You see the future. You know what's going to happen afterwards."[8] What she discovers is the extent to which her appreciaiton of life is a product of her retrospection, of her nostalgia, how different it is from her lived life.

With Wilder's play we may conclude this section in addressing an essential ambiguity of nostalgia. On the one hand, the nostalgic is an exile of the present, lost in the rush of lived experience, longing for a return to oneself, for a recovery of the self as lost in the passage of time. Nostalgia emphasizes human incompleteness in its temporal dimension – the way in which our finitude is conditioned by temporality. It is the self as divided and split temporally which is lamented in nostalgia. It is both my historicity and historicity itself which are lamented. But if the nostalgic lives under this fate of an ever-increasing distance from the past, he also experiences a kind of recovery. In nostalgia, distant time is brought near. Indeed, paradoxically, it may be nearer than when actually lived – as the lost moments of Emily's life were experienced so much more intensively in her retrospective vision of them. Thus the ambiguity of nostalgia – an overcoming of history which is enjoyed only at the end of history. We are left wondering whether the recovery of lost time, which is achieved in the nostalgic evocation, represents a retrospective deception or a retrospective insight, whether it is unreal or real. We will hold this question for later.

III

In moving now to a psychoanalytic perspective on nostalgia, let me begin with two brief clinical examples. The first involves a young man in the midst of a separation and divorce. In a therapy session he reports a dream which depicts his wife and himself together in several loving, playful scenes. He describes these as typical scenes which did or might have taken place. They fill him with a sense of regret and nostalgic longing for the lost relationship. But as we look more closely at the dream, what emerges is that the relationship was never quite as depicted in the dream. Even at the beginning, such idyllic scenes were clouded with a portent of conflict. It becomes clear that he is nostalgic over a relationship which never actually existed as represented in the dream. The second example concerns a nineteen-year-old young man who is attending school away from home. He spends his summer afernoons walking the streets of the small town of his school, glancing over hedges to catch a glimpse of other peoples' lives. He yearns for family rooms, patios, barbecues, swimming pools – all the markers, which for him, define a family. His father died at an early age, and his relationship with his mother has always been troubled. He also appears to be longing for something which never existed.

These two vignettes serve to direct our attention to the different perspective which psychoanalytic theory will bring to our topic. To begin with, there is a methodologic shift. We are now studying the experience of nostalgia from the vantage point of the consulting room. Subjective reflection has been replaced by interpersonal dialogue and the speculations based on it. In this setting, nostalgia emerges in the context of otherness. It is now the lost other who is longed for. Distance is now absence. Nostalgia is now a lament not over distance but over absence, an attempt not to bring the distant near but to render the absent present. Exile is now separation, the return reunion.

The second feature which emerges in these examples is the unreal quality of the nostalgic quest. The longed-for figures tend to dissolve under analysis into phantoms. This phantom-like character of the nostalgic objects is related to the psychoanalytic tendency to devalue direct experience in the effort to burrow beneath it for unconscious meanings and objects; and at the same time it is the psychoanalytic equivalent of the devaluation of present, lived time described in the previous section.

These features are readily present in a majority of the psychoanalytic papers dealing with nostalgia. These authors treat nostalgia as a fantasied response to loss through an imagined recreation of the lost object. They note, however, that the nostalgic fantasy of fulfillment and the accompanying sense of satisfaction, is based on a past fulfillment which was real – namely, in the early life of the individual. The obscurity of the nostalgia is based on the repression of the early object, a repression required for growth and separation from the mother. The repressed object has in fact been named differently by the various authors. Thus Freedman discovers in the nostalgically recalled places where his patient has been taken as a child the traces of pregenital mother.[9] The preoccupation of Sterba's patient with her old dribbling cloth, associated with nostalgic feelings, points to the mother's breast as the repressed object of nostalgic longing.[10] And the manner in which Fodor's patient recalls longing at eighteen months for a previous life suggests a location of the nostalgic object in the prenatal state.[11]

These papers are of limited interest, as they suffer from the worst aspects of psychoanalytic reductionism. A complex phenomenon is reduced to its genetic precursors, and all later manifestations are interpreted as merely screens for the earlier phenomenon. A more sophisticated treatment is offered by a French analyst, Dominique Geahchan, who locates the absent object of nostalgia not in another person but rather in the nostalgic's ego-ideal.[12] The nostalgic object thus represents a narcissistic structure of the personality. The nostalgic cannot relinquish his search for the lost object because that would represent giving up his own narcissistically invested, grandiose self-image. He projects the narcissistic ideal onto others, who always disappoint him because they are not equal to the grandiose expectations placed on them. The interest of Geahchan's paper for us is that it is now not simply the absent, repressed mother who is longed for nostalgically, but rather the mother as internalized into a personality structure. The entire theory of internalization is thus introduced into the discussion of nostalgia. Geahchan presents this as an internalization into the ego-ideal, an amalgam of self and other in which the mother becomes somewhat depersonalized but at the same time more deeply imbedded in the personality. In the case of the patient going through a separation from his wife, the illusory quality which pervades his longing reflects not just the hidden presence of his mother behind the figure of his wife, but even more the internalized structure containing an idea of himself that was supposed to be realized through his wife. Accepting the unreality of the relationship would mean giving up an image of himself.

While the article by Geahchan deepens the relationship of nostalgia to absence by focusing on internalization, I would like to take a further step in this direction by introducing a series of studies which have not been related to nostalgia but bear on the topic. These again have to do with separation, loss, and internalization, but internalization from another point of view. I will begin with Freud's now famous anecdote of his grandson's spool.[13] The child devises a game of throwing away and retrieving the spool, accompanying these gestures with the words, "gone," "here," − "fort," 'da." As the game appears related to the child's struggle to cope with the comings and goings of his mother, it offers an illustration of the birth of symbols and language. The struggle over the absence of the real mother is shifted into a symbolic order − and on two levels, that of the concrete object, the spool, and that of words, fort, da. It is now around the spool that the drama of presence and absence is played out. The mother, absent in reality, can now be made to be symbolically present.

A further step in the development of this theme of separation, loss, and symbolization was taken by the British analyst, D. W. Winnicott. In 1951 he first described the concept of the transitional object, that special piece of the material world – the security blanket, as we most commonly know it – which represents an intermediate area between self and nonself.[14] At the beginning the mother supports the infant's illusion of his own omnipotence – specifically that the breast is always available and therefore part of the self. It is on the way to accepting the breast – and the mother – as separate that the infant creates the transitional object. This object, symbolizing the lost breast, carries forward the illusion that a piece of the objective world is still subjective – still filled with subjective meaning and imbued with the power to comfort that has hitherto been placed in the mother. Winnicott develops his thought further. We eventually lose interest in the specific transitional object, but we do not give up the transitional realm. In fact that realm is expanded into the whole of symbolic, cultural experience.

Further work on the relationship of separation and loss to symbol formation has been done by two other British analysts, Wilfred Bion and Hanna Segal, both of whom were influenced, as was Winnicott, by the work of Melanie Klein.[15] Relating the origin of verbal thought to Klein's depressive position, they connect the recognition of the mother as whole and separate with the establishment of verbal thinking. Language then substitutes for the absent mother. In Segal's words;

> The symbols are also created in the internal world as a means of restoring, recreating, recapturing and owning again the original objects. . . . The capacity to experience loss and the wish to recreate the object within oneself gives the individual the unconscious freedom in the use of symbols.[16]

These notions, adumbrated by Freud and developed by these later analysts, may be directly related to our theme of nostalgia. If the transitional object and language have the original and intimate connection with absence just described, they may be seen as inherently nostalgic phenomena. The transitional object – concrete, unarticulated, preverbal – and embodying for the infant the lost state of oneness with the mother – may be thought of as the earliest precurson of nostalgia. And language, developing out of separateness and always involving a making present of the absent, is to be considered of itself a nostalgic act.

In this pursuit of psychoanalytic nostalgia we have reviewed three levels of psychoanalytic speculation: that of the mother as the repressed and unconscious object of nostalgia, that of the ego-ideal, a personality structure based on internalization, and that of the transitional object and language. These phenomena comprise the archeology of nostalgia, to use Freud's and Ricoeur's term.[17] They are the fundamentals on which adult nostalgia is constructed. They all imply absence, require absence, and compensate for absence. Because of this complex relationship to absence they remain highly ambiguous. Language, for instance, is founded on absence, on a lack; but it turns lack into a presence which threatens to be more real than the missing presence which it replaces. My patient, for instance, wanders the streets searching for a home. The word "home" calls into presence something, a sense of family, which is missing in his life. If no family experience he has had or will have is equal to his idea of family, we say that this is because his idea of family reflects an earlier, preverbal experience of maternal oneness. But this earlier experience is after all a conjecture, a vision of presence made on this side of the fateful separation . Since the polarity of presence and absence arises only with the first separation, the presence which is yearned for in psychoanalytic nostalgia is in a way the creation of that nostalgia itself. This parallels the manner in which, in the previous section, the nearness which was achieved in nostalgia – my childhood experienced as a childhood – was seen to be a creation of the nostalgic evocation.

IV

In this concluding section I would like to review and contrast the two perspectives on nostalgia already outlined. On the one hand, phenomenonogically, nostalgia is seen as a response to distance from the spatial-temporal world – a distance in which temporal factors predominate over spatial ones – and as an attempt to bring this distance near. On the other hand, psychoanalytically, nostalgia is seen as a response to the absence of the other, and as an attempt to make the absent other present. In both cases we are dealing with a kind of negativity of the present – the nostalgia expressing a regret over the fact and the necessity of the negativity. Further, in both cases the nostalgia reveals the negative present and virtually creates the anterior state of plenitude.

In underlining the differences between the two views let me again remark on the different methodology – on the one hand, a reflection on the direct experience of nostalgia, on the other hand, a series of conclusions drawn from an interpersonal therapeutic situation. The conclusions of both aim at the distant precursors of the adult phenomenon and at the same time focus on aberrant variants of the adult phenomenon, specifically on nostalgia as manifested in the irrational pursuit of the maternal derivatives under the pressure of the repetition compulsion. While we may grant the methodological differences and the different interpretations which emerge from them, we may still question whether the latter cannot be reduced, whether each interpretation does not in some manner imply the other. At least in some measure we can demonstrate such a merging of interpretations. If nostalgia posits a world which fades into the distant past, that past does not just involve myself but must include the network of others who were my life at that time. The distance from that time thus implies an absence of others − and even an absence of those aspects of myself which have remained attached to the departed others. And, on the other hand, the absence of the other on which we base psychoanalytic nostalgia likewise implicates the past, the past of this vital relationship and of its sundering, and my past as a participant in that process. I do not just long for the absent other but for myself as temporally estranged in that epoch.

What remains of the difference between these two interpretations of nostalgia? I will suggest that there does remain a fundamental difference, based ultimately on the different experiences of world in the two disciplines and on the different myth of origin from which each evolves. The notion of world is taken from the lexicon of phenomenology and has only limited applicability to psychoanalytic thought, which is oriented, by its methodological strictures and its therapeutic aim, to expound only a world of interpersonal relationships. The driving force in this world is the wish, which motivates actions and determines the endless permutations of the self-other relationship. The background of this world is the maternal-infant unit, out of which self and other evolve. This original unit is the myth of origin of psychoanalysis, the source of its world. It is the plenum from which separated existence develops. But the plenum is never experienced as such; it is only recognized later, from the vantage point of its absence − and, we will say, from the vantage point of nostalgia. Nostalgia, then, in this psychoanalytic reading, reveals a world of interpersonal separateness and harkens back to an imagined world of preseparation. The poignancy of my patients' nostalgias derives from the hopelessness of their search, from the fact that each approach to the supposed object will prove it to be less than the sought-for unity.

To this psychoanalytic reading we may contrast the phenomenologic experience of nostalgia and the world which it unfolds. If the lost Eden of psychoanalytic nostalgia is maternal oneness, for phenomenologic nostalgia it is the unreflective world. This is the plenum which forms the background of individualized experiences and to which nostalgia will now point us. It cannot be simply an object of reflection, as it forms the background of all reflection. In reflection we are forever trying to get back to it. To quote Merleau-Ponty; "The task of a radical reflection, the kind that aims at self-comprehension, consists, paradoxically enough, in recovering the unreflective experience of the world."[18] He multiplies expressions in trying to point to this world of unreflective experience. It is our "prehistory," "a kind of original past, a past which has never been present," "the horizon of all horizons, the style of all possible styles," "the native abode of all rationality,"[19] "wild being," and the world of "perceptual faith."[20] That this litany is so extensive, and could be further extended, points to the difficulty in conceptualizing this primordial world. It is to this world which nostalgia points. It is near because it is everywhere, yet distant because it must be approached through the categories of reflection. To quote Rilke again, whose eighth elegy is devoted entirely to this theme, we are "spectators always, everywhere, looking at, never out of, everything," whose destiny is "being opposite, and nothing else, and always opposite."[21] Now the experience of the nostalgic world as described in the first section – in terms of memorialized time, precious moments, irrecoverability – is an experience of reflection. it is Wilder's Emily *reflecting* on her childhood. The experience is indeed hypocritical, in the same manner that Merleau-Ponty says of the feeling for eternity that it is hypocritical, because it "feeds on time."[22] But it is genuine inasmuch as it represents the nostalgic's attempt to articulate a recovery of the unreflective source of experience. When Emily, at the end of the play, says, "Good-by, world . . . Good-by to clocks ticking . . . and Moma's sunflowers. And food and coffee. And new-ironed dresses and hot baths,"[23] she is evoking the unmediated presence of her world. That she is able to do this only retrospectively and nostalgically attests to the difficulty of directly experiencing this world. it must always be recovered, returned to. In her evocation of her world, Emily's estrangement from her lost childhood merges with the reflective distance which is always separating us from a direct experience of the world. She longs for an overcoming of both.

Nostalgia in this sense, a lament over our condition as spectators of life and a longing for recovery of immediate contact with the world, remains different from nostalgia as a yearning for maternal oneness. It is the difference between the recovery of oneness and the recovery of the world as one.

Notes

1. See G. Rosen, "Nostalgia: a 'Forgotten' Psychological Disorder," *Psychological Medicine* 5 (1975), 340–54; M. Bachet, "Etude sur les Etats de Nostalgie," *Ann. Med. Psych.* 108 (1950), T.I., 559–87, T.II., 11–34; J. Hofer, "Medical Dissertation on Nostalgia," *Bull. Hist. Med.* 2 (1934), 376–91.

2. Hofer, "Medical Dissertation."

3. For discussion of this process see J. Starobinski, "The Idea of Nostalgia," *Diogenes* 54 (1966), 81–93.

4. Developed at length in V. Jankelevitch, *L'Irreversible et la Nostalgie* (Paris: Frammarion, 1974).

5. E. Straus, *The Primary World of Senses*, trans. J. Needleman (London: Free Press of Glencoe, 1963), 383.

6. E. Minkowski *Lived Time*, trans. N. Metzel (Evanston: Northwestern University Press, 1970).

7. R. Rilke, *Duino Elegies*, trans. J. Leishman and S. Spender (New York: W. W. Norton and Co., 1939), 71.

8. Thornton Wilder, *Our Town* (New York: Coward McCann, 1938), 114.

9. A. Freedman, "The Feeling of Nostalgia and its Relationship to Phobia," *Bull. Phila. Assn. Psychoanal.* 6 (1956), 84–92.

10. E. Sterba, "Homesickness and the Mother's Breast," *Psychoanal. Quarterly* 14 (1940), 701–7.

11. N. Fodor, "Varieties of Nostalgia," *Psychoanal. Rev.* 37 (1950), 25–38.

12. Dominiue Geahchan, "Deuil et Nostalgie," *Rev. Fran. de Psychanal.* 32 (1968), 39–65.

13. Sigmund Freud, "Beyond the Pleasure Principle" (1920), in *The Standard Edition of the Complete Psychological Works of Sigmund Freud* (London: Hogarth Press, 1955), J. Strachey, ed., 18; 14–16.

14. D. Winnicott, "Transitional Objects and Transitional Phenomena" (1951), in D. Winnicott, *Through Paediatrics to Psycho-Analysis* (New York: Basic Books, 1975), 229–43. See also D. Winnicott, *Playing and Reality* (London: Tavistock Pub., 1971).

15. See Wilfred Bion, "Second Thoughts," *Selected Papers on Psycho-Analysis* (London: Heinemann Medical Books, 1967); Hanna Segal, "Notes on Symbol Formation," *Int. J. Psycho-Anal.* 38 (1957); also Melanie Klein, "The Importance of Symbol Formation in the Development of the Ego" (1930), in Melanie Klein, *Contributions to Psycho-Anal.*, 1921–1945 (London: Hogarth Press, 1948).

16. Segal, "Notes," p. 395.

17. Sigmund Freud, "The Interpretation of Dreams" (1900–1901), in *Standard Edition*, 5; P. Ricoeur, *Freud and Philosophy: An Essay on Interpretation*, trans. D. Savage (New Haven: Yale University Press, 1970), 459.

18. Maurice Merleau-Ponty, *Phenomenology of Perception*, trans. C. Smith (New York: Humanities Press, 1962), 241.

19. Ibid., p. 240, 242, 330, 430.

20. Maurice Merleau-Ponty, *The Visible and the Invisible*, trans. A. Lingis (Evanston: Northwestern University Press, 1968), xxxv, 3.

21. Rilke, *Duino Elegies*, 69–71.

22. Merleau-Ponty, *Phenomenology of Perception*, 423.

23. Wilder, *Our Town*, 124.

7. Nostalgia:
Experiencing the Elusive

E. B. Daniels

"She was one of those tireless wanderers who go to bed
night after night to dream of bacon-lettuce-and-tomato
sandwiches. . . ."
   – John Cheever, "A Woman without a Country"

One winter afternoon in New York City, the mezzo-soprano acclaimed as *prima donna assoluta* of La Scala, the Metropolitan Opera, Covent Garden, and other opera houses, gave a bravura recital of arias and lieder by Rossini, Vivaldi, and Mahler. Then, in the glittering gold-and-white house at Lincoln Center, this same woman, Marilyn Horne, born in the rural hills of Bradford, Pennsylvania, sang these words by Stephen Foster to her audience, known by all her fellow countrymen since childhood:

I long for Jeanie with the day-dawn smile,
Radiant in gladness, warm with winning guile;
I hear her melodies, like joys gone by,
Sighing 'round my heart o'er the fond hopes that die:
Sighing like the night wind and sobbing like the rain,
Waiting for the lost one that comes not again:
Oh! I dream of Jeanie with the light brown hair,
Floating, like a vapor, on the soft summer air.

Thus, dreaming, I return to my mother tongue, my homeland, my heartland, so real, so ephemeral, so elusive.

In an earlier paper, it was suggested that nostalgia, hovering at the crossroads of imagination and memory, was "a moment of reaching out, itself reaching out toward the infinite horizons of past and future; an immanent moment always yearning to transcend itself in its rich horizons of melancholy, menace, sentiment, dream" (Daniels 1982, 7). Nostalgia is "truly *Heimweh*: the yearning to return to an experience of community . . . of family . . . we imagine hidden in home – all the homes, where like the pot of gold at the end of the rainbow, we think we will find our lost home: the home of our everyday-life world, our world-as-community, and the community of our world-as-home" (Ibid., 10). Inherent in the elusive nature of nostalgia is the difficulty in evoking it through description; nostalgia, like home, "means different things to different people . . . home means one thing to the man who never has left it, another thing to the man who dwells far from it, and still another to him who returns" (Schütz 1945, 370). But this very evanescent, transitory quality is characteristic of nostalgia: in grasping it, like cotton candy, it disappears. In Andrew Wyeth's painting, "Christina's World," the vibrant moment of Christina's reaching out, struggling upward from the brown field to the house on the horizon, seems forever captured. But on a visit to the house years following Christina's death, after it had been bought and restored by the movie producer, Joseph E. Levine, the initial glad surprise at still finding the house of the painting turns to shock as one discovers that the original weathered siding has been replaced by a modern, cleverly painted sham; that the house is empty, lifeless, only a shell.

A visit to a farmhouse in upstate New York, owned by nostalgia buffs, does not reveal nostalgia. I look at the beautiful antiques, the old pictures, the little framed homilies harking back to the friendship of simpler times. I sit helpless on the old horsehair sofa, surrounded by ancient fringed pillows, the teddy bears, the collectible toys and souvenir glass, all the dreams of my elderly, smiling hosts, and the gossamer vapor of nostalgia fades into the sweet, sickly air of decay. Through the open kitchen door I see the perfectly clean linoleum floor, covered by a spotless rug, the rug in turn covered by a freshly laundered terrycloth towel. Dust and dirt, the hard stuff, the realities of change, the veil of time, have been lifted in this living museum.

In the towns of southeastern Connecticut, fine old colonial homes are bought and lovingly restored; tourists come to catch a glimpse of the new owners: June Havoc, Sylvia Sidney, now themselves objects of nostalgia. In his book, The Stepford Wives (1972), Ira Levin captures the nostalgia of the men living in these towns of skyscraper and saltbox, these high-tech executives who, helpless to find their own dreams, grow fascinated with the manufactured nostalgia of television: grandmas with homey, clean houses and kitchens, ruffled aprons, homecooking, families staying together watching television. Nostalgia becomes demonic as the men of Stepford, with the power of the new technologies at their disposal, create perfect robot replicas of their wives, programed to behave like the television grandmas, with which they replace their murdered wives. The Stepford men, driven crazy by nostalgia, in a fantastic attempt to recreate the community of their nostalgia, capture only a horrible illusion. But do we, in our shock and anxious laughter, know why we are nostalgic, for what we search? Do we, like Cheever's swimmer (Cheever 1980), begin exhilirating Sunday afternoon lark swimming through the neighbors' pools, only to find ourselves in a grim, compulsive journey through every pool in the county on an eight-mile trip home, wondering why we make the journey, and finding the house empty after we arrive? What is this desire for home, the desire of dreams and nightmares, or the desire for gladness and suffering? Thus,

> in continuing the quest for a word that most nearly captures the "tone," the "feel," the "texture" of the subjective state of nostalgia, one is, ironically, drawn closer and closer to the "diagnosis" made by Dr. Johannes Hofer some three centuries ago, to wit: homesickness. . . . There is perhaps no word that better evokes the odd mix of present discontents, of yearning, of joy clouded with sadness, and of small paradises lost (Davis 1979, 29).

While the present-day tendency in examining nostalgia has been to consider it "modified by an understanding that for moderns it is a homesickness severely stripped of connotations of geographic place and psychopathology" (Ibid.), a qualification that is not necessarily helpful in elucidating this elusive phenomenon. The Swiss physician, Johannes Hofer, made it quite clear in his dissertation of 1688 that the sickness for one's native land manifested itself both psychically and physically:

> including a tendency to melancholy arising from the individual's nature, an aversion to foreign customs and social gatherings, intense annoyance and anger at any jokes aimed at the individual, as well as the slightest injustice or inconvenience, and constant expressions of praise for his native land coupled with disparagement of other regions. The actual occurrence of nostalgia is revealed by a continuing melancholy, incessant thinking of home, disturbed sleep or insomnia, weakness, loss of appetite, anxiety, cardiac palpitation, stupor, and fever (Rosen 1975, 342).

A revised edition of Hofer's dissertation, published by Theïssen Zwinger during Hofer's lifetime, emphasized the connection of these bodily sufferings to the longing for one's country by substituting the word "pothopatridalgia" for nostalgia (Hofer 1688, 376). This eighteenth century pothos remains a part of contemporary nostalgia, as emphasized quite recently by Hillman (1974) in an article on nostalgia entitled, "Pothos"; and the symptoms Hofer described resulting from this desire, while perhaps no longer considered a disease process of organic etiology, remain embodied in ways quite familiar to any boot-camp sergeant or summer-camp counselor.

Thus, attempts to pin down nostalgia are akin to chasing a dream, while standing back and allowing the full weight of its historicity, its bodily antecedents to emerge, reveal a phenomenon of incredibly rich and varied horizons. While these horizons can only be hastily sketched at the present time, it should benoted that neither a formal noetic-noematic analysis nor a hermeneutic explication can wholly grasp a desire that can become sickness. Only the suffering of experience, of return to experience, will serve to restore nostalgia to the fulness of meaning of which it has been "stripped" in the twentieth century: its birth in the body, in the primary world of the senses. With these remarks, let us again look more closely at what it means to be sick for home.

Few composers, in speech and music, evoke more explicitly, more vividly, the desire for home, for one's native land, for *patria*,then Guiseppe Verdi. Here, nostalgia does not culminate only in community-as-family. Despite the profound family relationships, the intensely interpersonal conflict and longings present in Verdi's operas, what the family members are singing about to one another is striking: Aîda with her father, longing for her native land of Ethiopia; the elder Germont reminding his son of their homeland in Provence; the conflicts between erotic and patriotic passions besetting Don Carlos. And finally, in *Nabucco*, the breathtaking chorus where an entire nation, whether the community of Italians of *Risorgimento* times, or the community of Hebrews in captivity in Babylon – cries out in a revelation of nostalgia:

Va, pensiero, sull'ali dorate;
Va, ti posa sui clivi, sui colli,
Ove olezzano tepide e molli
L'aure dolci del suolo natal!

. . . Oh mia patria si bella e
    perduta!
O membranza si cara e fatal!

Go, thought, on golden wings;
Go, rest yourself on the slopes
    and hills,
Where, soft and warm, murmur
The sweet breezes of our native
    soil.

. . . Oh my country so beautiful
    and lost!
O memory so dear and fatal!

(Verdi 1842, Part III)

And so, too, this vast efulgence of nostalgia swells from a peaceful murmur, a reverie, to the golden, fortissimo shout that sweeps across chorus to orchestra brass, transcending opera house, to become the dream of a nation. Here is not an individual looking for community, but community looking for home. And yet this search also takes place at the most intimate, the most personal level, so poignantly captured by John Cheever in describing the elusive search for home:

> It was time to go home, and she got a plane for Orly that night and another plane for Idlewild the next evening. She was shaking with excitement long before they saw land. She was going home; she was going home. ... They circled the field once and came down. She planned to find a lunch counter in the airport and order a bacon-lettuce-and-tomato sandwich. She gripped her umbrella (Parisian) and her handbag (Sienese) and waited her turn to leave the plane, but as she was coming down the steps, even before her shoes (Roman) had touched her native earth, she heard a mechanic who was working on a DC-7 at the next gate singing [the hated song that had finally driven her from her country so many years before].

> She never left the airport. She took the next plane back to Orly and joined those hundreds, those thousands of Americans who stream through Europe, gay or sad, as if they were a truly homeless people. They round a street corner in Innsbruck, thirty strong, and vanish. They swarm over a bridge in Venice and are gone. They can be heard asking for ketchup in a Gasthaus above the clouds on the great massif, and be seen poking among the sea caves, with masks and snorkels, in the deep waters off Porto San Stefano. She spent the autumn in Paris. Kitzbühel saw her. She was in Rome for the horse show and in Siena for the Palio. She was always on the move, dreaming of bacon-lettuce-and-tomato sandwiches (Cheever 1980, 505).

The promise of the promised land remains elusive. Hofer noted, in his seventeenth century account of nostalgia, that patients could be cured not only by actually returning home, but by being given the promise of returning home. One wonders what actually happened to those who did return home; promises kept are not always promises fulfilled. As Schütz had pointed out,

> in the beginning it is not only the homeland that shows to the homecomer an unaccustomed face. The homecomer appears equally strange to those who expect him, and the thick air about him will keep him unknown. ... From the point of view of the absent one the longing for reestablishing the old intimacy − not only with persons but also with things − is the main feature of what is called "homesickness" (Schütz 1945, 373–76)

Nostalgia presents a problematic of intimacy - an intimacy with persons and things, community and country, an intimacy with a world which is not me but of which I am yet a part. Memorabilia – traces – of a world remembered with a fond, but bittersweet, golden glow, become more profound in homesickness; the longing for the intimacies of my past world pulls at my guts; but if I return in reality to my native land, I may be confronted with strangeness; in fantasy, as in *The Stepford Wives*, dream becomes nightmare, and the confrontation is with horror. Elusive pothos becomes confusion in space and time – even the space and time constituted within my own body.

So an experience, nostalgia, in its mundaneity at times appearing so lightweight, so trivial as to be nothing more than the sentimental, the embarrassment of the cliché, reveals at other times a desire for a return to an intimacy so profound as to paralyze an individual or fire a nation. Straus (1962, 31), speaking interestingly enough of memory traces, says "we have to learn again the mother tongue of human experience. We must practice grasping correctly the meaning of such expressions as the wondrous 'I was' and the 'again.'" Experience is the stuff of philosophy and of psychology. Nostalgia is most assuredly of concern to psychotherapists who seek in experience to move beyond questions of psychopathology and of *techne* to wonder, why psychotherapy? Why now? Why in this world? The intimacy of human experience, and its estrangement, was what interested Freud, what interested an Irish-American farmboy from Chenango County, New York – Harry Stack Sullivan – what possessed Stephen Foster, whose nostalgic quest was sung and dreamed again by a famous diva in return to her American roots at Lincoln Center. Regardless of the source of their difficulties in biogentic and environmental interactions, it is what brings patients to the consulting room – the crazy, the sad, the lonely, the frightened, the angry. And it is a search for intimacy – an intimacy with things and with persons – that will characterize the effort in the consulting room; for as Freud's twin discoveries of the resistance and the transference continue to reveal, there will be no psychotherapy without confronting the problem also raised by nostalgia: how to come to terms with a desire constitued in the space and time of my own body to return to intimacy with the world – a world of people, of things, of the psychotherapist. It was not theoretical statements, no matter how abstruse, how arcane, which resulted in Jacques Lacan's expulsion from the International Psycho-analytical Association, but a simple, direct, even violent gesture toward intimacy, the intimacy of the transference: varying the length of the sessions over the course of an analysis (Turkel 1978, 105-118).

Can we still look again at this fragile but powerful phenomenon; this dream of intimacy as insubstantial as a "vapor, floating on the soft summer air," but a dream with a sensibility to move people and nations. Nostalgia is not simply a reverie, but has a certain momentum. The walls of the familiar old farmhouse where I write "come at" me – not in an overpowering or stultifying way, à la Sartre, but in a rush of supporting solidity, in a heft of durability permeated by warmth and the smell of the patina of ages. There is an insistent quality to the sounds of the wind sighing through the pines in the windbreak. I cannot ignore these things; they precede reflection. In nostalgic experience, I become aware of the timelessness of the eternal Cosmos; and at once also aware of my temporality, my own ever-changing body. Gathered up in the moment of nostalgia, I am carried in a rush from now to then and back to now, and in that whirl of time I know with Schütz that "others become older, die, and the world continues on (and I in it.) It is indeed one of my basic experiences that I become older. I become older; thus I know that I will die and I know that the world will continue" (Schütz and Luckmann 1973, 47). And in an effort to stop change – to stop my rush toward the end of intimacy – I try to stop the world. Thus in another farmhouse, the gentle, elderly ones transfix the world: stuff it with the objects of nostalgia, the teddy bears and throw pillows, the antiques and old photographs, but it is a creation that pleads with others to see it, to be in it, to lend it validity, lest it collapse into the filth and decay that accompanies the hoarding of the miser – the miser, who "paralyzed by fear of the future, holds onto the past" (Straus 1970, 157–79). And yet nostalgia offers not only the immanence of my own end but, in some strange way, the possibility of its transcendence. Christina, reaching perpetually toward the house, that shining house transfigured beneath its weathered siding, stretches endlessly toward past and future, reaches in this moment beyond time.

But nostalgia is always changing, always evanescent – it is memorable, but without the heaviness of the memory of the depressed; it has a fullness and vibrancy not to be found in the moment of reminiscence; there is a momentum lacking in the frozen moment, the suspension of time, in fascination. How fleeting nostalgia is: on a nondescript day during the February thaw, I drove past the Amish house where last summer the quilts, shoofly pies, and gentle warmth of these simple people seemed caught up even in the homely stuff of their clothes to create a golden ambiance in which my own little blond daughter met the little Amish girl in her prayer bonnet, with all the innocence of two babes from other ends of the world and time (Daniels 1982, 8–9). This particular day there is no nostalgia. The shop is closed, buns and quilts gone. There is only a very old house, painted a preposterous chartreuse. Modern farm implements and an old buggy stand incongruously outside among the brown weeds, grim leafless trees, and dirty half-melted snow. Nostalgic reveries give way to unpleasant reflections on ugliness and decline, to last night's news where the governor of a western state, in a moment of nostalgic madness for the cowboy ethos, welcomes MX missiles to his environs. And then I return to the Amish house this summer, once again in the warm summer glow of an August day — and there it is: the house is alive, the bread actually is hot, the quilts are not polyester imitations, the grandmother really is a wonderfully simple, warm person with whom to talk. Looking around the side of the house, I see the little Amish girl in her prayer bonnet, and her brother with his suspenders and bowl-cropped hair, walking on the rungs of a ladder stretched across two small barrels. She slaps him through the rungs, gives him a swift whack on his head, and then turns with a grin running over to my intrigued daughter. I spot the mutual look of possibilities for fresh devilment pass between them; so does the pouting brother who panics and heads to the kitchen for his mother. I retrieve my daughter and leave before further mayhem takes place; the sweet nostalgia of last summer is no longer here. Not now. But there was. And can be again. There is something about presence — presence of the world — of things, and of others — that has to do with nostalgia. The Amish house, like a church supper, has a living, changing quality. The other farmhouse has stopped: it is filled with nostalgic trinkets like some museum of the mundane, its occupants the haunted keepers of the house. In nostalgia I touch the presence of the past; I long for its return. The world — the other — greets me not with the deadliness it held for Sartre in the horror of fascination, nor even with the authoritative but competitive heft of Straus's Allon. It greets me with the lightest of embraces, but one which I can never forget, and of which I dream. How often the dream is caught up in the house, that house for which Christina — and everyone — yearns. In this, nostalgia has a mythic quality, noted by Eliade:

Rocquet: And it isn't only the house that is "sacred," or the temple, but the territory, the land itself, the homeland.

Eliade: Every homeland constitutes a sacred geography. For those who have left it, the city of their childhood and adolesccence always becomes a mythical city. For me, Bucharest is the heart of an inexhaustible mythology. And through that mythology I have succeeded in getting to know its true history. And my own too, perhaps (Eliade 1982, 30–31).

Indeed, this mythology is captured in Wyeth's paintings of the Olson family, which extend over a twenty-year period. The seeming solidity of the house itself, of the Maine coast where the Olsons lived, did not change Wyeth's feeling "that it's all going to blow away" (Gilbert and Holt 1976, 3). Christina Olson, herself the subject of the most famous of this series, "Christina's World," when asked why she favored this particular painting, replied, "In ["Christina's World"] Andy put me where he knew I wanted to be. Now that I can't be there anymore, all I do is think of that picture and I'm there" (Wyeth 1982, 272). Nostalgia is a dream, a fantasy about return; and not necessarily a return to something that never was. It is a fantasy about what was, and now is lost. Because it is a dream, nostalgia is, in a sense, about neither what was, nor what never was; it masquerades as memory. Thus, there is in nostalgia not simply a sensibility, a yearning for what appears past and beyond return, but a feeling now of what is to be lost in the future. In the solidity of the farmhouse walls, I dream of the past sedimented in them; but as I touch them, I am aware that this moment also will pass, and that tomorrow, not yet here, will also come and pass, and I will leave the old house. In nostalgia, I dream also now of returning to what I shall lose in the future. Wyeth conveyed this in some of his final studies of the Olsons, most noticeably "Room after Room." "All that summer Wyeth was working almost constantly at Olsons', perhaps because he sensed there there would be a dramatic change if [Christina's brother] had to be moved away or hospitalized" (Wyeth 1982, 235). The painting itself is a view through the shed, into the kitchen and pantry, where Christina, partially hidden, is seated, and then, through an open door, into the dining room beyond. And beyond. And still beyond. Like many of Wyeth's paintings, the seeming realism masks the surrealistic quality, in this case, the infinite regress of the rooms beyond, like a series of mirrors endlessly reflecting themselves, so that there is a sense of an endless future, but already a future as becoming past. In nostalgia, there is a sense of ambiguity to the present moment; a sense also mirrored on the Maine coast as the morning fog lies out at sea so that the horizon disappears, a sense sometimes heightened by the appearance of islands, islands as a Stonington woman put it, "suspended in the air" (Hance 1983). And yet this suspension has a dynamic quality, like catching one's breath; in "Christina's World," a flash of pink on her dress, or, in "Room after Room," a bolt of blue on the door, electrify these otherwise somber colors, so that caught up in the moment of now are the hidden horizons of past and future whirling through. Indeed, it is not simply intimacy − a return to a lost intimacy − which characterizes transference in psychotherapy, but a living through time in a tumult of lost and misplaced effects. Neither catharsis nor interpretation, nor both together, can be the components of psychotherapy, but rather also a reliving now of the dream to return to what was and what will be, veiled in the horizons of time. "'Home is where one starts from,' says the poet. 'The home is the place to which a man intends to return when he is away from it,' says the jurist. . . . Where I come from and whither I want to return is my 'home'" (Schütz 1945, 370). But the home of my dreams, for which I search in the therapist's office, lies, always, beyond the horizon, beyond, in the sense toward which Levinas (1969) strives, the horizon of horizons.

Can we glimpse beyond this home of which I dream – "not merely the homestead – my house, my room, my garden, my town – but everything it stands for" (Schütz 1945, 370) – can we glimpse beyond the horizon? I step from within the Maine woods; the soft earth and spruce needles, the lush ferns, the fragrances are now disturbed by another smell from further away, the small briny tidewater pools. The salt air rushes at me, and I step into the sunlight and out onto the rocks; in an instant the enveloping softness of the pine woods rushes away, sweeping out across the transparent, mirror surface of the sea to meet the blinding, sunlit horizon. The horizon breaks up and melts in the morning fog at that zenith – and there, suspended beyond the horizon, are the islands. Caught up, I too rush out, skimming across the sea to approach the horizon moving toward me, enveloping me, and moving beyond it – for there, beyond the horizon, lies the dream, and nostalgia's pothos bursts and is transfigured in a moment of gladness. For indeed, it is in these ambiguities of boundary, this horizon where sea and sky meet in the ambiguity of fog, in the ambiguity of the sea's surface, that the ambiguity of nostalgia is transcended. Here, the hardness of the gray rocks and cliffs on which I sit disappears into the liquid movement of the sea. Here gravity is both felt and suspended. My body is both my home and my horizon. The sun glints on the sea with the "lightness of fireworks" (Eng 1966, 74–83); and there, suspended like a dream beyond that illuminated horizon, are the islands of my home, my world. All is caught in this brief, evanescent, always changing moment of sea's end and fog – even the ambiguity of boundary where earth meets sea, not in the plangent crash of surf, but in the still small ripples, the little sounds of the ever-moving tides. Motherland, fatherland – a mythic moment, yes, but a moment grounded in body and earth, these heavy rocks, appearing beneath the surface of the water, so clear, so transparent – so different than the rocks on which I sit; the sea, like the fog, transfigures. Even the fog itself, the very essence of ambiguity, is transfigured. In the sunlight, the fog glints and reflects, like a snowbank. This is not a gray fog shrouding, but a fog which in hiding the horizon, reveals what lies beyond in a flood of light. Like Wyeth's paintings, there is a flash of light, but here at the sea, it is a refulgence which envelops and embraces, before leaving. And all of this is so fleeting — the lost horizon momentarily revealed in a glad rush of recognition, disappears, not into the fog, but into everyday life, leaving, like fading fireworks, a renewed nostalgia (Eng 1966, 77). The fog, a vapor in the soft summer air, dissipates, and the islands remain, still beautiful, still evocative. But no longer beyond the horizon, but set here in the sea of earth, my home, this side of that once and again lost horizon.

Nostalgia, then, moves toward hope — the hope for ourselves, our home, our earth — the same hope that despite initial despair, anger, or madness, brings anyone into the therapist's office. As Baldini points out, the artistry of Verdi's *Nabucco* lies in more than a powerful analogy of the Italian *Risorgimento* with the story of the captive Hebrew nation under Nebuchadnezzar:

> It is better to say that in . . . Nabucco . . . one observes both an overwhelming desire and, at the same time, a nostalgia for affections which have been lost, or are soon to be lost, as well as anxiety to recover them, and joy at doing so. . . . The "Va, pensiero" chorus depicts, with unusual intensity and expressive power, an overwhelming longing for a lost good, and this ultimately raises itself into the shining nobility of hope. . . . But the chorus is no more beautiful merely because it can be interpreted as referring to a specific current situation; at best, it becomes more beautiful because these feelings, which are always present within the human spirit even when there is no oppressor — oppression can be a completely interior fact — are so fully expressed that they *also* include the suggestion of an analogy with actual living fact (Baldini 1980, 53–55).

Though the evocation of the artist, nostalgia can be shared: my hearth, my home, my family are transcended in my community, my people, my country. And yet, always here at its heart is this moment of intimacy occurring now. Whether for myself or for humanity, nostalgia hides within itself, in its apparent yearning for the past as it was, or never was, or the future as it may be, or may never be, the desire for an intimacy-at-home-now. The swirling, moving horizons of nostalgia, horizons of space and time, veil my desire. Thus, nostalgia blurs consciousness, blurs memory: after leaving the nostalgic setting of the Oyster Bar in Grand Central Station where I saw the wonderful old photograph of the turn of the century liner, "SS Majestic" in New York harbor, I find myself unable to remember whether the proud old ship

was setting sail or returning home. Similarly, Verdi nostalgically recalled the circumstances under which he wrote *Nabucco* some forty years
later in a letter to Giulio Ricordi:

> On my way [home] I feld a sort of indefinable malaise, a deep sadness,
> a pain which welled up in my heart! . . . I arrived home, threw the [lib-
> retto] onto the table with an almost violent gesture, and stood in front
> of it. As it fell on the table, the book opened; without knowing how, my
> eyes fixed on the page which lay before me, and I caught sight of this
> line: Va, pensiero, sull'ali dorate (Baldini 1980, 50).

And so he resumed composing, he says, after having only recently suffered the loss of not only his son and daughter, but his wife as well.
It has been noted that in this letter Verdi "puts his son's death before
his daughter's. He also telescopes the death of his wife and two children
into a three-month period. Actually, of course, they died over a period
of three years" (Martin 1963, 95). But then, nostalgia is a dream, and
as in all dreams, the horizons of space and time are altered. Nostalgia,
like transference, deals with dreams, with their creation, their shatter-
ing, their apotheosis. These are dreams of intimacy occurring in the
time, the space, of my lived body, and its mystery of growing older.
They are dreams, riddles, of the lost. Again with John Cheever, we
return to the sea:

> Each year, we rent a house at the edge of the sea and drive there in the
> first of the summer. . . . Our affairs are certainly not written in air and
> water, but they do seem to be chronicled in scuffed baseboards, odors,
> and tastes in furniture and paintings, and the climates we step into in
> these rented places are as marked as the changes of weather on the beach.
> . . . Sometimes the climate of the place seems mysterious, and remains
> a mystery until we leave in August. Who, we wonder, is the lady in the
> portrait in the upstairs hallway? Whose was the Aqualung, the set of
> Virginia Woolf? Who hid the copy of *Fanny Hill* in the china closet, who
> played the zither, who slept in the cradle, and who was the woman who
> painted red enamel on the nails of the claw-footed bathtub? What was
> this moment in her life? . . .

> But outside the windows we hear the percussive noise of the sea; it shakes
> the bluff where the house stands, and sends its rhythm up through the
> plaster and timbers of the place, and in the end we all go down to
> the beach — it is what we came for, after all — and the rented house
> on the bluff, burning now with our lights, is one of those images that
> have preserved their urgency of their fitness. Fishing in the spring woods,
> you step on a clump of wild mint and the fragrance released is like the

essence of that day. Walking on the Palatine, bored with antiquities and life in general, you see an owl fly out of the ruins of the palace of Septimius Severus and suddenly that day, that raffish and noisy city all make sense. . . . After dark we shake up a drink, send the children to bed, and make love in a strange room that smells of someone else's soap – all measures taken to exorcise the owners and secure our possessions of the place. But in the middle of the night the terrace door flies open with a crash, although there seems to be no wind, and my wife says, half asleep, "Oh, why have they come back? Why have they come back? What have they lost?"

(Cheever 1980, 568–70)

The riddle of what is lost is the riddle of what we shall find. "The homecomer is not the same man who left. He is neither the same for himself nor for those who await his return. . . . Each homecomer has tasted the magic fruit of strangeness, to be sweet or bitter" (Schütz 1945, 375). Beyond the horizon lies the lost and the yet to be found. Nostalgia's dream is its own answer:

Eliade: One rediscovers the whole past in space: a street, a church, a tree. Suddenly time past has been regained. That is one of the things that make traveling such an enrichment of self, of one's own experience. One finds oneself again, one can communicate with the person one was fifteen, twenty, years before. One meets him, one meets oneself, one meets one's time, one's historical moment, of twenty years ago.

Rocquet: Might one say that you are a man of nostalgia, but of joyful nostalgia?

Eliade: Yes. Yes! That's very well put, and you're quite right. I rediscover precious things though such nostalgia. And in that way I feel that I never lose anything, that nothing is ever lost.

(Eliade 1982, 101)

And so in the dream of nostalgia lies the elusive lost, appearing and receding in the soft vapors beyond the horizon, beckoning in an ever-renewed nostalgia. There is in the present, through the incarnate grace of my endless horizons into past and future, a past that was, transfigured in a present epiphany coming to greet me from a future that will never be – a future always too future – and then receding in a blinding flash, the blazing fog of the present, dissipating into a past becoming what never was – a past always, and infinitely, too past.

References

Baldini, Gabriele. 1980. *The Story of Guiseppe Verdi.* Cambridge, Eng.: Cambridge University Press, 1980.

Cheever, John. 1980a. "A Woman Without a Country." In John Cheever, *The Stories of John Cheever*, 499–505. New York: Ballantine Books.

_____. "The Seaside Houses." In Cheever, *Stories*, 568–78.

_____. "The Swimmer." In Cheever, *Stories*, 713–25.

Corn, Wanda M. 1973. *The Art of Andrew Wyeth.* New York: Little, Brown.

Daniels, Eugene B. 1982. "Nostalgia and Hidden Meaning," unpublished paper.

Davis, Fred. 1979. *Yearning for Yesteryear: A Sociology of Nostalgia.* New York: Free Press 1982.

Eliade, Mircea. 1982. *Ordeal by Labyrinth: Conversations with Claude-Henri Rocquet.* Chicago: University of Chicago Press.

Eng, Erling. 1966. "The Lightness of Fireworks." In *Conditio Humana*, edited by Walter von Baeyer and Richard M. Griffith, 74–84. New York: Springer Verlag.

Gilbert, Katherine Stoddert, and Joan K. Hold, editors. 1976. *Two Worlds of Andrew Wyeth: Kuerners and Olsons.* New York: The Metropolitan Museum of Art.

Hance, Ebba. 1983. Personal communication.

Hillman, James. 1974. "Pothos: The Nostalgia of the Puer Eternus." In *Loose Ends: Primary Papers in Archetypal Psychology*, 49–63. Dallas: Spring Publications, 1975.

Hofer, Johannes. 1688. *Medical Dissertation on Nostalgia.* In *Bulletin of Historical Medicine*, 1934, trans. Carolyn Kiser Anspach, 2, 376.

Levin, Ira. 1972. *The Stepford Wives.* New York: Random House.

Levinas, Emmanuel. 1969. *Totality and Infinity: An Essay on Exteriority.* Pittsburgh: Duquesne University Press.

Martin, George W. 1963. *Verdi: His Music, Life and Times.* New York: Dodd, Mead.

Rosen, George. 1975. "Nostalgia: A 'Forgotten' Psychological Disorder," *Psychological Medicine* 5; 340–54.

Schütz, Alfred. 1945. "The Homecomer," *American Journal of Sociology* 50; 367–76.

Schütz, Alfred, and Thomas Luckmann. 1973. *The Structures of the Life-World.* Evanston, Ill.: Northwestern University Press.

Straus, Erwin. 1962. "On Memory Traces," *Tijdschrift voor Philosophie* 24e Jaargang, Nr. 1, 1-32.

———. 1970. "The Miser." In *Patterns of the Life-World.* ed. James M Edie, et al., 157-80. Evanston: Northwestern University Press.

Turkle, Sherry. 1978. *Psychoanalytic Politics: Freud's French Revolution.* New York: Basic Books.

Verdi, Guiseppe. 1963. *Nabucco.* English translation by George W. Martin in *Verdi: His Music, Life, and Times,* New York: Dodd, Mead. (1842).

Wyeth, Betsy James. 1982. *Christina's World.* Boston: Houghton Mifflin.

8. The Sources of
Experienced Temporal Features

Peter K. McInerney

E xistential phenomenological ontology, following in the tradition of Kant, has sought the sources of the temporal features of the world of experience in the temporalizing activity of human being, rather than in the temporal character of things-in-themselves. A transexperiential, ontologically real time has been denied primarily because it has been thought unnecessary to account for the temporal character of experienced entities. The most basic time has been claimed to be that of the temporal features of the activities of human being (and consciousness), which activities constitute the world of experience. In Husserlian terminology, it is the activities, such as passive synthesis, on the noetic side of consciousness that are the source of the temporal structure and temporal features of experienced entitites.

Existential phenomenologists are not alone in claiming that activities that are definitive of human being (and consciousness) are an important determinant of the temporal features of the world of experience. Many psychologists and other philosophers would agree that human cognitive and motivational activities, such as those of retaining information and of projecting it into the future, strongly influence the ways in which humans experience and understand the temporal features of things. Theorists who want to distinguish the experienced temporal characteristics of things from the ontologically real temporal characteristics (perhaps as described by scientific theory) will have to appeal to something about the structures, capacities, and activities of human experience in order to explain why humans do not directly experience the ontologically real temporal characteristics.

The major difference between this more psychological thesis and the existential ontological position is in the postulation of an onto-

logically real time. While admitting that the activities of human consciousness play a major role in structuring the temporal features of
experienced entitites, proponents of the more psychological position
maintain that appeal to ontologically real temporal features that are not
directly experienced is necessary in order to account for some aspects
of the temporal features that are experienced.

This essay will examine the phenomenological grounds for Sartre's
thesis in *Being and Nothingness* that temporality is an ontological
structure only of what exists for itself.[1] Sartre's phenomenological
descriptions of the temporality of experiencing and of the temporality
of experienced things, although sometimes difficult to separate from
the ontological points with which they are intermingled, provide
essential support for his ontological claim about temporality. After
explicating how Sartre's phenomenological accounts support his ontological thesis and summarizing these phenomenological accounts, I will
argue that his attempt to locate the sources of all the temporal features
of the world of experience in the temporalizing activity of Being-for-
itself nevertheless fails.

I

In at least one straightforward way, phenomenological description
is relevant to an ontological theory. Phenomenological descriptions
provide a pretheoretical organization and clarification of the subject
matter for which an ontology has to account. For a subject matter as
complex as temporality, this clarification can be very significant;
structures of experienced temporality can emerge (or fail to be noticed)
that give direction to an ontological account.

A phenomenology of time needs to describe both the (experienced)
temporal features of entities that appear to consciousness and the
temporal features of the *experiencing*. Both the objects of consciousness
and the noetic acts are temporal; a phenomenology should describe
these temporalities and how they are coordinated with each other. The
temporal character of noetic acts is sometimes neglected in discussions
of time. That a retentive act of a previous event is itself past or present
according to some (usually unrealized) version of pastness or presentness is an important phenomenological fact. Only when the temporality
of experienced acts becomes explicit can issues be raised about the
relationship between this temporality and the temporality of the objects
of consciousness. This relationship between the temporalities has
significant implications for any ontology of time.

Sartre's distinctive phenomenological claim about temporality is that the *temporality of experiencing is different from the temporality of the objects of consciousness*. The "original temporality of the For-itself" is different from the "time of the world," and this difference is disclosed phenomenologically. Yet the two temporal characters are coordinate with each other. Consciousness must be past in order to be conscious of past states of the world and must be future in order to be conscious of future states of the world, even though the character of the pastness and futurity of experiencing is different from that of the object of experience.[2]

Sartre's phenomenological claims about the two different temporalities provide the major support for his ontological claim that all temporal features of the world derive from the temporalizing activity of Being-for-itself.[3] Sartre claims *to find phenomenologically* that the temporality of experiencing is *more basic than* and *the source for* the temporality of the objects of consciousness. The experienced temporal character of objects of consciousness is found, Sartre claims, to be a hybrid of the temporality of the For-itself with the a-temporality of the In-itself.

> Nevertheless the a-temporality of being is *represented* in its very revelation; in so far as it is grasped through and in a temporality which temporalizes itself, the *this* appears originally as temporal; but in so far as it is what it is, it refuses *to be* its own temporality and merely *reflects* time. . . . It is not true therefore that the non-temporality of being escapes us; on the contrary, it is *given in time* . . . [4]

The description of this "hybrid temporality" in terms of Being-for-itself and Being-in-itself is, of course, a description at the ontological level; however, the evidence or basis for this ontological summary is phenomenological description of the two temporalities.

If the temporal character of the objects of consciousness was indeed found phenomenologically to be completely derivative of the temporality of consciousness itself, this would make very plausible Sartre's ontological thesis (which is just one form of his general thesis that all *determinateness* of the objects of consciousness, such as quality, quantity, potentiality, and spatiality, derive from Being-for-itself because they all include negation or relation). To evaluate this phenomenological basis, Sartre's phenomenological accounts of the temporality of consciousness and of the temporality of the objects of consciousness must be separated off from his ontological arguments. All too frequently Sartre claims to be doing phenomenology when he is actually arguing ontologically that since the being of the object of consciousness is Being-in-itself and Being-in-itself contains no internal relations or negations, the object of consciousness cannot contain some specific internal relation or negation (such as quality or potentiality). After summarizing in the next two sections Sartre's phenomenological descriptions of the two temporalities, I will evaluate in Section IV and V the strength of his phenomenological argument.

II: Temporality of the Objects of Consciousness

According to Sartre, the world that is experienced is composed primarily of instrumental things, that is, of distinct enduring things with qualities that are related to each other in terms of their possible instrumental uses together in achieving some desired state of affairs (composed of instrumental things) through action. Instrumental things are experienced (at any given time) as being past, present, and future, and as being immersed in the passage of time from future to present to past.

A. Instrumental things as past, present and future.

1. Instrumental things as past
   a) having been present[5]
   b) contributing to the meaning of what is present[6]
   c) being completely determinate and without possibility[7]
   d) cannot be used as an instrument or perceived

2. Instrumental things as present
   a) presence to perception either as focus or as background[8]
   b) presence to action (part of the instrumental complex being used)[9]
   c) being in motion[10]

3. Instrumental things as future
   a) what will be present (determined future)[11]
   b) what might be present[12]
   c) what is to be made present[13]

4. Categorial connections of instrumental things as past with instrumental things as present.

5. Categorial connections of instrumental things as future with instrumental things as present.

B. Instrumental things as immersed in the passage of time.

1. Instrumental things as present becoming past
   a) displacement of what is present by the new present (which was future)
   b) becoming fully determinate and without possibility[14]

2. Instrumental things as future becoming present
   a) "slipping by of In-itself instants"[15]
   b) what is lacking in the present situation being made present[16]

A. Most of the temporal features of the instrumental thing require little explication.

1. (a) It is obvious that what is past has been present, and it is experienced as formerly being present.

   (b) The past states of instrumental things affect what the thing now is in at least two ways. Firstly, it makes a difference that there are past states at all; otherwise the current state would be that of a newly existent thing. Secondly, the specific past states make a difference concerning whether the current state is usual or unusual and whether it is an enduring characteristic or part of a process of change; for example, if brightly colored autumn leaves dangling from a tree were always that way, trees would be quite different things.

   (c) The past of instrumental things is completely determinate and without possibility. States of things and states of affairs that could have been different are now fixed and unalterable.

   (d) Sartre does not discuss the notion that instrumental things as past cannot be used instrumentally or be perceived, but these features follow from the fact that the past is no longer present.

2. (a) States of instrumental things and states of affairs involving several instrumental things are present in so far as consciousness is present to them either as the focus of perception or as the context (ultimately including the entire world) from which the focus stands out.

   (b) States of instrumental things and states of affairs involving several instrumental things are present in so far as acting consciousness uses them in its simple action to attain its goals.[17] A simple action is one that is experienced as an undivided unit, as not composed of a series of shorter term actions. What is used in the course of a longer term action (which is composed of a series of simple actions) need not be present.

(c) Sartre also claims that the present of universal time is defined by the motion of enduring things from place to place. His thought is that being in motion requires a type of "exteriority to itself" that is the appropriate reflection onto Being-in-itself of the For-itself's present. This claim appears not to be at all phenomenologically based, however. Certainly not all motion is experienced as in the present. If a body moves uniformly for ten days, we can inquire concerning which temporal part of that motion is present.

3. (a) The essence of an instrumental thing includes all of the characteristics that it will have (assuming that it is not destroyed by human agency). What will be present includes both those characteristics that are permanent through time and those characteristics that result from inevitable change. However, none of these characteristics really exist according to Sartre until they are present; they are "being beyond being."

(b) Within the essence of the instrumental thing there is also a range of possibilities concerning characteristics of things and states of affairs. One or another of these possibilities will come about, either through human action or through the mere passage of time.

(c) Humans experience instrumental things as composing a "world of tasks" where certain states of affairs are to be brought about through action. What is to be made present is that which the present states of affairs lack.

4. In terms of the above features of instrumental things as past and as present, there do appear to be some obvious categorial connections between them. Pastness is partially defined by having been present (A1a), and what it is that is present is partly defined by its past (see A1b). Furthermore, being completely determinate and without possibility (A1c) seems to characterize the present as well as the past of instrumental things, although this does not make them mutually constitutive.

5. There also appears to be some obvious categorial connections between instrumental things as future and as present. All three features of futurity are defined with respect to the present. Conversely, the future characteristics of a thing seem to affect its pre-

sent by partially defining what it is that is present (by defining the essence, just as a thing's past does). Furthermore, present states of affairs are lacking only in constrast with future more perfect totalities, and instrumental complexes are used and usable only in order to bring about future states of affairs.

B. According to Sartre, there is very little to be said about instrumental things as immersed in the passage of time other than that they do change from future to present to past. There is nothing in the instrumental thing itself to require or to make intelligible this becoming; the future states of instrumental things just slip by into the present and thence into the past. The passage of time is dependent entirely on the activity of acting consciousness.[18]

1. (a) States of instrumental things and states of affairs become past by being displaced from the present by new present states. What is displaced does not disappear entirely but slips by into the past.
   (b) The transition from present to past is the acquisition of the distinctive characteristics of being past. Sartre describes consciousness' transition from presentness to pastness as a matter of becoming factual, that is, fully determinate and without possibility. However, instrumental things are already factual in the present. For instrumental things, becoming fully determinate and without possibility (A1c) best describes the transition from future to past, since both the present and the past are factual. The inability to be used as an instrument or to be perceived (A1d) best distinguishes the past from the present.

2. (a) States of instrumental things and states of affairs also become present through the apparently external slipping by of instants. What will be present (A3a) and part of what might be present (A3b) move from the future to the present in this way.

   (b) However, there is a second type of transition from future to present, that in which acting makes some desired state of affairs present. The lack of relationship between present and future does provide some basis for the transition from future to present. However, if value is indeed consciousnes-dependent, both this lack of relationship and the action motivated by it derive from consciousness as Sartre's thesis claims.

III: Temporality of Acting Consciousness

That which experiences the temporality of instrumental things is human being, what I will call "acting consciousness" in order to avoid the ontological features of Sartre's term "Being-for-itself." The phenomenological essence of acting consciousness is such that at any given time there is necessarily a pastness, presentness, and futurity of consciousness and an activity wherein the futurity is becoming present and the present is becoming past.

Sartre's phenomenological descriptions of the temporality of acting consciousness cover some features that are not directly concerned with the experiencing of other temporal things; for example, there are features of the pastness of acting consciousness that are not directly concerned with being conscious of the past of instrumental things. However, these do ultimately play a role in being conscious of the temporality of instrumental things. It should also be emphasized that the experiencing of instrumental things (with their temporal features) is not a matter of interestless perception. Both perceiving and using these types of experiencing, and each refers to the other.

A. Acting consciousness as past, present, and future.

1. Acting consciousness as past
   a) having been present in perceiving or using to _____[19]
   b) acting consciousness as fact (ontologically: the For-itself-become-In-itself)[20]
   c) having to be its past; responsibility[21]

2. Acting consciousness as present
   a) being present perceptually to _____[22]
   b) being present through action to _____[23]

3. Acting consciousness as future
   a) having projects; what I am to be[24]
   b) projects as possible (freedom)[25]
   c) possible presence to _____[26]

4. Categorial connections of acting consciousness as past with acting consciousness as present.

5. Categorial connections of acting consciousness as future with acting consciousness as present.

B. The basic activity of consciousness as the source of time's passage.

1. Acting to bring about projects is the part of the activity whereby the future becomes present.[27]

2. Displaced presence to _____ becoming consciousness-as-fact is the part of the activity whereby the present becomes past.[28]

C.1. Sartre does not explicitly distinguish three forms of pastness, but it is important tha they be distinguished in order that the question of their interrelations can arise. I will indicate how the three forms can be interpreted so as to be mutually consistent, although I will not explore this issue in detail.

(a) Having been present to _____, which Sartre also describes as "past presence to a past state of the world,"[29] is Sartre's replacement for Husserl's retention. It refers to our previous experiences of things *as informing* our current perceiving and acting. It is the understanding of what things are like *through* our prior being present to them. For example, in order to perceive the eighth chime *as* eighth when a clock strikes 8 o'clock, we have to be conscious of the present chime as following in sequence seven other chimes, each of which is present when it occurs. Sartre's phenomenological claim is that acting consciousness is *still conscious through* each of the former acts of being present to one chime but in the mode of "having been." We are present to the eighth chime and have been present to the seventh, sixth, fifth, etc. All practical or empirical knowledge of what things are like, for example, that an automobile endures relatively unchanged through short stretches of time or that it will crush a leaf in its path, is based on having been present to _____[30] as is all extended action (where we *have been* the earlier steps of an extended action).

(b) There is a second type of pastness of acting consciousness, its solidifying into facticity. Acting consciousness-as-fact is its former perceiving, thinking, or acting as viewed externally, rather than being conscious through it (C1a). It is past actions, thoughts, emotions, etc., as facts back behind the present, as past episodes in which we no longer participate.

Ontologically, Sartre describes acting consciousness-as-fact as "the For-itself-become-In-itself." If this feature of the pastness of acting consciousness is to be made consistent with the "having been present to _____" feature, many of our past experiences must be still in the process of solidifying. Given Sartre's ontological account of consciousness in terms of nihilation, there must still be nothingness in the For-itself-become-In-itself if we are to be *conscious through* former acts of presence to _____.

(c) The third form of pastness, having to be its past, is the way that at any time acting consciousness is defined by its *attitudes towards* its past-as-fact (C1b). Having to be its past is an obligation or responsibility to appropriate past actions, thoughts, emotions, etc. We appropriate them as something *outside of* our current consciousness; they are factual episodes of past acting consciousness towards which we now take some stance (which stance affects our current action and outlook on the world). Sartre is rather vague about what various forms of appropriation are available to us. Presumably, attitudes such as "being ashamed of" or "being proud of" or "being guilty for" or "feeling entitled to something because of" are what he has in mind. Even considering our current self *not to be responsible* for parts of our past is claimed to be a form of appropriation.[31]

It is obvious that this third form of acting consciousness as past depends upon the second. What is less obvious, although I think that Sartre intends this, is that the second form itself depends upon the third. What I think that Sartre wants to maintain is that acting consciousness-as-fact is the past of current acting consciousness *only if* the current acting consciousness has to be this past, and is thus partially constituted by these past facts. It is the obligation to appropriate these past facts that makes them the past of the current consciousness.

2. Presence to _____ is the basic form of intentionality according to Sartre. Its very basicness makes it difficult to describe phenomenologically, and Sartre says very little specifically about it.

(a) Perceptual presence to _____ is the awareness of some appearance (profile of an enduring thing) or set of appearances against the background of the less determinate field of other (present) appearances. The experience is of "not-being" or of standing over against the appearance-in-context. Ingredient in not-being the appearance-in-context is the nonpositional awareness (of) the type of not-being the appearance-in-context. In addition to our positional awareness of the appearance-in-context, there is a non-positional awareness of the variety of our conscious awareness of it. This is the basis for Sartre's ontological thesis concerning the reflection-reflecting form of nihilation.

(b) Since Sartre conceives perceiving and acting to be interdefined, there should be a type of being present through action to _____. Our making use of something or acting upon something to attain our goals seems also to be a form of presence to it.

3. Sartre portrays the futurity of consciousness in several ways without explaining specifically how these are related to each other. Since I have elsewhere explored many of the relations between these different forms of futurity, as well as how they are grounded in the ontology of nihilation, I will not examine these relations in the present essay.[32]

(a) Having projects, conditions or states of acting consciousness that are *to be attained*, is one form of the futurity of consciousness. By having projects there is a future with which acting consciousness is in the process of uniting itself through its acting. The ultimate project of consciousness is to be an In-itself-For-itself, but short of this there are "qualified futures" that consist of consciousness being in a certain state or condition, such as being dancing, being generous, or being successful. Projects provide the ends or goals of action; their reflection on the object of consciousness is what is to be made present in the world.

(b) Once acting consciousness has a future to be attained, it is not forced to continue to pursue it. Freedom possibilizes the projects of consciousness. The future that we are currently acting to unite ourselves with need not remain our future over time because we are always free to develop new projects. The futurity of acting consciousness is essentially possibility because being free requires that any project can be revised or abandoned before being attained.

(c) Possible presence to _____ (being beyond being) describes the future of acting consciousness as present to _____. It depends upon both C3a and C3b. Since consciousness is essentially intentional, the future condition of consciousness that is to be attained is also present to _____. However, since the future condition of consciousness is only possible because of freedom, possible presence to _____ results. Which appearance-in-context we will experience is now undermined because our future courses of action (including how we align our senses) are now only possible.

4. The pastness and the presentness of acting consciousness are mutually constitutive. The past is defined by formerly being present, and the present is affected in two ways by its past. Firstly, having been present to _____ (C1a) affects being present to _____ by partly defining *what it is* (the essence of) that we are present to. This is especially obvious for action; what we have already done qualifies what we are now doing. Secondly, the attitudes towards our past consciousness-as-fact that are required to be our past (C1c) affect our present action and outlook on the world. Both of these affects of its pastness on its presentness are instances of how "surpassed facticity" provides a point of view.

5. The presentness and futurity of acting consciousness are also mutually constitutive. All the forms of futurity are defined with respect to presentness, as either what is to be made present or what might possibly be present. The presentness of consciousness is itself defined with respect to futurity as *lacking* the qualified completeness that the attainment of a project would accomplish. The present of consciousness is deficient with respect to the future condition of consciousness with which we are to unite ourselves. This deficiency is the motivation for action; present acting is to attain a future goal.

D. For Sartre the passage of time is equivalent to the basic activity of consciousness that he describes phenomenologically.[33] This basic activity can be divided for explanatory purposes into two parts.

1. Acting consciousness is always engaged in pursuing its projects, that is, in uniting itself with some more ideal state or condition of consciousness that its current presence to _____ lacks (see C5). The process of making the future condition of consciousness present is how the future becomes present.

2. In making its own future present, the basic activity displaces its lacking presence to _____. This former present does not disappear entirely but becomes factual, a special type of fact, consciousness-as-fact, results. In ontological terms, the presence to _____ is reabsorbed by Being-in-itself, which produces the For-itself-become-In-itself.

IV: Temporality of Experience as the Source of All Temporal Features

The basic move in Sartre's argument that the temporality of the instrumental-thing can be seen to be entirely derived from the temporality of consciousness is to analyze the instrumental-thing into a series of appearances. Each individual appearance will show itself to be a-temporal and to be just what it is, and the seriality or temporal relations of appearances to each other will show themselves to be *external* relations that do not define the appearances themselves but which are the mere reflection onto what exists In-itself of the temporality of consciousness. The temporal relations between appearances are supposed to show themselves to be derived from the temporality of consciousness; they exist only *for* an observing consciousness.[34]

> Permanence, as a compromise between non-temporal identity and the ekstatic unity of temporalization, will appear therefore as the pure slipping by of in-itself instants, little nothingnesses separated one from another and reunited by a relation of simple exteriority on the surface of a being which preserves an a-temporal immutability. (E 281, F 246)

> The cohesion of Time is a pure phantom, the objective reflection (reflet) of the ekstatic project of the For-itself towards itself and the cohesion in motion of human reality. But this cohesion has no *raison d'être*. If Time is considered by itself, it immediately dissolves into an absolute multiplicity of instants which considered separately lose all temporal nature and are reduced purely and simply to the total a-temporality of the *this*. (E 293, F 257)

The argument for the derivativeness of the temporality of the instrumental thing starts from presentness. The present of the instrumental-thing is defined directly in terms of consciousness being present to the thing. Given Sartre's claims in the Introduction that the object of consciousness is a series of appearances, that its essence is just the principle of the series, and that the mode of existence of the appearance is Being-in-itself, it is plausible to claim that the presentness of the instrumental-thing consists of consciousness being present to an a-temporal appearance. If each appearance is a-temporal and exists as self-contained, the series of appearances that constitute an object should be a series of self-contained, a-temporal "atoms." We thus arrive at time as a series of instants (a-temporal "atoms"). Since each appearance is self-contained (not defined by relation to anything else), the appearances themselves do not provide for their being related in a temporal series.

The seriality of the appearances is external to the appearances themselves; the source of the temporal relations between instants must be elsewhere, ultimately, from the temporalizing activity of acting consciousness.

The argument continues by claiming that according to the phenomenological description of the temporality of the instrumental-thing, its past is external to its present. The present of the instrumental-thing does not "have to be its past." Whereas the present of acting consciousness is defined by its past which it has to be (see C1c), the past of instrumental-things just exists as a self-contained fact behind the present. The present of the instrumental-thing is connected with its past only by the experiencing consciousness which brings past appearances together with present appearances into a series. The temporal relation of the present of instrumental-things to its past exists *only for* acting consciousness; it is constructed out of the a-temporality of the appearances and the temporality of acting consciousness.

Similarly, the future of the instrumental-thing is external to its present. The present appearance does not "have to be its future"; it does not strive to unite itself with its future, as the present of acting consciousness does. Not only is the future of the instrumental-thing dependent upon acting consciousness to unite it in a temporal series with the present, but it is totally dependent upon acting consciousness for its being. Whereas past states of instrumental-things exist on their own, though not *as past*, future states do not exist at all until they are present. *Qua* future, they exist *only for* an experiencing that is defined by its future. Temporal relations again appear to be derived from the temporality of acting consciousness.

There *is* a feature of instrumental-things as future that essentially connects the present and the future, what is to be made present (A3c). Present and future states of affairs of instrumental-things are mutually defined by the "lack" relation. However, as I have already indicated under B2b, this "lack" relations is itself consciousness-dependent; it too is derived from the temporality of acting consciousness.

The final point of the derivation argument focusses on the passage of time. Since the past, present, and future of instrumental-things are all external to each other, there is nothing in the instrumental-thing as past or as present or as future to account for its transition to being more past or just past or present or less future. The passage of time is an external flow in which the self-contained appearances slip by. This passage of time is dependent upon the basic activity of acting consciousness. It is only as a reflection of consciousness' changing what it is present to through making its future present, that present appearances become past and future appearances become present.

V: Problems with the Derivation Thesis

The derivativeness of the temporality of the instrumental-thing requires that the essence of seriality of the series of appearances *not be based* in the appearances themselves, which are supposed to be self-contained and non-relational. As I noted earlier, Sartre frequently smuggles in undefended ontological premises into his supposedly phenomenological arguments. I will not object to his claim that an appearance exists independently of the consciousness that is present to it; he does argue for this point in the Introduction. However, the notion that an appearance is non-relational and self-contained is based on a mere ontological postulation about Being-in-itself. The phenomenological evidence does not support this claim. The instrumental-thing does not fall apart into self-contained "atoms" that are only externally related.

1. In explicating Sartre's phenomenological argument in Section IV of this essay, I noted that he claims that the past of the instrumental-thing is external to its present because the present of the instrumental-thing does not "have to be its past." While this is true, there is another way in which the past of an instrumental-thing defines its present, namely, by partially defining the essence of what is present.[35] As described earlier in A1b and A4, there is a categorial connection between the past of an instrumental-thing and its present appearances; what it is that appears in the present appearance is partly defined by the past.

Similarly, Sartre claims that the future of the instrumental thing is external to its present becuase the present appearance does not "have to be its future." Despite this, the future of the instrumental-thing does partialy define the present appearance. What characteristics of the thing will be present (A3a) and the range of possible characteristics of the thing that might present (A3b) affect what it is that is now present. Even assuming that the essence of the instrumental-thing is consciousness-dependent, the present appearance is itself defined by the essence, which depends upon the past and the future of the thing.

Since the appearances that constitute a thing are internally related in terms of their essence, there is no phenomenological evidence for the "a-temporality of the In-itself" in the object of consciousness. The result is that at the phenomenological level there is an essential *correlation* between the temporality of experiencing consciousness and the temporality of the object of consciousness. In this correlation, neither is more basic than the other; there is no indication that the temporality of consciousness is *more basic than* and the *sole source for* the temporality of the object, which on its own would be a-temporal.

2. Assuming with Sartre that appearances exist on their own (as transcendent of consciousness), the phenomena of "abolitions and

apparitions"[36] indicate that there is some type of temporality to the thing-in-itself. Apparitions and abolitions are the coming into existence and the passing into complete pastness (or passing out of existence, in ordinary language terms) of instrumental-things, conceived as containing within their essence the whole sequence of their appearances.[37] Sartre himself admits that the beginning and the end of the sequence of appearances that constitute an object is not brought about soley by the temporality of consciousness. In effect, this is to introduce a basis *within the appearances-as-transcendent* for the uniting of individual appearances into a temporal series to form an object. The beginning and the end of the series of appearances is not totally dependent upon consciousness because there is this basis in the appearances-as-transcendent for their being united with other appearances in a temporal series to form one object. Although there are alternative ways of conceptually structuring the world into objects, there are constraints in the *appearances-as-transcendent* upon which other appearances they can be united with in a series to form a temporally extended object.

This characteristic of individual appearances that makes them "fit together" in a temporal series with some other appearances but not "fit together" with others is the reason that the beginning and end of things seems to derive from the In-itself. Sartre recognizes that the In-itself *as he has portrayed it* can not contain such temporal features. Yet he admits that abolitions and apparitions do involve a "quasi-after" and "quasi-before" within what appears. The "quasi-temporality" of abolitions and apparitions is claimed to be a contingent metaphysical fact that is not explainable in terms of the ontology of Being-in-itself and Being-for-itself. This is to admit the failure of the program of tracing all temporal features of instrumental-things to the temporalizing activity of Being-for-itself.

3. A third problem concerns the derivativeness of the futurity of the instrumental-thing from the futurity of acting consciousness and the derivativeness of the passage of time. These are essentially connected because the meaningfulness of the notion of futurity requires that there be a passage of time. Recall that under A3 the futurity of the instrumental-thing is entirely defined in terms of variations on becoming present.

In Sarte's theory the futurity of the instrumental-thing is entirely derivative because it does not *exist as fact* (the being of the In-itself) until it becomes present. *Qua* future, this future is entirely dependent upon the futurity of consciousness. The futurity of the instrumental-thing becomes present only because it is the correlate of the futurity of consciousness that is made present through acting.

The problem with this is that it does not explain why the specific future characteristics of things are destined to be the way they are or why these specific characteristics and states of affairs should become present. It is plausible to think: (a) that both the determined future of a thing (A3a) and the determined range of its possibilities (A3b) have some basis in the thing-in-itself, and (b) that it is something temporal about the thing-in-itself that accounts for the determined future of a thing (A3a) becoming actual. After all, almost all the specific characteristics of the future of the world seem to become present independently of human action. While I have not attempted to prove (a) and (b), Sartre's derivation thesis appears unable to give an account of temporal passage without attributing a time-like future to the instrumental-thing as thing-in-itself.

There are further problems concerning the present becoming past. Consciousness' presence to _____ being reabsorbed by Being-in-itself seems to require some activity or force on the part of Being-in-itself. However, since this problem concerns the ontology of temporalizing, I will not develop it here.

Notes

1. I will not discuss Sartre's other ontological argument that to be temporal requires being "diasporic" or "ekstatic," which only Being-for-itself is.

2. Sartre's claims about the pastness of the For-itself being the same as the pastness of objects in the world are obviously partial truths. See part III of this essay.

3. See note 1.

4. E 280–281; F 246. Jean-Paul Sartre, *Being and Nothingness*, trans. Hazel Barnes (New York: Washington Square Press, 1966). *L'Etre et le Néant* (Saint Amand: Gallimard, 1979). "E" refers to this English translation; "F" refers to this French edition.

5. E 281; F 246–47.

6. E 200–01; F 180; E 268–69; F 236.

7. E 614–15; F 534–35; E 637–38,. F 553–54.

8. E 176–79; F 159–62.

9. E 422; F 368; E 424–25; F 370.

10. E. 290–91; F 254–55.

11. E 183-84; F 165-66; E 265-66; F 233-34.

12. E 269-71; F 237-38.

13. E 273-74; F 240-41.

14. E 285; F 249-50.

15. E 294; F 257-58; E 436-37; F 380.

16. E 273-75; F 240-41.

17. I develop this notion of a "simple action" in considerably more detail in "Sartre's Nihilations," *The Southern Journal of Philosophy* XX (Spring 1982), especially pages 101-02.

18. In many respects Sartre's analysis is very similar to that of philosophers such as Grunbaum and Mellor who claim that McTaggart's A-series (past, present, and future) is consciousness-dependent. However, unlike Sartre, these philosophers accept the transcendental reality of McTaggart's B-series (the tenseless relations 'earlier than' 'simultaneous with,' and 'later than').

19. E 170; F 154-55; E 207; F 185-86.

20. E 173-74; F 157-58; E 277; F 243.

21. E 172; F 156-57; E 638-39, F 554.

22. E 176-79; F 159-62.

23. E 422; F 368; E 424-25; F 370.

24. E 182-84; F 165-66; E 578-79; F 503-04.

25. E 185-86; F 167-68; E 598; F 520.

26. E 279; F 245; E 292; F 256.

27. E 209-10; F 187-88; E 272-73; F 239-40.

28. E 175; F 158-59; E 206-08; F 185-86.

29. E 207; F 186.

30. E 269; F 236.

31. E 168-69; F 153.

32. "Sartre's Nihilations," op. cit., especially sections 1 and 2.

33. In following out Sartre's phenomenological argument, I will not discuss his ontological account of the For-itself's temporalizing in terms of nihilating activity. I examine nihilating activity as explaining the future's becoming present in "Sartre's Nihilations," op. cit.

34. See also E 253; F 223-24.

35. This corresponds to another way in which the past of acting consciousness defines its present, through having been present to _____ (C1a).

36. See E 282; F 248.

37. "Each *this* is revealed with a law of being which determines its threshold, its level of change where it will cease to be what it is in order simply not to be. This law of being, which expresses 'permanence' is an immediately revealed structure of the essence of the 'this'. . . . E 282; F 248.

Part III.
Phenomenology
and the Artful

9. Toward a Phenomenological Aesthetics of Environment

Arnold Berleant

Aesthetics, as a discipline, retains a bond with its eighteenth-century origins, when it was named the "science of sensory knowledge."[1] Much has come to supplement this sensory base, such as meaning, memory, metaphor, symbol, and history, but it is important to reaffirm the central place that sense perception holds in aesthetic experience, for the senses are essential and, indeed, central to the study of art and natural beauty. Of course the early emphasis on beauty has changed with the evolution of the arts, and today the field embraces a wide range of qualities and features of perceptual experience that may be termed, in some fashion, aesthetic. These may include the ugly, the grotesque, the comic or playful, as well as the conventionally pleasing or beautiful. In fact the concept of beauty may itself be extended to cover such as these, insofar as they enable us to participate in experience that can be regarded as aesthetic.

The nature of such experience has understandably been the subject of much discussion. Aesthetic experience has been approached from the naturalistic standpoint by Dewey, Prall, and Langfeld, from the analytic perspective by Beardsley and Aldrich, from the phenomenological by Merleau-Ponty and Dufrenne. In fact, so important has the notion of experience been in theories of art that it may be taken as the seminal concept in modern aesthetics. Drawing from many of these sources, I shall attempt to develop some ideas that hold significant implications for an environmental aesthetic.

The usual form in which aesthetic perception is described is in visual terms: we are given not an aesthetic of experience but an aesthetic of appearance. The sense of sight has a long history in the West, and throughout the twenty-five hundred years through which the philosophic tradition extends, visual perception has been dominant and sight has been associated with cognitive activities and results. This is seen clearly in the standard stock of visual metaphors that provide the usual vocabulary to denote acts of thought and cognition. These are so familiar that their reiteration is tiresome, from Descartes' "inspection by the mind" which confirms that ideas that the mind perceives as "clear and distinct" in "the light of nature" are true, to the multitude of metaphorical commonplaces reflected by the many ordinary expressions denoting comprehension. This convention has been transferred readily to the arts, so that sight, along with the other distance receptor, hearing, are the only senses admitted to legitimacy in aesthetics. Early on Plato proposed that only the pleasure apprehended by sight and hearing is aesthetic,[2] and this conviction has been affirmed repeatedly without serious question until recent times.

I shall not review the long and tedious history, from classical times to the present, during which visual perception reigned as a cognitive standard for art and aesthetic experience. It is a history that describes a multitude of diverse forces that our understanding of the arts by standards other than those than can be obtained from our perceptual experience of those arts. Religious, metaphysical, historical, and epistemological criteria provided the governing principles by which art was to be made, understood, and judged. When the study of art finally achieved its emancipation and identity late in the Enlightenment, this intellectualist visual model was not abandoned. It became, instead, the governing metaphor for the explanation of aesthetic experience, which emerged as a contemplative attitude for appreciating an art object for its sake alone. It was only in the present century that the hegemony of this account was challenged by explanations such as those based on empathy or pragmatic functionalism.

My purpose, however, is not an historical one in this instance. That is a task I have undertaken elsewhere.[3] I should like rather to elaborate three models of aesthetic experience, two of which have appeared since the emergence of aesthetics as a discipline and a third which is still nascent. And further, since I propose to illustrate and examine these in specific instances, the better to explain and test them, and since the full range and complexity of these ideas is well beyond the possible scope of an essay such as this, and since environmental perception offers a peculiarly rich and distinctive field for the consideration of such an issue as aesthetic experience, I shall direct myself towards environmental aesthetics for the illustration of elaboration of these models.

The contemplative model of aesthetic experience is so securely established as to assume the status of an official doctrine. Resting on

a philosophical tradition that extends back to classical times, it appears
to many to be the very foundation of modern aesthetics, axiomatic and
unchallengeable. First formulated in the eighteenth century in the
writings of Shaftesbury, Hutcheson, and others of the British school
and embodied in a systematic philosophical setting later in that period
by Baumgarten and Kant, a doctrine emerges that identifies the art
object as separate and distinct from that which surrounds it, isolated
from the rest of life.[4] Such an object requires a special attitude, an attitude of disinterestedness that regards the object in the light of its own
intrinsic qualities with no concern for ulterior purposes. Disinterestedness thus became a tenet echoed regularly through the halls of academe
by such phrases as Bullough's well-known notion of "psychical distance"
and Ortega's less gracious "dehumanization." More recently, the interest
in the formal properties of art objects, in their peculiarly distinctive
nature, in the definition of art in terms of these properties, and in
psychologistic theories of aesthetic perception that develop distinctive
ways of looking at art are all theoretical manifestations of the same
impulse to disengage art from the social experiential matrix and assign
it to a removed, albeit elevated, position.[5] Stolnitz sums up two centuries of discussion when he defines the aesthetic attitude as "disinterested and sympathetic attention to and contemplation of any object
of awareness whatever, for its own sake alone."[6]

There are numerous instances throughout the history of landscape
painting that offer a clear reflection of this doctrine of separation and
distance. These derive from a conception of space modeled on the space
of the physicist, more specifically the eighteenth-century physicist.
Space here becomes an abstraction, a medium that is universal, objective, and impersonal, independent of the objects that are situated in
it and move through it. Such an objective space leads to the objectification of things which are then regarded from the stance of an impersonal observer. What is common to landscapes that assume this notion
of objective space is the depiction of a scene observed from some vantage point. The observer is removed from the scene, contemplating it
from a distance. Such cases illustrate the usual definition of a landscape
as "a picture representing a section of natural, inland scenery" that
reflects the conception of a landscape as "an expanse of natural scenery
seen by the eye in one view."[7]

There are pictorial features characteristic of these works, features
which present an objectified space and encourage an attitude of
disinterestedness. The space of the painting is separated sharply from
the space that surrounds it, including that of the observer. the landscape space is also discontinuous with the viewer. It begins abruptly
in the foreground, originating at the picture plane. While it may lead

into the space of the painting, that space is often divided into deparate, uncommunicating areas, the objective and divisible space of classical physics. And indeed, the desideratum seems to be to regard the painting as a totality, visually objective and complete. Division, distance, separation, and isolation are equally the order of the art and the order of the experience, for the features of the painting shape the character of our perception.[8]

Custom and occurrence, to be sure, give great weight to the classical view. So philosophically coherent a position is formidable and has received no successful challenge to its hegemony from the scholarly camp. One is reminded here of Laurence Sterne's ironic observation on the use we commonly make of such ideas:

> It is the nature of a hypothesis, when once a man has conceived it, that it assimilates every thing to itself, as proper nourishment; and, from the first moment of your begetting it, it generally grows the stronger by every thing you see, hear, read, or understand. This is of great use.[9]

The objectification of art is the predictable product of an intellectualist tradition, one that grasps the world by knowing it and that controls the world by subduing it to the order of thought. Such a strategy may have secured the assent of philosophers but it has not won over the ranks of artists.[10] Wallace Stevens' response, in the last of his "Six Significant Landscapes," is eloquent as it is explicit:

> Rationalists wearing square hats
> Think, in square rooms,
> Looking at the floor,
> Looking at the ceiling.
> They confine themselves
> To right angled triangles.
> If they tried rhomboids,
> Cones, waving lines, ellipses –
> As, for example, the ellipse of the half moon –
> Rationalists would wear sombreros.[11]

While much in the modern arts moves deliberately in a contrary direction, one can reconsider a great deal of the art of the past and discover that it lends itself to different modes of experience and to different explanations. Landscape in the visual arts provides a particularly telling illustration.

There have been attempts since the eighteenth century to develop alternatives to the classical world of aesthetic experience. Some romantic theories stressed the sympathetic feeling of the appreciator while others proposed an emphathetic identification with the object.[12] These intepreted the experience primarily in psychological terms, emphasizing an attitude of absorption rather than separation. During the past fifty years, however, despite the continued dominance of the classical theory, some proposals have appeared that have gone well beyond the psychological locus of the prevalent nineteenth-century alternative. These offered to overcome the passibity and separation of the standard theory by depicting the aesthetic perceiver more as a multisensory, active rather than through the traditional disengaged vision. These new accounts offer a more promising direction for this discussion and have been developed in various forms, two of which I shall consider now here.

Let me call the first the "active model." Versions of this may be found in the aesthetics of pragmatism, especially in Dewey's *Art as Experience*, and in the phenomenological aesthetics of Merleau-Ponty and others. What is common to the various forms of the active model is the recognition that the objective world of classical science is not the experiential world of the human perceiver. Thus there is a sharp difference to be drawn between space, as it is presumably held to be actually and objectively, and the perception of that space. A theory of aesthetic experience must thus derive from the latter rather than the former, from the manner in which we engage in spatial experience rather than from the way in which we objectify and conceptualize such experience.

Dewey emphasizes this difference. At the outset Dewey argues that "the actual work of art is what the product does with and in experience,"[13] a condition that makes art difficult to understand. Aesthetic experience must base itself on ordinary experience, experience that is "determined by the essential conditions of life." (AE 13) Foremost among these conditions is that "life goes on in an environment; not merely *in* it but because of it, through interaction on with it. . . . The career and destiny of a living being are bound up with its interchanges with its environment, not externally but in the most intimate way." (AE 13) He insists that just as life goes on through interactions of an organism with an environment that engages all the scenes, art requires the full capacities of the organism to restore "the union of sense, need, impulse and action characteristic of the live creature." (AE 29) Art stirs into activity those inherent dispositions to an intimate relationship to the surroundings that the human being has acquired through his evolutionary and cultural development. (AE 26) Such activity comes as an impulsion of the organism, which appears in art as an act of expression. (AE 58) This idea is central, for it is such an act that constitutes the work of art, an act in which there is a simultaneous transformation of materials and feelings. (AE 60, 65) Indeed, a work becomes artistic to the extent that two transformations take place, one of the materials of the artist's medium and a second of the artist's ideas and feelings. (AE 74–75) There is, however, a difference between the art product, a painting or statue, and the work of art. The work of art is the object working, interacting with the energies that emerge from the experience. Thus, Dewey, holds that the work of art in its actuality is perception. (AE 162) It is clear that in this portrayal of the experience of art the organism is an activator of the environment. Perception is not purely visual but rather somatic: it is the body that energizes space.

One discovers a curious resemblance between these ideas of Dewey, ideas that share something with the radical empiricism of William James, and the phenomenological aesthetics of Merleau-Ponty. Resembling Dewey, Merleau-Ponty argues for synaesthesia, for a unified collaboration of all the senses, including touch, in a manner in which they are undifferentiated from one another.[15] For him, too, perception starts with the body; the presence of the body as *here* is the primary reference point from which all spatial coordinates must be derived. Thus the perceived object is grasped in relation to the space of the perceiver. Yet it does not stand as a discrete material object. "Perception does not give me truths like geometry but presences."[16] There is, so to say, an "intentional arc" which supports consciousness, through which we are situated temporarlly, physically, socially, and in the realms of meaning. The subject who perceives "is my body as the field of perception and action." Indeed, "the perceived thing . . . exists only in so far as someone can perceive it." Indeed, the human body occurs through a blending of sensing and sensible, a blending in which vision is not just of, but in things.[17] Moreover, as Merleau-Ponty continues, space is not, as it was for Descartes, "network of relations between objects" that can be seen from the outside by an impartial observer. "It is, rather, a space reckoned starting from me as the zero points or degree zero of spatiality. I do not see it according to its exterior envelope; I live in it from the inside; I am immersed in it. After all, the world is all around me, not in front of me."

O. F. Bollnow develops an account of space in a similar fashion. Like Merleau-Ponty, he rejects the mathematical conception of space which is characterized by a pervasive homogeneity. Here all points and all directions are of the same importance; none is distinctive and none preferred. Mathematical space allows the construction of an orthogonal axis system in which any point can be the coordinating zero point and every direction can become the coordinating axis. But this sense of space, as Heidegger puts it, "contains no spaces and no places. We never find in it any locations.[18] Instead of the homogeneous space of mathematics, Bollnow proposes the notion of "lived-space." Here the human body becomes the originating point of an axis system of vertical and horizontal planes. Yet the natural zero point of that system is not necessarily where the concrete living person happens to be; it is the natural place to which he belongs. It is his house that is "the reference point from which he builds his spatial world," and this becomes the coordinating zero point of his reference system. Thus "all live movement in space occurs as a going away from or a coming back" to the home.[19]

Bellnow sees the inner space of the house as a private and safe space that is separated from the outer space of danger and abandonment. That world beyond the protective boundaries of the house is characterized by breadth or unrestrictedness, strangeness, and distance, yet it is opened up by roads and paths through which people structure their space as a reflection of the "lines of force" along which they move. This world beyond is not undifferentiated, however. There is a middle point which is the space of the group, and ultimately the space of the nation, to which the individual belongs. Spatial egocentrism has long been believed and practiced, and so such outer space becomes a space of vulnerability, a place of danger and abandonment. Only in the inner space of the house is one safe and hidden. Distance, too, is not mathematical but lived. My concrete life situation produces "lines of force" which structure the space I experience. Distances within lived-space, moreover, depend on a person's disposition at the time. Fear contracts space, for example, while love generates it.[20]

The notion of the lived-body develops further this sense of lived-space. It takes the body as the vital center of our spatial experience. From the body we view existential space, determine its directional axes, and measure existential distance.[21] To conceive the spatiality of the lived-body is to recognize that places and movements are perceived in relation to the body, seen as here or there. The discernment of places with their value and meanings occurs in relationship to the central position of the body. "The proper and improper places of utensils, objects, and persons are defined within the context of these regions and territories." Moreover, the world is not composed of objects and instruments for the lived-body; it is also a social world. The body's field of action must recognize and take into account the presence of the other. Yet the egocentricity of this conception remains, for the space surrounding the body is territorial, a space surrounded and limited by the space of others. The lived-body dominates its surroundings, marking out territorial space over which it exercises control.

Phenomenological views as these treat space in its relationship to the body and the environment, not as an independent quantity, but as an intentional object in relation to the perceiving body. This goes far beyond Amiel's observation that "every landscape is a state of mind." The landscape is generated out of more than an act of consciousness; it emanates from the perceiving body and is infused by that body with its meaning, force, and feelings. It is such an awareness as this that he led some recent authors to characterize architecture as "a matter of extending the inner landscape of human beings into the world in ways that are comprehensible, experiential, and inhabitable.[22]

Yet this is not enough. Environment is not wholly dependent on the perceiving subject; it also imposes itself in significant ways on the human person, engaging one in a relationship of mutual influence. Not only can the environment not be objectified; it cannot be taken as a mere reflection of the perceiver. Recognizing the influence of specific features in the environment makes it necessary to extend the active model of aesthetic experience to include such factors. The consciousness of self, of the lived-body and of lived-space must be complemented by a recognition of environment as exerting influences on the body, as contributing to the shaping of the body's spatial sense and mobility, and ultimately to the definition of its lived-space. This leads us to consider a different conception of aesthetic experience of environment. In this view the environment is understood as a field of forces continuous with the organism, a field in which there is a reciprocal action of organism on environment and environment on organism and in which there is not real demarcation between them. Such a pattern may be regarded as a participatory model of experience.

It is perhaps easier to understand the forces that emanate from the body as it thrusts itself into the environment than it is to grasp the magnetism of environmental configurations as they exert a subtle influence on the body. We sense our own vitality more directly than we apprehend the actions of spaces and masses. While the body and the environment extend mutually interacting forces, what distinguishes the participatory model of aesthetic experience from the active model is its recognition of the way in which environmental features reach out to affect and respond to the perceiver. This phenomenon is not new; artists and architects have long utilized it. What has been missing, however, is an articulation of the manner in which environmental activity occurs and which offers a conceptual formulation of this phenomenon within the frame of an aesthetic theory. I propose to suggest such an account here, for I believe that the participatory model is no special case, an exception to the prevalent observational mode in aesthetics that is required by the unique conditions of environmental experience. Rather this is a model that can be applied successfully to other, indeed, all modes of art in the form of a general theory of aesthetic experience.

Some psychologists have tried to take note of the influence of environmental features on the body, although they are prone to regard these influences as derived from and dependent on individual psychology. Kurt Lewin's field theory is a most helpful instance of this. Lewin's topological psychology represents the framework in which events can occur within a life space. The magnitude of such events requires the use of the concepts of psychological force and field of force, and leads Lewin to develop a vector psychology.[23] Lewin regards the psychological environment of an individual as directly governing behavior. Distance and direction are properties of that psychological environment, and tendencies for or against our goals are forces exerted on a person. Since such forces concern possible courses of action or of paths within our life space, Lewin calls such space "hodological" (from the Greek hodos, way, or path). Situations possess dynamic properties, and Lewin develops concepts such as positive and negative valence to denote the attractive or repulsive properties of a region; vectors or psychological forces that directly produce the reaction of a person;[24] barriers or barrier-regions which may exist in the life space of an individual; and the boundary zone of the life space[25] Although Lewin did take somewhat into his account facts that impinge on the life space, its foreign hull, as he put it, he did not devote much attention to them and was content largely to treat them in the light of their influence on the psychological environment. Lewin's vector psychology is, then, a psychology of motivation, not of environment, but it displays the value of revealing the interpenetration of consciousness and environmental perception. However, Lewin made some use of what he called the *aufförderungscharakter* or the *aufförderungsqualität* of a barrier region, which may be translated as "invitational quality", an influence that environmental features exercise on us.[26] It is a suggestive concept and has been used by some writers in art history and town planning. More recently the perceptual psychologist James J. Gibson has spoken of "affordances for behavior," a term which he apparently derives from Lewin, and by which he means features in the environment that influence our behavior and lead us to act in certain ways.[27]

As is properly the case in such matters, artists' works have anticipated the theoretical formulation of a participatory aesthetic and, indeed, is a basis for developing such an account. One can find numerous instances of invitational qualities in the visual arts by the use of features designed to elicit a participatory response in the viewer, a response often imaginative, to be sure, but perceptual and thus genuinely experienced. While the contemporary arts are rich with a multitude of ingenious uses of viewer participation, one might think that this trait is a recent innovation and anomalous in the history of the arts. This, however, is not at all the case, and so to make my claim the stronger, I should like to point to a number of historical examples of the use of such invitational features.

Portraits of the Madonna and Child in late Gothic and early Renaissance art, beginning with Cimabue and Giotto, typically place these figures on a throne which rests on a dais approached by several steps. While these personages are flanked by angels or other figures, the steps are typically empty; they face the viewer as an invitation to mount them.[28] Similarly, Bernini's design of St. Peter's Square opens up to invite us in, and once in, surrounds us in a columnar embrace. Michelangelo's Campidoglio works in a similar way, with an entering staircase that welcomes one into a stately enclosed square. Caravaggio's paintings often operate in like fashion, seeking to engage the spectator directly in the action. In some of his early works, "Caravaggio's youths do not merely address themselves to the spectator – they solicit him.[29] In both *The Lute Player* and *The Musician*, for example, he places a violin and a bow in the foreground of the picture with the neck of the violin facing outward toward the spectator – an invitation to join the musicians in their music making.[30] In Rubens' landscape of his villa, the viewer is drawn into the space as an invitation to visit, just as in Vermeer's view of the artist painting, the spectator peers over the artist's shoulder to view his work in progress. This last is emulated more recently by Cartier-Bresson's photographs of people in the act of viewing something, making us join the crowd as we gaze at the photograph.

Paintings of landscapes offer a particularly effective illustration of environmental action, for they contain the same kinds of features that environmental designers must fashion and thus they become instructive models. Landscape paintings often incorporate the perceiver into their space, compelling involvement. The road or river does more than organize the landscape and provide visual interest and variety. It does even more than serve to draw the eye into the painting. As a path it becomes the occasion for the virtual movement of the living body into the landscape. The road beckons to the viewer, just as a spoken word commands our attention and a question compels an answer. Artistic license was not the reason for Cezanne's claim that a picture contains within itself even the smell of the landscape;[31] it was his proposition that through the effective use of pictorial qualities a painting creates the total sensory field of experience. Again, the use of perspective in visual art of the eighteenth to the early twentieth centuries is an implicit recognition of the position and hence the participation of the observer. By moving in toward the painting, perspective opens up the pictorial space and includes us in it, just as molded figures emerge from the flat canvas when we step back. Our action then, activates the life of the painting, the more so as we leave the observational mode.

It is a mistake of the observational attitude to think that as viewer we must encompass the entire painting in our visual field. Many landscape paintings have to be seen from too close a position to do this, and whatever the physical distance to the canvas, the participating landscape requires that we look into the space, enter it, so to say, and become a part of it. In the interior forest of Ruisdael's "A Forest Marsh," for instance, the trees must be looked through and seen as overhead. In one of Guardi's landscapes, to take another case, we stand in the shadow of the central group of twisted trunks which, from a distance, appear to dominate the painting, but when seen from up close are looked through and past. When they are seen in this way, a remarkable inversion of importance takes place and the rest of the landscape becomes central. Paintings with exceptionally large canvases force this involvement on us. In Monet's *Nymphias*, "the presence of the figure would define the scale of the picture from the *inside* in terms of the proportions of the human body, while "the picture's scale depends on its relation to the human body of the spectator *outside*." Thus the picture "is no longer a window to a world but *the* world immanent and antonomous."[32] One can see the same action on the viewer in portraits. The type and direction of the subject's gaze tends to elicit an appropriate response in the eyes of the viewer. An averted gaze makes one look tentatively at the person so as not to be too forward or bold, while a downcast gaze evokes a look of superior strength.

When paintings are regarded experimentally active they come to exemplify the workings of features that occur outside art. Landscape photography joins painting in achievement what art in general may do – revealing aspects and dimensions of human experience with a clarity and force that are absent under ordinary circumstances. Moreover, what is true of our perception of painting and photography when understood in this fashion may hold true for our perception of the physical environment, for the same features in both can act in similar ways. Let me explore this possibility by considering several such features of the physical landscape.

Perhaps the most apparent case is the path. Paths, of course, are especially rich in significance. They are not experienced as cognitive symbols but, if one insists on using that concept, as living symbols that embody their meaning, symbols that make us act, make us commit our bodies, ourselves, to choices, one can. As Malcolm Lowry says:

> There has always been something preternatural about paths . . . for not only poetry but folklore abounds with symbolic stories about them: paths that divide and become two paths, paths that lead to a golden kingdom . . . paths that not merely divide but become the twenty-one paths that lead back to Eden.[33]

But what is most striking is the way in which paths, as features of the environment, act on us. In describing the hiking path, Bollnow comments that "the path does not shoot for a destination but rests in itself. It invites loitering. Here a man is *in* the landscape, taken up and dissolved into it, a part of it. He must have time when he abandons himself to such a path. He must stop to enjoy the view."[34] Roads, like paths, act on us in diverse ways, inviting us to move down them or putting us off. Thus routes are often unidirectional, more appealing in one direction than in the other. On a round trip that we make regularly, we are likely to follow one course going and a different one returning. Similarly, the habitual behavior with which we take a customary route may be explained as the largely unattended attraction of environmental cues that act on us to lead us regularly in the same direction.

Places, plazas, parks, and gardens may be inviting and discouraging in much the same manner. Participatory spaces encourage entry; they evoke our interest and draw us in. Instead of offering a harmonious formal array that has visual appeal when regarded from a distance, there may be comfortable irregularity and disorder. Great open spaces are divided into smaller protective ones, and enclosure replaces exposure, providing an easy habitation for the body that is sharply different from the monumental forms and spaces of such places as the federal area in Washington, D.C., City Hall Plaza in Boston, and Brazilia.[35]

Buildings may also offer opportunities for participation, and when they do contrast sharply with the usual treatment of architectural structures as visual objects. Visual buildings may display a symmetrical structure, they may stand apart as a monumental object, they may be primarily a facade whose third dimension is an incidental and unrelated appendage, or they may devolve into pure surface, as in the curtain-wall skyscraper.[36] The building that encourages participation possesses human scale; it is no isolated object that opposes the perceiver, mounted on a rise in the ground apart from its surroundings. It is instead a part of the landscape that evokes our active interest and welcomes our approach.

Nowhere is this invitation to take part more pronounced than in the case of entrances, doorways, and stairs. These can put one off or bring one in, in ways that may be subtle or obvious. An effective entrance or doorway draws one in rather than putting one off. It does not erect obstacles to be overcome or confused shapes to be identified, or present either intimidating or insignificant ways of passing into a place or a building. Rather, such an entrance is easily and clearly recognized, appropriate to the body, inclusionary in its perceptual character, welcoming in its affective qualities. So, too, can a staircase invite ascent, pulling the body upward through its own rising movement. A visual staircase becomes a pedestal to support an imposing structure; a participatory staircase beckons us upward.

Now these invitational qualities are not like traditional primary qualities, features inherent in an object like mass, weight, and shape. They resemble more the secondary qualities of empiricists, features of objects that excite certain perceptual responses in the viewer, like color or small. Neither inherent in objects nor originating in consciousness, such qualities are rather characteristics to which perceptual consciousness is receptive and to which it responds. They emerge only in the intimate reciprocity that is central to experiencing an environment aesthetically.

The recognition of such traits requires us to rethink what we mean by environment. Its etymology notwithstanding, the perception of environment is not a perception of an alien territory surrounding the self. It is rather the medium in which we are, of which our being partakes and comes to identity. Within this environmental medium occur the activating forces of mind, eye, and hand, together with the perceptual features that engage these forces and elicit their reactions. Every vestige of dualism here must be cast off. There is no inside and outside, human being and external world, even, in the final reckoning, self and other. The conscious body moving within, and as part of, a spatio-temporal environmental medium becomes the domain of human experience, the human world, the ground of human reality within which discriminations and distinctions are made. We live, then, in a dynamic nexus of interpenetrating forces to which we contribute and to which we respond.

Marcel urges us to say not that I have a body but that I am my body. So we can say, similarly, not that I live in my environment but that I am my environment. As the body can be considered an extrapolation from the unity of the self, so can the environment be regarded. Thus the concept of the environment must be altered to assimilate the lived-body on the one hand and broadened to embrace the social on the other. The social is, however, not only the institutions with which the self participates; it includes the cultural meanings with which it is infused. We need to include, then, not only a study of physical environmental features that participate in a reciprocal fashion with the self but a correlative study of the semiotics of environment that would explore the meanings inseparable from such features.

The environment, then, is a perceptual-cultural system that embraces person and place. The features of the world we fashion can create such a condition of harmony or they can discourage it by separation and ultimately alienation. Heidegger writes of the bridge as creating the banks that lie on either side, bringing "stream, banks, and land into each other's neighborhood." The bridge actually "gathers the earth as landscape around the stream."[37] More than this, it "gathers to itself . . . earth and sky, divinities and mortals. We must, then, dispense with the notion of space and consider location instead. And it is through dwelling, belonging in a place, that the human relationship appears. Thus it may be that the absence of spaces which speak to us and to which we belong may be the most egregious failure of mass industrial society. With the sense of place so often lacking, it may be why with home and hearth we still wander yet homeless and unwarmed.

A participatory model of experience thus provides a key to environmental understanding. It enables us to grasp the environment as a setting of dynamnic forces, a field of forces that engages both perceiver and perceived in a dynamic unity. What is important are not physical traits but perceptual ones, not how things are but how they are experienced. In such a phenomenological field the environment cannot be objectified; rather it is a totality continuous with the participant. An environment can be designed to work in this mode or it can be structured to oppose it. It can be shaped to encourage participation or to inhibit, intimidate or oppress the person. When design becomes humane it not only fits the shape, movements, and uses of the body; it also works with the conscious organism in an arc of expansion, development, and fulfillment. This is a goal which a consciously articulated aesthetic can help accomplish, and the challenge of such an aesthetic can be a powerful force in the effort to transform the world we inhabit into a place for human dwelling.

Notes

1. Alexander Gottlieb Baumgarten, *Aesthetica*, 1750.

2. *Greater Hippias*, 299.

3. Arnold Berleant, "The Historicity of Aesthetics," in V. Tejera and T. Levine, eds., *Against Anti-History in Philosophy*, M. Nijhof, forthcoming.

4. Anthony, Earl of Shaftesbury, *Characteristics of Men, Manners, Opinions, Times* (1711) (New York: 1900), esp. I; 94, II; 130–31, 136–37; Francis Hutcheson, *An Inquiry into the Origin of Our Ideas of Beauty and Virtue* (1725), 3rd ed. (London: 1729), Sect. II, Para. 1, 3. Thomas Reid, *On the Intellectual Powers of Man* (1785); "Of Beauty," in Immanuel Kant, *Critique of Judgment* (1790). Sects. 11, 43, 45.

5. Berleant, "Historicity of Aesthetics."

6. Jerome Stolnitz, *Aesthetics and Philosophy of Art Criticism (Boston; Houghton, Mifflin, 1960)*, 35.

7. *Webster's New World Dictionary*, College ed. (Cleveland and New York: World, 1959), 820.

8. In "Perception of Perspective Pictorial Space from Different Viewing Points," *Leonardo* 10; 4 (Autumn 1977), 283–88), Rudolf Arnheim illustrates the tendencies (1) to allow the geometry of perception to dominate the phenomena of perception (see p. 287, 286) and (2) to objectify the spatial object so that it is disparate to the viewer's space. See also M. H. Pirenne, *Optics, Painting and Photography* (Cambridge: Cambridge University Press, 1970). Arnheim refers also to H. Maertens who determines "that from a distance twice the length of a painting's longer dimension, the whole will be seen comfortably at an angle subtending about 27°." Arnheim seems to aver that "unless the total visual pattern is comprehended within this range, it cannot be seen and judged as an integrated whole. See his *The Dynamics of Architectural Form* (Berkeley: University of California Press, 1977), 128.

9. Laurence Sterne, *Tristram Shandy*, Vol. II, ch. 19.

10. This is not the place to offer a survey of tendencies and works by artists of this century that contradict the classical model of aesthetic perception. That is a project I have done elsewhere. See Arnold Berleant, "Aesthetics and the Contemporary Arts," *Journal of Aesthetics and Art Criticism* XXIX; 2 (Winter 1970), 155–68; "The Visual Arts and the Art of the Unseen," *Leonardo* XII (Summer 1979), 231–35; and "The Historicity of Aesthetics."

11. *The Collected Poems of Wallace Stevens* (New York: Knopf, 1954), 75.

12. Eugene Véron and Leo Tolstoy are instances of the first; Theodor Lipps and Vernon Lee of the second.

13. John Dewey, *Art as Experience* (New York: Minton, Balch, 1934). p3.

14. *Ibid.*, 3, 13, 25, 29, 58, 60, 65, 74–75, 162.

15. Maurice Merleau-Ponty, *Phenomenologie de la perception* (Paris: Gallimard, 1945), 119–58; Eugene F. Kaelin, *An Existentialist Aesthetic* (Madison: University of Wisconsin Press, 1966), 239–40.

16. Maurice Merleau-Ponty, "The Primacy of Perception," in *The Primacy of Perception*, ed. J. M. Edie (Evanston: Northwestern University Press, 1964), 14, 16.

17. "Eye and Mind," in *The Primacy of Perception*, 163, 178.

18. Martin Heidegger, "Building, Dwelling, Thinking," in *Poetry, Language, Thought* trans. Albert Hofstadter (New York: Harper Colophon Books), 155.

19. O. F. Bollnow, "Lived-Space," in *Philosophy Today* V (1961), 31–39.

20. Bollnow, *op. cit.* 39.

21. Calvin O. Schrag, *Experience and Being* (Evanston: Northwestern University Press, 1969), 136, 137, 170, 192.

22. R. C. Bloomer and C. W. Moore, *Body, Memory and Architecture* (New Haven: Yale, 1977), 105.

23. Kurt Lewin, *Principles of Topological Psychology* (New York: McGraw-Hill, 1936), 205.

24. Robert W. Leeper, *Lewin's Topological and Vector Psychology* (Eugene, Oregon, 1943), 14, 33–36, 37, 63, 65.

25. Melvin H. Mark, *Psychological Theory* (New York: Macmillan, 1951), 311.

26. Leeper, *op. cit.*, 33–90, 66, 115–118.

27. James J. Gibson, *The Perception of the Visual World* (Cambridge, MA, 1950), *The Senses Considered as Perceptual Systems* (Boston: Houghton, Mifflin, 1966), *Ecological Approach to Visual Perception* (Westport, CT: Greenwood Press, 1979).

28. I am indebted to the painter and art historian Palko Lukaçs for this example.

29. Donald Posner, "Caravaggio's Homo Erotic Early Works," *Art Quarterly* 1971, 11, 24, 26.

30. Ibid.

31. Mentioned in Merleau-Ponty, *Phenomenology of Perception*, 318–319.

32. E. C. Goosan, "The Big Canvas," in *The New Art*, G. Battcock, ed. (New York: Dutton, 1973), 63, 65.

33. Malcolm Lowry, *Hear Us O Lord from Heaven Thy Dwelling Place* (London, 1969), 272.

34. Bollnow, "Lived-Space," 38.

35. See Fritz Steel, *The Sense of Place* (Boston: CBI Publ., 1981), 187.

36. "Its potential for pulling us into the realm of a movement or sound game is almost nil. We can neither measure ourselves against it nor imagine a bodily

participation." Robert J. Yudell, in Bloomer and Moore, *Body, Memory, and Architecture*, 61.

37. M. Heidegger, *op. cit.*, 152, 153, 156–157.

10. The Ethical Function of Architecture

Karsten Harries

Architecture is in a confused state. The long taken-for-granted authority of the masters of modern architecture has been challenged. There is an openness to past architectural styles that recall the eclecticism of the nineteenth century and with a refreshing appreciation of popular architecture; but the other side of such welcome willingness to experiment is an often depressing lack of focus and direction. Christian Norberg-Schulz claims that "the schools have shown themselves incapable of bringing forth architects to solve the actual tasks,"[1] but do we know what the "actual tasks" of architecture are? Is the prevailing uncertainty linked to an uncertainty as to how this question is to be answered? One could of course point to the needs generated by our way of life and look to scientists, especially to social scientists, to state these needs with a precision that would allow engineers to offer solutions that would best meet them. But are buildings machines? Surely they should be more than that. Corbusier, to whom we owe the often repeated determination of the house as "a machine for living in," at the same time also insists that architects be more than just engineers, that they also be artists. Should buildings then be machines *and* works of art? As Arthur Drexler remarks in *Transformations in Modern Architecture*, "we are still dealing with the conflict between art and technology that beset the nineteenth century, and which the modern movement expected to resolve."[2] The present confusion is inseparable from the disappointment of that expectation.

Confusion invites critical reflection. Not surprisingly, architects have shown a new receptivity to philosophy and to philosophical ideas. Unfortunately much of what philosophers have had to say about architecture has proven to be as much of a hindrance as a help in arriving

129

at a determination of the tasks of architecture. Architecture has traditionally been considered one of the arts, and its philosophy appears
as part of the philosophy of art. Art has often been understood as
granting a particular kind of pleasure. Following Kant, I shall use an
approach to art that emphasizes the pleasure generated by the beautiful
aesthetic. I will show that if philosophy is to make a significant contribution to the ongoing discussion of building and its tasks, it first has
to free itself from aesthetics and recognize what I shall call the "ethical
function of architecture."

Aesthetics should not be taken here as simply synonymous with
the philosophy of art. If today we understand the philosophy of art first
of all as aesthetics, then we are the heirs of an approach to art that in
the eighteenth century finally triumphed over an older approach that
could not grant autonomy to the work of art. This older approach placed
beauty in the service of the need to represent the order that assigns
to human beings its character or place, its ethos.[3] The establishment
of aesthetics as one of the main branches of philosophy is bound up
with the weakening of this older approach. The term itself belongs to
the eighteenth century. It derives from Alexander Gottlieb Baumgarten's
dissertation of 1735, which helps to remind us that the aesthetic
approach to art is part of that somewhat questionable legacy left to us
by the Enlightenment.

A suggestive characterization of the aesthetic approach is provided
by one of Baumgarten's similes: a successful poem, he tells us, is like
a world, more precisely like the world as described by rationalist
philosophers, by Leibniz for example, who understood the cosmos as
a perfectly ordered whole having its sufficient reason in God.[4] In that
best of all possible worlds nothing is superfluous nor is anything
missing. The same ought to be true of a poem, and, more generally,
of any work of art. It, too, ought to be a perfect and, therefore, self-
sufficient whole. Its integrity should be such that to add or subtract
anything would be to weaken it. The beautiful object, on this view,
presents itself to us being as it should be. Nothing is missing; nothing
is superfluous. Baumgarten's simile, quite traditional in its understanding of the artist as a second God, seems innocent enough. After
all, ever since Aristotle, unity has been demanded of works of art. To
be sure, to demand unity is not to deny complexity, tension, and incon-
gruity, but, in the end, order should triumph. Baumgarten, too, cites
the familiar definition of beauty as sensible perfection: to speak of
beauty as *sensible* perfection is to insist that a work of art be sensuous
and concrete; the beautiful has no being apart from experience. To speak
of it as sensible *perfection* is to insist on the autonomy of the art work.

A beautiful object does not refer beyond itself. Because of this there is no point to calling it true or false. It is experienced as a self-sufficient presence. This presence is what really matters.

To the self-sufficiency of the aesthetic object corresponds to the self-sufficiency of the aesthetic experience, which, if only for a time, gives us a sense of existing as we should exist and thus lifts the burden character of time. Herein lies the magic of that disinterested satisfaction which, according to Kant, lets us judge the object that grants it beautiful. Kant's characterization of the beautiful as the object of an entirely disinterested satisfaction asserts the autonomy of the aesthetic realm, distinguishes it from the moral realm and separates it from our usual desires.[5] The aesthetic object is essentially dislocated. Such dislocation is a necessary part of the appreciation of the self-sufficiency of the genuine work of art. Art, in this view, brackets the concerns of the everyday. These brackets may be exclusive or inclusive; but even when they are inclusive and our concerns are preserved in the aesthetic experience, such preservation nonetheless also implies a distancing that frees us from their burden and transforms them into material for aesthetic enjoyment. Art is for art's sake.

But if art is for the art's sake, it is difficult to find much architecture that can be considered art. Architecture cannot rise to the purity found in the other arts, for as Kant observes, "the suitability of a product for a certain use is the essential thing in an *architectural work*."[6] Architecture, in Kant's view has to be both practical and beautiful, where the former must be given priority. Its beauty appears as something added on to what need dictates. Indeed, if beauty demands aesthetic purity, it is difficult to understand how architecture can ever yield unalloyed beauty. Buildings are more than objects for aesthetic contemplation; the architect has to take into account the uses to which a building will be put, while those using it will not be able to keep their distance from it. To the extent that we measure buildings by aesthetic conceptions of what constitutes a complete work of art, architecture has to be considered deficient and impure, a not quite respectable art. Pure works of art are uninhabitable. Aesthetic self-sufficiency is incompatible with the requirements of a dwelling.

All of this would be of little importance were it only a matter of some philosophers arguing about the essence of architecture. But the rise of aesthetics is only one aspect of a more deeply rooted change in sensibility that in the name of reason has divorced pragmatic and aesthetic considerations and placed the architect uneasily between the two: on the one hand, the uses of architecture have been emphasized; on the other, architecture is supposed to be beautiful. And who could quarrel with the demand that buildings be both practical and beautiful? Unfortunately, the hopes of the modern movement notwithstanding, there is not only no assurance that an economical and efficient solution to a practical problem will also be aesthetically pleasing, but given the aesthetics of purity, there is no chance that the marriage of engineer and artist will be free of tension and compromise. Given the aesthetic approach, the beauty of a building has to appear as something added on to what is dictated by necessity, decoration that is given its special value precisely by its superfluity.

It is thus hardly surprising that, with the rise of the aesthetic approach in the eighteenth century, architecture should have entered a period of uncertainty and crisis from which it has not yet emerged. To be sure, there were attempts even then to raise architecture to the status of a pure art. The prophetic designs of Ledoux offer the most obvious examples. The architect here becomes an abstract artist who casts his forms, his cubes, pyramids, and spheres into the void. Not that the embodied self expresses itself in such an absolute and pure architecture, but as a purely aesthetic interest. Not surprisingly Ledoux's most daring designs remain on paper. The pursuit of aesthetic purity has to lead the architect to utopian fantasies unlikely ever to be realized. Reality demands compromises; aesthetic vision has to be tempered by nonaesthetic considerations. The nineteenth century thus clothed its often very practical architecture in a veneer of borrowed ornament and placed the architect uneasily between the *école polytechnique* and the *école des beaux arts*. Given such an approach, all beauty in architecture has to be considered, in a profound sense, just ornamentation. This is suggested by Ruskin's distinction between buildings and architecture. What transforms the former into the latter is essentially useless ornamentation. From this perspective Venturi's call for an architecture of ornamented sheds appears as not at all controversial, but rather as a call to accept and to affirm the compromises with what beauty demands that necessity enforces. From the aesthetic approach, architecture can claim the dignity of the other arts only to the extent that it liberates itself from building and become absolute. But for such an architecture we have no use.

II

I have argued that as long as the aesthetic approach guides architectural theory, architecture will appear as an impure art, haunted by utopian visions of an absolute architecture unfettered by concerns for function. As long as this approach continues to inform architectural practice, architecture will remain caught in the conflict between art and technology. If there is to be an escape from this bind it must be through a different approach. One obvious solution is to divorce art and building. One might thus call on architects to emancipate themselves from the seductive concept of architecture as an art. Hannes Meyer, who succeeded Gropius as head of the Bauhaus, attempted to lead architecture in this direction with his insistence that building be considered in no way an "aesthetic process."[7] Buildings should be machines. Meyer thus described the house as a "biological apparatus serving the needs of the body and mind." But does such a functional approach lead to an inhabitable architecture? What are the requirements of dwelling?

When we think of a dwelling we think first of all of shelter. By protecting us against weather and strangers, shelter provides for dwelling. Not that dwelling can be adequately understood as a being sheltered: we may be sheltered and yet remain homeless and displaced. Consider our mobile homes. In the undeniable success of the mobile home industry − in 1973 48 percent of all new houses in the United States were mobile homes − a guide to such homes finds proof that they offer what is demanded: basic shelter at modest cost.[8] There is a suggestion that what distinguishes the traditional house from the mobile home are just frills, extras easily dispensed with. But what kind of dwelling do such homes, reduced to basic shelter, invite? The term "mobile home" gives a first answer. Even if, as a matter of fact, mobile homes are difficult to move and rarely moved, they are yet mobile. Like a tent, the mobile home stands in no essential relationship to the environment in which it happens to be located. We have a home that does not belong to a particular place or region. Nor need this be seen as a defect. Given an increasingly mobile population this mobility may well be considered an attractive feature.

More disturbingly, the cited guide adds to the advantage of mobility another: the owner of a mobile home has the possibility of becoming a member of an instant community. "Many mobile home parks exist throughout the country. Each park lot has the necessary utilities, and many of these parks offer a variety of recreational and service facilities which can be attractive bonuses. In addition everyone living in a mobile home park lives in a mobile home, and some might find this reassuring."[9] Not only has the relationship of the home to the environment become accidental, but so has the relationship of the individual to the community of which he just happens to be a member. The instant community of accidental relationships is in a deeper sense not a community at all.

If there is no essential relationship between the mobile home and
its social and physical environment, there is similarly no essential relationship between the mobile home and those who happen to live in
it. Not only are all mobile homes "similar in appearance" and constructed
pretty much in the same manner," but, as the guide proudly proclaims,
the individual is provided with a "total living environment, fully furnished and decorated by the manufacturer. Even bath towels of suitable
pattern and color can be made part of the package."[10] To be sure, the
customer is offered a choice between different "decor packages." Thus
he may choose between a Spanish, early American, or contemporary
look. But the individual no longer needs to shape his environment; all
he needs to do is step into a total environment, designed for him by
some decorator. The relationship between the person and his home has
become accidental. This is the price that has to be paid whenever a
house is reduced to a "machine for living." That something is lost in
this reduction is suggested by the many attempts to appropriate mobile
homes and to make them real houses, for example, by adding fake shut-
ters or a pitched roof. A porch, patio, or garden may further help to
bind the home to the environment and give it roots. Such features cannot be dismissed as unnecessary ornamentation. They answer a need
for a sense of place that not only goes beyond the need for shelter, but
also beyond any merely aesthetic interest. What I have called the "ethical
function" of architecture answers to this need.

III

To make this function a bit clearer, let me turn to a very different
example. In *On Adam's House in Paradise*, Joseph Rykwert discusses as
protoarchitecture the ceremonial objects of certain Australian tribes,
tribes so primitive that they do not have even rudimentary buildings.
"The only shelters they put up for their own use are windbreaks of bush
and scrub which are made by weeding and trimming as much as by
piling up."[11]
In the initiation ceremonies of these tribes curious objects play an
important part. "They consist of one long stick – usually a spear –
and one or two cross-sticks, latched to it at right angles. On this
framework string is wound in dense parallel lines, so that the whole
object appears as a rectangle with a triangle at each of its short ends."
Each such *waninga* has a multiple significance; it "represents the totemic
animal or object," while its general form also represents some constella-
tions . . . and finally the *waninga* represents the coupling of the ancestral

pair." During the ceremony the initiate embraces this object, thus identifying with it and with the order that it represents. A link is established
between the individual and the world around him. I am not interested
here in the details of Rykwert's account. What matters is only that the
waninga articulates the world as a meaningful order and assigns the
initiate a place in it. He is brought to affirm himself as belonging to
the world, the world as belonging to him. The *waninga* thus helps to
establish the initiate's stance in the world – his ethos.

As I mentioned, Rykwert discusses these *waningas* as protoarchitecture; and, although not buildings in the sense that they enclose space
like temples or churches, they do establish space as a meaningful order.
While the mobile home lets us dwell by providing shelter, the *waninga*
lets the Australian aborigine dwell by assigning him his place in a larger
order. The latter, too, is a necessary requirement of genuine dwelling.
Building should meet both requirements.

This is the point of Heidegger's description of an old farmhouse
in the Black Forest and the kind of dwelling that shaped it.

> It placed the farm on the wind-sheltered mountain slope looking south,
> among the meadows close to the spring. It gave the wide overhanging
> shingle roof whose proper slope bears up under the burden of snow, and
> which, reaching deep down, shields the chambers against the storms of
> the long winter nights. It did not forget the altar corner behind the com-
> munity table – it made room for the hallowed places of childbed and
> "the tree of the dead" – for that is what call a coffin here: the *Totenbaum*
> – and in this way it designed for the different generations under one
> roof the character of their journey through time.[12]

As Heidegger describes the farmhouse, it not only offers shelter,
but it provides a dwelling for an articulating man; a place in an ongoing order that includes God, community, and nature. The farmhouse
edifies – the word still hints at the relationship between building and
ethics.

But is such an edifying building still possible to us? Must we not
dismiss Heidegger's description of the Black Forest farmhouse as a
romantically anachronistic idealization that fails to do justice to the
shape of our world?

To be sure, the farmhouse still speaks to us of a dwelling rooted
in a particular time and place. That our dwelling does not know this
sense of place cannot be denied. Nor can we deny that there is
something very moving about buildings that speak to us of such a
dwelling. What is not clear, however, is that this loss must be deplored.
Should it not rather be welcomed as a liberation from what may be

called the tyranny of place? A tendency to escape from the rule of place has always marked human existence; the story of the fall, a story of self-assertion and displacement, gives it paradigmatic expression. But if man has always tried to free himself from the tyranny of place and to overcome distance, technology has provided this effort with far more effective means. Consider the way modern means of communication have brought the distant close; or the automobile and the possibilities it has opened up of living and working in widely scattered places. This attack on distance has to be understood in its ambivalence. Certainly, it does bring with it a rootlessness which threatens not only a loss of place, but also a loss of community. The small, closed community of the Black Forest peasant has given way to the less sheltering, but also far less imprisoning community – or should we rather speak of communities – in which we find ourselves participating. Such participation depends on the means of communication that help to liberate the individual from the tyranny of place. But does such liberation not demand that architecture shed its ethical function? Is the essential mobility of our houses not the other side of our freedom?

IV

Both the aesthetic and the functional approach deny to architecture what I have termed its "ethical function"; both belong together and are linked to the ruling understanding of being as objective reality and to a conception of space that knows nothing of home or privileged places.

The understanding of being, as objective reality, rests on a twofold reduction of experience. First of all, we find ourselves caught up in the world. The way we encounter things is tied to the activities in which we are engaged; their presentation is bound up with mood and interest. The first reduction attempts to bracket both: The self loses its place in the world and is transformed into a disinterested spectator of what is. Being becomes presence to such a subject; the world appears rather like a picture. As Schopenhauer points out, lost in this reduction is the real significance of things, that "by virtue of which these pictures or images do not march past us strange and meaningless, as they would otherwise inevitably do, but speak to us directly, are understood, and acquire an interest that engrosses our whole nature."[13]

The second reduction compounds this displacement. The key to it is provided by a reflection on perspective that plays a central part already in Plato's thinking: is not the way we experience things subject to a point of view that is ours only because of the place in which we happen to be? Our experience of things is mediated by our body and thus subject to the accident of location. To seize things as they are, we have to overcome this accident. But is not spirit bound to the body? The perspective assigned to us by our location is not a prison. Not only can we move and thus gain different perspectives, but in imagination we can put ourselves in other places even without moving. And we can go even further and demand descriptions free from all perspectival distortion — objectivity. Truth is here opposed to perspectival appearance. Implied is the essential invisibility of reality: whatever is real cannot in principal be seen as it is. One may object that if the eyes do not see things as they are, the spirit does so even less; indeed, it does not see at all. In its search for the truth it can do not better than replace reality with its own constructions. This must be admitted. But these constructions are more than idle creations: they are reconstructions to be tested by experience and experiment. Technology demonstrates their power. The necessity of returning in this sense to the life world does not, however, challenge the thesis of the essential invisibility of reality so understood. Nor can this return be understood in any way as a homecoming. Objective reason knows neither ethos nor home.

It should be evident that such reason cannot know anything of an ethical function of art or architecture. Plato condemned art for being thrice removed from the truth. Essentially the same insight led Hegel to claim that "art is and remains for us, from the side of its highest vocation, something past." "We" are here, those whose spiritual situation is determined by the conviction that we gain proper access to reality only to the extent that our thinking has freed itself from the tyranny of perspective. Art "from the side of its highest vocation" is art that takes seriously its ethical function. Only such art is said to belong to the past. This cannot be said of an art that resigns itself to the limits implied by the aesthetic conception. Quite the contrary: such an art belongs to the present age.[14]

We would be making it too easy for ourselves were we to think that "we" referred only to a few philosophers who, by placing exaggerated trust in the power of thinking, distort both the being of the self and the being of things. This would suggest that Hegel's proclamation of the death of art in its highest sense is characteristic of the sort of things that philosophers are likely to say, given their professional prejudice. The suggestion is thus often made that to escape their dismal conclusions, including this one about art, all that one has to do is reimmerse oneself in the life world, in that reality that affects us with its colors and sounds, its tastes and smells. This easy opposition of the life

world to the fantastic flights of philosophers fails to do justice to the
fact that the world we live in has been shaped by technology. Technology
rests on science, while science presupposes the two reductions that I
have sketched. Technology has carried these reductions into the world
in which we live. They are bound up with our sense of freedom, with
our modern ethos. This must make every attempt to escape from the
aberrations of a supposedly too Cartesian philosophy to the life world
or to the language games of the everyday questionable. Much as we
may resent it, we live in the shadow of an ontology that finds its first
clear articulation in Descartes's determination of the being of things
as reality, of the being on nature as *res extensa*, of human being as *res
cogitans*.

But in what sense does this ontology support the aesthetic approach?
Why does it not lead simply to the suggestion that we no longer need
art at all? The answer has to be sought in the twofold deficiency of the
understanding of being that I have sketched. The first reduction robs
things of what lets them speak to us and engage our interest: no longer
are they infused with our emotions, interests, and values. The second
reduction robs things of their sensuous presence: what we see and hear
is interpreted as the mere appearance of a reality that is essentially invisible. The world is transformed into a collection of colorless, soundless
facts, which happen to be as they are. In that reality man cannot feel
at home. As Nietzsche saw, and understood, the pursuit of truth must
tend toward nihilism. There is something disturbingly right about his
suggestion that "since Copernicus man has been rolling from the center
towards x."

The earth itself has become a mobile home. But we continue to
dream of a more genuine home, of an architecture strong enough
to assign us our place and to rescue us from the meaningless homogeneity of space.

V

Is architecture still able to establish man's ethos? Should it be? What
stands in the way of such understanding is, as I have suggested, an
understanding of being that has made objective and dislocated reasons
the measure of what is real. Such understanding must assign building
an instrumental function. The house becomes a machine. Not content
with such a machine we may try to add decorative frills. Unable to hold
on to its traditional ethical function, architecture thus leads an uneasy
life between aesthetic and functional considerations. Where we actually
dwell becomes unimportant.

But does objective reason provide the measure of what is real? Do we have to consider our physical environment as material to be manipulated or controlled? Or can we, must we, learn to understand this environment as something that does not so much belong to us as that we belong to it and place architecture in the service of such belonging? I would like to suggest that it is such an understanding that genuine building, that is to say a building that permits a genuine dwelling, both articulates and preserves.

Notes

1. Christian Norberg-Schulz, *Intentions in Architecture* (Cambridge, MA: M.I.T. Press, 1965), 219.

2. Arthur Drexler, *Transformations in Modern Architecture* (New York: The Museum of Modern Art, 1979), 17.

3. See Martin Heidegger, *Uber den Humanismus* (Frankfurt: Klostermann, 1949), 41.

4. Alexander Gottlieb Baumgarten, *Relections on Poetry*, trans. and intro. by Karl Aschenbrenner and William B. Holther (Berkeley: University of California Press, 1954), par. 68.

5. Immanuel Kant, *Critique of Judgement*, trans. by J. H. Bernard (New York: Hafner Publishing Co., 1951), pars. 1–5. Kant's disagreement with Baumgarten's understanding of the beautiful as sensible perfection, spelled out in par. 15, does not extend to the aesthetic approach.

6. Ibid., par. 51, p. 166.

7. Hannes Meyer, "Building," in *Programs and Manifestoes on 20th Century Architecture*, edited by Ulrich Conrads, translated by Michael Bullock (Cambridge, MA: M.I.T. Press, 1970), 119.

8. Judith and Bernard Raab, *Good Shelter: A Guide to Mobile, Modular, and Prefabricated Houses, Including Domes* (New York: Quadrangle, 1975), 29.

9. Ibid., 27.

10. Ibid., 39.

11. Joseph Rykwert, *On Adam's House in Paradise* (New York: The Museum of Modern Art, 1972), 185–89.

12. Martin Heidegger, "Building, Dwelling, Thinking," in *Poetry, Language, Thought*, trans. by A. Hofstadter (New York: Harper and Row, 1971), 160.

13. Arthur Schopenhauer, *The World as Will and Representation*, trans. by E. F. J. Payne (New York: Dover, 1969), I: 95, par. 17.

14. See Karsten Harries, "Hegel on the Future of Art," *The Review of Metaphysics* 27; 4 (June 1974), 677–96.

11. The Subject in Sartre and Elsewhere

Peter Caws

My subject here is the subject, in Sartre because I have learned from him, but mainly elsewhere because he was only a beginning. Sartre has dealt with my subject, indirectly, in several texts; I shall concentrate on two of them. But first I should perhaps explain why I say *my* subject. I say "my subject," first of all, because I am always the one in question; if I said *the* subject, as if it belonged to some metaphysical or ontological category, I would be making it the object of my own thought and would thus precisely sacrifice its status as subject (as Lacan has said in connection with the human sciences).[1] Such a categorization, furthermore, would imply the possession by this subject of constant and enumerable properties, whereas it is quite possible that other people's subjectivity takes a quite different form from mine; where subjectivity is concerned, I know only one, and it is my own. Something similar happens in the case of other philosophical myths, such as mind, reason, *the* unconscious, even Man himself, categories with which I can never be acquainted except as they occur in me. It is obviously difficult to suppress such forms of expression and I shall use them (including "the subject" itself) freely, but it must be remembered from the beginning that they are not the names of objective givens.

Secondly, my subject is the subject as I understand it — that is: what permits the integral, continuous, and possibly repeated apprehension of the object, in the moment of this apprehension and abstracting from purely physiological conditions of perception ("object" does not necessarily mean "object of perception" — there can be other objects, imaginary, intentional, and so on). "Integral" does not require a total integration of the object in itself, even though every integration is total

141

in its way, and is (for me) precisely a totalization. And "continuous" does not require a very long time — but enough. Although there could theoretically be an "instantaneous subject" it would be difficult to imagine such a subject's recognition of an object as such. Continuity implies, one might say, a repetition from one moment to the next; the further possibility of the repetition of a whole episode of apprehension, the recognition of the same object after a more or less prolonged absence, and implies the "genidentity" of the subject as an individual and of its own point of view. The subject will sometimes say "I," sometimes "me," according to the grammatical situation — hence the temptation to identify the problem of the subject with the problem of the "I" or the "me," which is acceptable on condition that one never takes these categories to be objective.

Now Sartre had a horror of the "inner life" and went to great pains, in *The Transcendence of the Ego*, to eliminate the subject from philosophy. I shall not follow his whole argument but I cite the last few sentences of that work:

> In fact, it is not necessary that the object precede the subject for spiritual pseudo-values to vanish and for ethics to find its bases in reality. It is enough that the *me* be contemporaneous with the World, and that the subject-object duality, which is purely logical, definitively disappear from philosophical preoccupations. The World has not created the *me*; the *me* has not created the World. These are two objects for absolute, impersonal consciousness, and it is by virtue of this consciousness that they are connected. This absolute consciousness, when it is purified of the *I*, no longer has anything of the *subject*. It is no longer a collection of representations. It is quite simply a first condition and an absolute source of existence. And the relation of interdependence established by this absolute consciousness between the *me* and the World is sufficient for the *me* to appear as "endangered" before the World, for the *me* (indirectly and through the intermediary of states) to draw the whole of its content from the World. No more is needed in the way of a philosophical foundation for an ethics and a politics which are absolutely positive.[2]

On the one hand, Sartre, in this text, has completely *objectified* the "me," but, on the other, he has introduced, in spite of his own protestations, a new subject, preceded in its turn by the object, in the person (if I may so put it) of "absolute consciousness." And this "absolute consciousness" poses a much graver problem than the subject itself. We encounter here Sartre's answer to the question of the origin of the self, which surges up for him out of a sort of pre-personal field of consciousness. He adopts this solution in order to avoid the phenom-

enological doctrine of a "refuge," represented by Husserl's "transcendental ego."

Unfortunately it is just on this point that Sartre has totally
misunderstood Husserl's position. The idea of a "refuge" is that of a place
where one escapes from what is happening elsewhere, a part of the
world protected from the rest. The Husserlian doctrine of the transcendental ego effects an inversion of the subject-object (or subject-world)
relationship according to which the subject, far from being a part of
the world, contains it. I cite one or two short passages from the *Cartesian Meditations*:

> This Ego, with his Ego-life, who necessarily remains for me, by virtue
> of such epochè, is not a piece of the world; and if he says, "I exist, *ego
> cogito*," that no longer signifies: "I, this man, exist," No longer am I the
> man who, in natural self-experience, finds himself *as* a man and who,
> with the abstractive restriction to the pure contents of "internal" or purely
> psychological self-experience, finds his own pure *mens sive animus sive
> intellectus*, nor am I the separately considered psyche itself. . . .
> Just as the reduced Ego is not a piece of its world, so, con-
> versely, neither the world nor any worldly object is a piece of my
> Ego, to be found in my conscious life as a really inherent part of
> it, as a complex of data of sensation or a complex of acts. This
> *"transcendance"* is part of the intrinsic sense of anything worldly,
> despite the fact that anything worldly necessarily acquires all the
> sense determining it, along with its existential status, exclusively
> from my experiencing, my objectivating, thinking, valuing, or
> doing, at a particular time − notably the status of an evidently
> valid being is one it can acquire only from my own evidences,
> my grounding acts. If this "transcendance," which consists in be-
> ing non-really included, is part of the intrinsic sense of the world,
> then, by way of contrast, the Ego himself, who bears within him
> the world as an accepted sense and who, in turn, is necessarily
> presupposed by this sense, is legitimately called *transcendental*,
> in the phenomenological sense.[3]

Now clearly the Husserlian sense in which the subject "contains" the
world allows the world to exist without a subject − it is just that this
will not be *our* world (or, strictly speaking, *mine*). Husserl does not fall
into the megalomania of Hegel, who, when he says that "everything
turns on grasping and expressing the True, not only as *Substance*, but
equally as *Subject*,"[4] refers less to the individual subject (the one I know
because I am it) than to the Absolute, personalizing and subjectifying,

so to speak, the dualism of Spinoza. Hegel, as Kierkegaard often remarked, lost himself as an individual subject in conferring all reality on the System:

> Existence must be revoked in the eternal before the system can round itself out; there must be no existing remainder, not even such a little minikin as the existing Herr Professor who writes the System . . .
>
> The systematic Idea is the identity of subject and object, the unity of thought and being. Existence, on the other hand, is their separation. It does not by any means follow that existence is thoughtless; but it has brought about, and brings about, a separation between subject and object, thought and being. In the objective sense, thought is understood as being pure thought; this corresponds in an equally abstract-objective sense to its object, which object is therefore the thought itself, and the truth becomes the correspondence of thought with itself. This objective thought has no relation to the existing subject; and while we are always confronted with the difficult question of how the existing subject slips into this objectivity, where subjectivity is merely pure abstract subjectivity (which again is an objective determination, not signifying any existing human being) it is certain that the existing subjectivity tends more and more to evaporate. And finally, if it is possible for a human being to become anything of the sort, and the whole thing is not something of which at most he becomes aware through the imagination, he becomes the pure abstract conscious participation in and knowledge of this pure relationship between thought and being, this pure identity, aye, this tautology, because this being which is ascribed to the thinker does not signify that he *is*, but only that he is engaged in thinking.
>
> The existing subject, on the other hand, is engaged in existing, which is indeed the case with every human being.[5]

We have therefore to give a sense to this existence which will do justice to the fact that it thinks, without absorbing it in thought understood as adequation to, if not identity with, being. The pairs subject/object, thought/being, are *thought by* a subject, as it happens here and now by me, by you. To account for this we have to introduce a new dimensionality, which encroaches on the perfect and eternal unity of the System. I have used in this connection the term *orthogonality*,[6] which I understand as the incursion of *time* into *structure*.

Sartre himself, in the second text of which I shall make use here, envisages precisely such a temporal (because dynamic) aspect of consciousness if not of subjectivity. I refer to the text on the idea of intentionality in Husserl, which dates from some years before *Being and Nothingness* and which is of exceptional brevity and lucidity:

If you were able to do the impossible and enter "into" a consciousness, you would be caught up by a whirlwind and thrown outside again, next to the tree in the dust, for consciousness has no "inside"; it is nothing but the outside of itself and it is this absolute flight, this refusal to be a substance, that constitutes it as a consciousness. Imagine now a connected series of burstings-forth that wrench us out of ourselves, which do not even leave to something called "ourselves" the leisure to form itself behind them, but which on the contrary throw us beyond them, in the dry dust of the world, on to the rude earth, among things; imagine that we are thus rejected, abandoned by our very nature in an indifferent, hostile and stubborn world; you will have grasped the profound sense of Husserl's discovery expressed in this famous remark: "All consciousness is consciousness of something." To be, says Heidegger, is to-be-in-the-world. Understand this "being-in" in the sense of movement. To be is to burst into the world, it is to start from a nothingness of world and consciousness in order suddenly to burst-out-as-consciousness-in-the-world. If consciousness should try to take itself back, to coincide finally with itself. all warm and enclosed, it would annihilate itself. This necessity for consciousness to exist as consciousness of something other than itself is what Husserl called "intentionality."[7]

What I want to suggest here, not for the first time,[8] is that Husserl's "famous remark" is incomplete — it has to be complemented by another: "All consciousness is somebody's consciousness." Sartre's idea of an absolute, prepersonal consciousness seems to me to be a pure mystification. It is admittedly hard to see how individual or personal consciousness (I prefer "individual" because it is precisely not a question of the *persona*, the individual as seen by others, but, in the end, of biological individuality, a point to which I shall return) arises out of the materiality of the body, but it seems to me useless to invent a common source of human existence as prepersonal, certainly not as a form of *consciousness*. Whose consciousness? Who, in the text just cited, is *rejected* into the world, who is *subjected* to all that? It is also true that when I come to an awareness of *myself* (which is not when I — and the "I" is important — come to an awareness of the *world*, but much later) I do not grasp myself *as an individual* but *as a consciousness*. However it is I just the same; if I do not yet know who I am, this is not at any rate because I confuse myself with someone else.

It seems to me in fact that the denial of subjectivity, on the part of subjects, whether in Sartre or in the structuralists, like the denial by Derrida, at the beginning of a book, that what he has written is a book, can only be taken seriously under the form of a surrealist game: this is not a pipe. It is one thing, however, to show in this way the inadequacy of language to things, but quite another actually to use this inade-

quate language for philosophical purposes. "I am not a subject" is a pro-
nouncement that would require a quite different preparation, like M.
Waldemar's "I am dead" in Poe's story. For the moment, at all events,
I am one.

Even if all this is accepted, provisionally at least, the problem of
the nature and provenance of the subject remains. I now approach the
question from a quite different angle. To reflect on the problem of subjectivity is necessarily to engage in *auto*reflection, to commit oneself
to *reflexivity*. Now in the rhetoric of Quintilian there occurs a figure
known as *subiectio*, defined as follows: to give the answer to one's own
question. In full subjectivity I give *myself* as the answer to my own question. But what sort of being must I be in order to be able to do that?
One way of approaching this question is by a genetic strategy, rather
like Condillac's with his statue but without presupposing any interior
organization. One might imagine a series of ascending stages, beginning with a being for which no obvious interior-exterior relationship
holds, a stone for example. At the second stage might be found a very
simple animal, like an amoeba, whose behavior we could imagine to
consist of situating itself in a fluid of varying salinity; this animal would
merely be *reactive*, making random movements as long as the salinity
of the fluid was too high or too low but stopping when it was just right.
In this case there would have to be some interior trigger corresponding to an acceptable level of salinity. Let us specify interior and exterior *states* (S) and what I shall call the *matching* of these states, symbolized
by the operator " $\sim$ ":

$$S_{int} \sim S_{ext}$$

("Matching" is not a simple correspondence but has an active sense.
Among things that match are not just left and right gloves but also keys
and locks, musical phrases and their repetitions, bits of jigsaw puzzles
and the spaces they fit into, and so on, and above all the signifier and
the signified. As I will stress later, I consider matching to be the fundamental phenomenon of signification. The essential point is that the
things matched should have, in relevant respects, similar structures and
complexities.)
So far, no subjectivity, nor even consciousness. At the third stage
I introduce a being that is in principle *sensitive*, still reactive but now
furnished with an interior *representation* (R) of the exterior state. This
representation is determined by the exterior state itself, so that we have:

$$S_{ext} \rightarrow R(S_{ext}); \ S_{int} \sim R(S_{ext})$$

The matching is now *internal*, and the agreement or disagreement between its terms might well show itself through a sensation of pleasure or pain. But we would not want to say that this being was a subject, even though it would be conscious in a primitive way. Subjectivity emerges only at the fourth stage, where we have not only an interior representation of the exterior state, but also a representation of the interior state. I will now advance the hypothesis that subjectivity is created in the matching of two interior representations, one the projection of a state of the individual, the other the interiorization of a state of the world (or eventually, the representation of another state of the same individual), the first as it were "thrown under" (*jetee sous*), the second in such a way as to ground and fix it. The reason why we require a *representation* of the interior state, and not just that state itself, is that the state changes from moment to moment, fleeing toward the future just as Sartre says being-for-itself does (and thus being unable to exist self-identically), whereas representations can be fixed, at least briefly, so as to constitute a *present* with a certain thickness. This element of duration can also be regarded as the solution to the problem of *differance*: the slippage between subjectivity and objectivity is overcome to the extent that they are both prolonged long enough to allow a mutual overlapping to establish itself; this would be a true case of *presence* whose essential feature we could capture by saying that presence is realized in the apposition of two representations.

The case of matching that would be constitutive of subjectivity is thus expressed as follows:

$$R(S_{int}) \sim R(S_{ext})$$

or even:

$$R(S_{int})_1 \sim R(S_{ext})_2$$

The concept of matching clearly needs to be developed more rigorously and in greater detail, but in what follows I shall consider it to be established sufficiently for my present purposes.

I come now to a consideration of the complexity of the representations R and thus of the world of the subject in question. Note that the condition that the two sides of a matching must be of comparable complexity does not require that subjectivity as such must be complex; as I have shown elsewhere[9] it is often the case that two matched complexities yield a simple product. (For example if I observe that two complex objects are identical to one another – two twins perhaps, dressed in the same way – their identity presents itself as a simple fact, even though an adequate description of either would have to be extremely complex. A simple subject may live in a complex world.

What is the world of a conscious subject like? That depends on the conditions of its representation (for example, I understand that frogs do not notice anything unles it is moving). It seems clear that *my world cannot be more complex than the internal structure by means of which it is represented to me*; the aspects of *the* world that are not reflected or matched by this structure do not and cannot exist for me. What hides this truth from us is that we have at our disposal a structure whose complexity is such that it requires a tremendous effort of the imagination to take it in: ten million cells at the back of the eye, thirty billion in the brain. Without pursuing this idea into its furthest physiological ramifications (although I am absolutely convinced that any serious understanding of subjectivity *must* take this route) we can easily go one step further and claim that our interior world not only can but must be *far more* complex than the exterior world in which we appear to live.

To be in a position to match a given exterior situation I must have at my disposal a repertory of interior elements far exceeding the totality of the elements of that situation. It is a bit like reading (it is in effect a kind of reading): if I am to be able to read a given text I must know all the words it contains – and all the others. This principle of the "prepared reader" is very far-reaching (and this statement of it is already inaccurate, since some contextual understanding is possible), but I leave it aside here. It is worth remarking, however, that the principle explains, for example, the experiences of drug users who believe themselves to have discovered new worlds in their states of intoxication. If we are to be able to read the world in which we actually do live, we must have at hand the materials for reading other worlds, that is, for constructing the internal representations that would constitute consciousness of them if we lived in *them*, and it need occasion no surprise if the violence we are capable of doing to the brain by the ingestion of chemicals should occasionally produce such representations, although these, given their manner of production, provide of course no evidence whatever for the actual existence of the worlds in question.

In fact, the complexity of the apparatus at our disposal is such that many other questions are readily clarified by theories which take account of it. For the structure of the apparatus is not just determined by the physiology of the nervous system, but is acquired in large part from experience, mainly by reading, and above all by the reading of texts. (Note that this does not contradict the "prepared-reader" principle: I must have most of the elements at my disposal, but their relationships may be unexpected.) Subjectivity, I shall say, is the *animation* of this structure, its *scanning* (since there can obviously be no question of matching everything at once, we have to acknowledge *episodes* of subjectivity, partial animations of its extraordinarily rich resources). The structure is idiosyncratic in each of us, partly because of genetic differentiation but mainly because of *radical* differences in experience and in reading. And it allows of virtually unlimited extension. If I read a book, I borrow its structure, I lose myself in it, I am "buried" in it — a significant expression for the light of it throws on the relationship between daily life and the life of the imagination.

It was just this that André Breton understood when he wrote in *Surrealism and Painting*:

> Nothing prevents me, at this moment, from concentrating my attention on some illustration in a book — and what surrounded me no longer exists. Instead of what surrounded me there is something else because, for example, I am present without difficulty at a wholly different ceremony.[10]

"What surrounds me" may in fact be far less interesting than what I am reading — or what I find in myself, in my unconscious, my dreams, my hypnagogic images and phrases. As a subject, I have a whole domain to explore if only I can find the keys to it. But where then am *I*? It is not that I *inhabit* my body, rather as a conscious subject I *am* it. But I am it differently depending on the circumstances. Often I am the animation only of its physical structure or the structure of the surrounding world as this is delivered to me in perception. But often I am the animation of other structures, those of books or of the imagination itself. I cite Breton again, this time in the first *Surrealist Manifesto*:

> For today I think of a *chateau* which is not necesarily half in ruins; this chateau belongs to me, I see it in a rural setting, not far from Paris. . . . I will be accused of poetic falsehood: people will say that I live in the rue Fontaine, and that they won't swallow this story. Parbleu! But this chateau to which I welcome them, are they so sure that it is just an image? What if this palace existed! My guests are there to answer for it; their caprice is the luminous road that leads to it. Truly it is in our fantasy that we live, *when we are there*.[11]

Now we are always somewhere, we are there morally on the basis of what we are physically, even though this truth hides itself from us and may well continue to do so. There is enough going on in us to make boredom superfluous. Among other things, there are the second-order reflections we call criticism and philosophy, including reflections on the subject. If as a subject I traverse, as I have suggested, the labyrinthine structure of the *me*, this means that I inscribe in it my own history, I trace it as if it were a continuous line through this network of available subjective states. And if now I add to the idiosyncrasy of the subject its *linearity*, evoking in this way the doctrine of the sign, this will perhaps not come as a surprise. The matching, of which I have spoken, has been the trademark of the sign ever since Saussure, and that of the life of the subject should show itself to be a life of significance or of meaning seems altogether appropriate. "A life of meaning" might well replace "the meaning of life" as the goal of the quest for happiness or truth on which uneasy people are always embarking.

In conclusion let me add to the idiosyncrasy and the linearity of the subject something inevitably suggested by the latter, namely its *arbitrariness*. For the subject, like the sign, is arbitrary.[12] That *these* subjectivities, in *these* bodies, here and now, should be in question does not admit of reasons or explanations. They are not only our mode of access to reality, they *are* this reality; they contain their world. But as Husserl saw, this is not an asymmetrical relationship. I end therefore with a further passage from Breton:

> Everything I love, everything I think and feel, inclines me towards a special philosophy of immanence according to which surreality would be contained in reality itself, and would be neither superior or exterior to it. And reciprocally, for the container would also be the contained.[13]

One last word: the question "why this subjectivity, in this body?" is, on the one hand, extremely profound, on the other, completely empty. It is serious in the sense that with this body I might have been somebody else, or nobody, or in the very different sense that "I" could have had a different body. How and when does subjectivity *begin*, what are the necessary and sufficient conditions of its emergence? These are questions worth pursuing, perhaps with the resources of pathology: one might ask, for example, whether autism and schizophrenia might not be the effects of a lack, or as it were, a disconnection of subjectivity. But it would be logically absurd to ask "why am I myself?" It is quite enough for me to be it.

Notes

1. Jacques Lacan, *Ecrits* (Paris: Seuil, 1966), 230.

2. Jean-Paul Sartre, *The Transcendence of the Ego*, tr. Forrest Williams and Robert Kirkpatrick (New York: The Noonday Press, 1957), 105–6.

3. Edmund Husserl, *Cartesian Meditations*, tr. Dorion Cairns (The Hague: Martinus Nijhoff, 1960), 25-26.

4. G.W.F. Hegel, *Phenomenology of Spirit*, tr. A.V. Miller (Oxford: Clarendon Press, 1977), 10.

5. Soren Kierkegaard, *Concluding Unscientific Postscript to the "Philosophical Fragments,"* tr. David F. Swenson, Lillian Marvin Swenson, and Walter Lowrie, *A Kierkegaard Anthology*, edited by Robert Bretall (Princeton, N.J.: Princeton University Press, 1946), 204-5.

6. Peter Caws, "Parallels and Orthogonals," *Semioxtext(e)* I:2 (Fall 1974), 64.

7. Jean-Paul Sartre, "Une idée fondamentale de la phénoménologie de Husserl: l'intentionnalité," in *Situations, I* (Paris: Gallimard, 1947), 30-31 (tr. P.C.).

8. See Peter Caws, *Sartre* (London: Routledge and Kegan Paul, 1979), 60.

9. Peter Caws, "Science, Computers, and the Complexity of Nature," *Philosophy of Science* 30;2 (April 1963), 158-64.

10. André Breton, *Le Surréalisme et la peinture* (nouvelle edition revue et corrigee) (Paris: Gallimard, 1965), 2 (tr. by P.C.).

11. André Breton, *Manifestes du Surréalisme* (Paris: Pauvert, 1962), 30-31 (tr. P.C.).

12. See note 6.

13. André Breton, *Le Surréalisme et la peinture*, 46 (tr. P.C.).

12. Method and Madness in *The Family Idiot*

William Leon McBride

The book's flaws are too manifest to dwell on. It would have been useful if volume 4, concerning *Madame Bovary*, had actually been written, but I am skeptical about Sartre's oft-repeated claim that anyone who understood what Sartre was about could theoretically write that projected volume for himself or herself. Nowhere more than in *The Idiot*[1] is the lack of a responsible editor more keenly felt. Literary critics, such as Harry Levin, charge that some of Sartre's crucial reconstructions of Flaubert's early life either are unsupported by evidence or, worse, run counter to the evidence[2] – although Levin's closing salvo, to the effect that *The Family Idiot* constitutes an attack on literature itself, is so overblown as to arouse suspicion about his objectivity. Ronald Aronson, in devoting the closing chapter of his recent book on Sartre[3] to *The Family Idiot*, assembles many pieces of internal evidence to attempt to show that *The Idiot* amounts to a late Sartrean retreat into unreality, with a partly imaginary Flaubert living in an unreal world, and with this entire Sartrean enterprise being entirely removed from the exigent political realities of his times, to the involvement with which Sartre had once been so committed. I myself was particularly struck, when rereading these volumes, by what I feel to be the excessively French orientation of the book; Sartre could and should have said much more than he did about both the relationship and the applicability of the case of Flaubert and the Second Empire to other nineteenth- and twentieth-century cultures, at least to those most similar. The carpings, the expressions of reservations, could consume my entire allotted space.

I prefer, however, to explore two salient themes, that of method and that of madness, from *The Idiot*, in each case first explicating some aspects of Sartre's treatment and then raising a few questions about it.

I should explain that I have taken some literary license in naming the second one "madness," since I do not mean to speak of *folie* or certainly of *asiles* or *cliniques* primarily in a Foucaultian vein. (In fact, a comparison of Foucault's method in *Madness and Civilization* with Sartre's in *The Idiot* might be very interesting, but it is a task that I am not prepared to undertake.) Rather, I mean the sort of madness that is usually considered milder and for which the canonical Sartrean term in *The Family Idiot* is *névrose* – neurosis (although he does occasionally also speak of *folie* in volume 2).

As has frequently been observed, Sartre intended *The Family Idiot* to be an exemplification of the method of which it had been a question in *Search for a Method*. An important aspect of this method was to be the blending of regression with progression – roughly, the effort to dig below the surface of a phenomenon in its full-blown form, inverting chronological sequence, in order then to reconstruct the chronology with the aid of the explanatory elements that have been discovered. Although Sartre writes frequently about these topics of regression and progression in the first two volumes of *The Family Idiot* (not very much in the third volume), and although some of Sartre's discussions of Flaubert's *juvenilia* are good, clear illustrations of what he means by regressive analysis, it is not this aspect of his method on which I wish to dwell. What interests me more is the way in which Sartre attempts to synthesize Freud and Marx, and the extent to which he may or may not have succeeded.

Of course, I do not mean the precise doctrines of either one, Marx or Freud. Although Sartre's painfully detailed discussion of Flaubert's childhood seems closer to Freud in language and assumptions than anything else Sartre wrote, including *The Words*, and although readers are left with the very strong question as to just how, if all the alleged facts that Sartre has marshalled are true, Flaubert could have become anything very different from what he did become, still we may say with confidence that first, Sartre rejected to the end what he considered Freud's metaphysical apparatus, especially the structures of id, ego, and superego; and second, that Sartre continued to the end, to uphold some notion of individual free choice, as opposed to Freud's determinism. As for Marx, Sartre mentions him rarely by name in *The Family Idiot*, but tosses about a few Marxian phrases, such as ideology (to which I will return later), with his usual disdain for adhering to precise original meanings, and sounds as contemptuous of later Marxist oversimplifications (see, for example, III:423–24)[4] of reality as he did in *Search for a Method*. Besides, we must admit that, in addition to being a philosopher and some other things, Marx was also an economist;

whereas Sartre, in *The Family Idiot*, exhibits considerably less knowledge of economic phenomena than does Flaubert when Flaubert describes the details of Emma Bovary's financial ruin!

No, the synthesis of which I am speaking is the synthesis of the psychoanalytic domain (to the understanding of which Freud has contributed the most basic categories), with the sociohistorical (for the understanding of which we are most beholden to Marx). Or, to put the matter even more simply, as Sartre does in his section titles, it is the synthesis of the subjective with the objective – subjective neurosis with objective neurosis, Flaubert, the individual, with the objective spirit of his culture. This is the heart of Sartre's answer to the question of what would constitute an adequate, fully explanatory anthropology. It yields the universal singular. In Flaubert's case – and it must be remembered that the whole analysis of Flaubert is supposed to be taken as just an illustration – it shows us why the neurotic younger child of a prominent provincial physician, the sources of many of whose ideas and attitudes went back to the early part of his century, and who therefore might not have appeared as a particularly good candidate to express the spirit of the Second Empire, nevertheless came to do so, whereas seemingly more "with it," more forward-looking contemporaries, such as Lecomte de Lisle, did not. As Sartre says at one point (III:425 – my translation, here and throughout):

> Gustave undertakes his readings [as an adolescent] when he is, if not striken with neurosis, at least in a preneurotic state; for this reason his poetic [attitude] will fully coincide with Neurosis-Art. Lecomte de Lisle, by contrast, interiorizing the demands of Absolute-Art, is not, however, affected with psychosomatic problems; in other words, he lives this abstract madness of failure in full health of body and mind; for that reason, he writes his work – and misses with it.

Now, it seems to me that the real paradox to which Sartre is alluding here is just the sort of paradox with which we are constantly confronted when we try to understand the first things about history and about our society. Behavioral methods will certainly not come close to explaining what actually happens, but neither, by themselves, will those approaches that take all historical actors to be simply prime candidates for the psychoanalyst's couch. Just think of all the paradoxes that are ingredients in the fact of Ronald Reagan's being the current president of the United States: the older man who presides over a society which shows little sympathy for its elderly and who threatens to cut their existing benefits; the product of a quite impoversihed background whose style is to flaunt wealth and to surround himself with advisors who obviously have contempt for poverty with a self-righteousness based on self-serving economic principles; the former labor union president who is dedicated to weakening the powers of unions; and so forth. Some of Reagan's detractors, both here and abroad, make a major point of his being a professional actor. This is important for understanding him, to be sure and Sartre, who was always fascinated by the actor's role (and who, even in *The Family Idiot*, makes much of the young Flaubert's interest in plays and in play acting) would have found it a fascinating circumstance. But, by itself, the observation that Reagan is an actor is superficial, totally inadequate to account for his role in the larger drama of contemporary society.

What I conclude is that, if we are to achieve an understanding of universal singulars, something like the synthetic method that Sartre tries to exemplify in *The Family Idiot* it is what we must follow. (And so, to this extent at least, the book is by no means a failure.) This method cannot be given the kind of precision that is appropriate to a mathematical equation; it is open ended; it must be partly anecdotal; it must involve a certain amount of reconstruction – of employment, if you will, of *imagination* on the part of the person who is using it – and yet it makes sense. It starts from *lived experience*, that notion that Sartre claimed, in an interview,[5] really to have discovered only later on in his career, and that plays a prominent role especially in volumes 1 and 2 of *The Family Idiot*.

But there are a number of philosophical difficulties, as one might suspect, with Sartre's own instantiation of this method in that work. I shall mention a few of them. It goes without saying, of course, that, if the method is to have any practical value, the explainers of social events must learn to use it with more conciseness than Sartre did. Beyond that, however, there is the question of just how to *balance* the two aspects, the psychoanalytic and the sociohistorical. In *The Idiot*, Sartre's balance, from a sheer content standpoint, is skewed in the direction of the spychoanalytic – far too much so, in my opinion. Peter Caws, in his book, *Sartre*,[6] seems to me to be suggesting that volume 3, the shortest of the three, in which what I have been calling the sociohistorical domain is emphasized, is the most philosophically interesting, and I certainly agree with that.

Another, deeper problem, is that of the relationship between the two synthesized domains. By the very structure of his presentation, Sartre seems to me to be assuming a greater separability between them than is warranted by lived experience itself. In fact, he usually seems to equate *le vècu* with the psychoanalytic, including those elements of the psychic life that are sometimes called "the subconscious." There are

problems not only with this very terminology but also with the way
– far too narrow, in my opinion – of identifying lived experience. (I
have written about this elsewhere[7].) Now, it is true that the typical
childhood, the time on which, as Sartre and Freud agree, one must focus
in order to understand the psychoanalytic aspects of individuals, has
for the modern bourgeois child traditionally been lived largely in apparent isolation from the sociohistorical. This was true in the ninteenth
century with Flaubert, just as it was true in the twentieth century with
Sartre. But the very reality of the complex practices of the bourgeois
family, within which a neurosis such as that of *The Family Idiot* can
develop, is itself an unique sociohistorical phenomenon, rather than
being an eternal, fixed given, as writers from Engels on have taken pains
to show. So you cannot, in principle, separate the psychoanalytic from
the other dimension, even at the beginning of the individual's life. Now
it is obvious that, when writing, an author can only deal with one topic
at a time; even a Sartre requires some order of presentation. But it seems
to me that his separation of the two dimensions goes considerably
beyond what is required by the rules of orderly presentation. For
instance, he uses, as I have mentioned, the adjectives, "subjective" and
"objective," as a means of identifying the distinction between the two
domains. I find this very disturbing. It seems to me to point back to
some fundamental conceptual errors, or at least oversimplifications, of
which Husserl's method, still a strong influence on Sartre in *The Family
Idiot*, had the merit of attempting to overcome.

    Having made, then, a few comments that may be of use for a discus-
sion concerning Sartre's overall method, I now turn to my second chosen
topic, madness. Out of considerations both of limited space and of personal interest, I shall confine my remarks mostly to what Sartre has
to say about "the objective neurosis" – the madness of the society at
large. First of all, just what was this neurosis, in the case of Flaubert's
society? Sartre, for purposes of understanding Flaubert, focuses mostly
on the notion of what he calls "Art-Neurosis," the pessimistic idea, very
common at the time, that good writing must be the product of some
nervous disorder. But there are other strains in the objective spirit of
the time that, in turn, help account for the popularity of this idea –
for instance, the fact that there had been a revolution in 1848, sup-
pressed with considerable bloodshed, leading to the anomalous situation of a national bourgeoisie, which had come to dominance in the
very radical revolution of 1789, grimly concluding that its interests could
only be protected by an *imperial* form of government. Notions of what
is healthy activity and what is not, where art falls under the latter
category, can be shown to be intimately related to this highly confused
historical state of affairs.

Without entering further into the details of these interconnections, or into the way in which Sartre attempts to show the linkage between teh epoch's objective neurosis and the subjective neurosis of Flaubert, or into the reasons why *Madame Bovary*, recalling a slightly earlier period of the century but at the same time depicting the neurotic aspects of provincial life as fated, inevitable, and unchanging, was such a success in the Second Empire public, I wish to raise some questions about the general status of this key Sartrean concept of objective neurosis.

First of all, can every period be characterized as having some such neurosis? Sartre's own answer is clearly no. As he says early in volume 3 (pp, 36–37), "Shall we say that every ideology is a collective neurosis? That would be singularly to abuse a rigorous concept." He goes on to discuss the ideals of healthy rationality which prevailed during the period of the Enlightenment, even though, as he says, "that society is nourished on false ideas: false is the idea of Nature, of human nature, of natural right; false is the fundamental conception of a bourgeoisie which takes itself for the universal class."

Now, if indeed Sartre is right in his answer to this question, then what he has done by writing *The Family Idiot* may not, after all, be very helpful. For if what makes the universal singularity of Flaubert what it is is the coexistence of his particular personal neurosis with a *uniquely* neurotic moment in the history of French society, then how can we generalize Sartre's approach in studying Flaubert to the study of other significant individuals – for example, Ronald Reagan in our society? It would seem that the terms of the inquiry would have to be so very different, incommensurable with Sartre's.

This is especially true if the one more general concept with which we have to work is "ideology," at least as Sartre has treated it. For his use of this concept is anything but rigorous. True, he inserts a footnote (III:212) in which he demonstrates his recognition of "the Marxist sense of the term," and in which he says that he has been using it in this passage for the sake of convenience, that it is not at all used in the same as the sense in which he used it in *Search for a Method*. There, as he now puts it, he used it to refer to "the practice of post-Marxian philosophers, who look for what is true beginning with Marxist philosophy, and whom I named ideologists . . . to indicate that they were attempting to specify in its details a philosophy that they did not create." He might have added, but does not, that in *Search for a Method* he took his own existentialism to be a prime example of ideology in this sense. But the other sense, the actual Marxist sense, is one that Sartre now claims to be employing for convenience, wihtout really examining with philosophical care what it means; he only mentions that it is a "practico-inert determination" – which is not a great deal of help. Certainly Marx and Engels were quite vague about indicating the term's precise meaning, and many interesting scholarly controversies rage about the meaning today. So it is by no means a well-honed intellectual tool with which to go about applying Sartre's method, as exemplified in *The Family Idiot*, to other individuals and epochs.

But is Sartre really correct about the uniqueness of objective neurosis to the Second Empire period, and perhaps to a few other periods scattered through history? Doesn't every age have its own illusions, as well as its own delusions? The Enlightenment, for example, with its allegedly healthy, optimistic rationality, can be said to have suffered form a sort of society-wide delusion of grandeur. Indeed Hegel, in his discussion of the Enlightenment in the *Phenomenology of Mind* – the dialectical struggle of insight with superstition, the triumph of the former, its turn to the principle of utility, its assertion of absolute freedom and eventual dénouement in terror – has rather well captured some of the sicker, one might as well say neurotic, aspects of that period. So Sartre's contrast between it and the supposedly unique neurotic mid-nineteenth century begins to break down.

The fundamental philosophical difficulties with Sartre's treatment of neurosis become even more serious when we consider the complementary issue of what this word, *neurosis*, a kind of madness, implies. It implies that we can, in fact, *rigorously* (Sartre's word) distinguish neurotic from healthy behavior, both in individuals and in societies. Is this really true? A very extensive recent literature, particularly in this country, has been devoted to putting this implication into question in the case of individuals; the notion of a society-wide neurosis, except perhaps as it might be applied to a contemporary society, regarded as a so-called sick society, has generally not been taken seriously enough by scholars to warrant refutation.

Flaubert, as he emerges in the first two volumes of *The Family Idiot*, has something of the monstrous about him. Years before, Sartre made something of a monster, too, though obviously a monster for whom he had more admiration than he did for Flaubert, out of Genet. (I am convinced that he tried valiantly, but I think failed, to do the same with the child Jean-Paul in *The Words*.) In any event, Flaubert does not seem generally to have been seen as a monster by those who knew him; even the rather ridiculous prosecutor at the trial in which an unsuccessful attempt was made to censor *Madame Bovary*, the transcript of which I recently had occasion to read, did not depict Flaubert as a fearsome, deeply neurotic creature. Similarly Genet, despite the devastating events of his early life, which Sartre has recorded, turned out to be a successful author, quite capable of conducting himself in a conventional manner among other human beings, as I myself once observed.

My point is not, of course, to deny the real peculiarities of behavior, centered around the tendency to severe seizures of an apparently psychosomatic nature, that characterized Flaubert, It is rather to express agreement with that recent literature which has challenged the rigidity of the line drawn, as it was by Freud, and as it is, rather surprisingly in light of the very convincing arguments against traditional notions about fixed character traits in *Being and Nothingness* by Sartre, and in *The Family Idiot*, between the neurotic and its opposite — call it the "normal," if you will. Sartre himself is said to have acted in a bizarre way, for instance, with respect to money, sometimes dispensing it with an astonishingly insouciant bountifulness. Was this neurotic behavior? Once one has begun to examine the meaning of the term, the question itself loses much of its force.

The same can be said, with even less hesitation, concerning questions about allegedly neurotic societies. A society in which it was commonly held that one must in some sense be mad in order to be a significant writer was indeed a society characterized by deep contradictions. But the same can certainly be said of a society in which economic considerations are commonly taken to outweigh in importance virtually all other human objectives, so that a figure such as the moneylender in *Madame Bovary*, transposed into this society, would be treated as a hero of "free enterprise"; such is our American society today. At the same time, however, I am dubious about the explanatory or practical value of dwelling very much on just how sick we are collectively.

In *The Family Idiot*, Sartre has exemplified a methodology that will enable future writers to better identify the profound, interrelated social and individual contradictions that account for salient behaviors in a nonbehaviorist fashion, and for that reason this mammoth, unwieldy book must be considered a landmark and a significant part of our philosophical heritage. But in carrying out this project with respect to Flaubert and the Second Empire, he placed, I believe, undue emphasis on the idea of *neuroses* as being peculiar, respectively, to that individual and that epoch, thus unnecessarily denigrating both is own earlier views about the fluidity of human personality and the rich possibilities of generalization inherent in the method that he has proposed.

Notes

1. Gustave Flaubert, *The Family Idiot*, tr. by Cosman, (Chicago and London, University of Chicago Press, 1981.)

2. *Journal of the History of Ideas* XXXIII; NO. 4 (October–December 1972), 643–49.

3. *Jean-Paul Sartre – Philosophy in the World* (London: NLB and Verso Editions, 1980), 325–54.

4. All page references to Sartre in this paper are to *L'Idiot de la Famille: Gustave Flaubert de 1821 à 1857* (Paris: Editions Gallimard, 1972).

5. "The Itinerary of a Thought," in Jean-Paul Sartre, *Between Existentialism and Marxism*, trans. by J. Mathews (New York: William Morrow, 1976), 41–42.

6. *Sartre* (London: Routledge & Kegan Paul, 1974).

7. "Sartre and Lived Experience," *Research in Phenomenology* XI (1981), 75–89.

Part IV.
Phenomenology
and the Sciences

13. Natural and Artificial Intelligence

Elmar Holenstein

After the fascinating initial successes with computer models in psychology and neurology, there has been a sober awakening in recent years. It has become increasingly apparent that the blank spaces on the map of both sciences cannot be explored merely by developing ever more intricate versions of current computer models, but rather only by the promotion of radically different ones. This paper proposes the mode of functioning of natural languages as such an alternative model.

Natural human languages, like brains and minds, are sytems endowed with the possibility of development and their actual development is under constraint of success. Successful adaptation to the tasks required of the organism by its environment is rewarded. In the following, such systems are called natural systems.

Natural languages are opposed in their mode of functioning to present-day computers in a significant respect. The mode of functioning (the functional structure) of computers is independent of the (chemical-physical) matter (the material structure) of which they are made. Natural languages are, however, in their meaningful usages manifestly dependent upon the (usually phonic) matter of which they are made. Another salient property of natural languages is intimately tied to this dependency upon matter, their plurifunctionality.

Thus the two theses set forth in this paper read as follows: (1) the mode of functioning of the brain is not independent of the particular matter of which it consists, of its particular chemical-physical structure, and (2) the structures of brain and mind are plurifunctional. Inasmuch as the plurifunctionality of a system is related to the dependence of functional structure upon material structure, the two theses are also related.

The import of these two theses – and thus of the model of natural language – is considerable for the Philosophy of Mind. In their wake, two common assumptions of recent Philosophy of Mind prove to be dogmas. They are the assumption of the underdetermination of neural or mental structures in relation to the output of the brain or mind, and the assumption of a stable functionlessness of epiphenomenal structures.

In spite of its being diametrically opposed to computer models, the model of natural language, seen from a certain perspective, is a continuation of computer models. It is an indisputable, although in recent philosophy of science little reflected fact that computers in turn owe their creation to the model of a natural system, namely the mode of functioning of human acts, concrete acts such as a goal-oriented hurling of missiles and abstract acts such as computation and other mental problem solving.[1]

The simulation of specifically human acts in technical systems led to a startling discovery. It suddenly became possible – to the surprise of both proponents and opponents of phenomenological philosophy – to be a *phenomenologist* (in the sense of non-materialist, non-mechanist) without being a *mentalist* as well. Computer models imply a phenomenological attitude.

The anti-materialist, anti-mechanist interpretation of computers and computer models in psychology and neurology (e.g. by G. Klaus and H. Putnam), however was not pursued with explicit recourse to phenomenological terms and theses. On the contrary, the most outspoken critics of computer models in psychology and neurology (e.g. H. Dreyfus) were the ones who recurred to phenomenological ideas. But the two theses presented here, the interrelatedness of function (sense) and matter (substance), and the plurifunctionality of structures, are also phenomenologically inspired. They are most explicit in Prague structuralism (particularly in R. Jakobson), i.e. in that branch of structural linguistics that makes frequent reference to Husserl.[2]

Since the (partial) phenomenological continuity between computer models and the model of natural languages is just as remarkable as their (partial) contrast, I shall proceed with a brief phenomenological interpretation of computer achievements. This is followed by an exemplary introduction to the two theses of the interrelatedness of function and matter and of plurifunctionality. In the last section the two dogmas of the underdetermination of neural and mental structures and the stable functionlessness of epiphenomena shall be subjected to critical examination.

1. The Phenomenological Interpretation of Computer Models

The historical point of departure of phenomenology was the demonstration of the autonomy of the laws of logic vis-a-vis those of psychology. This was seconded and, in the subseqent development of phenomenology, soon dominated by the thesis of the autonomy of the laws of psychology vis-à-vis those of physics. The opposing doctrines commit dire categorical mistakes. And it is precisely this view which has also become commonplace in a field deemed profane by traditional phenomenology, namely the computer sciences.

The solution of a logical problem and no less the solution of a psychological problem, e.g., the choice between two conflicting actions with regard to a system of preferences, are in principle independent of the physical constitution of the computer. The same program and thus the same problem-solving strategy can be realized in an infinity of systems with quite different physical-chemical constitutions. As Fodor puts it: "Physically *different* structures may obey the *same* psychological theory."[3] Or in Putnam's more vivid formulation: "The question of the autonomy of our mental life does not hinge on and has nothing to do with that all too popular, all too old question about matter or soul-stuff. We could be made of Swiss cheese and it wouldn't matter."[4]

The truly phenomenological character of this insight within the computer sciences becomes evident upon consideration of the shift in categories that accompanied it. The categories predominant in modern physics at the beginning of this century were *thrust, pressure, attraction, repulsion, tension, load, impulse*, and the like. Naturalist psychology, repudiated by phenomenology, had adopted these categories and augmented them with analogies such as *reinforcement*. Common to all of these categories is their implication of the notion of *force*. Not pioneered by any philosophers, cybernetics and information theory introduced entirely different categories into technology, categories such as *goal, selection, regulation, representation, program, model, signal, information*, and the like. In contrast to the first-named categories, the latter have nothing to do with force. Rather, they imply generic concepts such as *structure* and *sense* (i.e. goal-directedness).

Modern science owes its great success to the exclusion of just these humanist or – more generally – idealist categories. It has now become clear, however, that they are ontologically neutral and thus allow both a mentalist and a physicalist interpretation (i.e. realization). Even if, in the domain of the humanities, their mentalist interpretation were to prove superfluous, two aspects are still worthy of note: (1) the great advances made in this century in neurology and in biology quite generally have been possible only through the adoption of these originally humanist categories by the natural sciences, that is, through the reversal of a 300-year trend of dislodging humanist categories from more and more subject areas, and (2) there is still a categorical distinction between the first list of notions and the second, even upon a physical interpretation of the latter. The proponents of Artificial Intelligence are justifiably charged – and the philosophic ones among them readily admit it – with adhering to a radical dualism when they insist that the same (functional) program can be realized by (materially) totally different physical systems. This new dualism is not, as in Descartes, a dualism between two substances, mental and physical, but rather between material structure (matter/energy) on the one hand and functional structure (function/sense) on the other, in other words a dualism between energetic and hermeneutic categories. This kind of dualism is perfectly familiar to phenomenological circles, at the latest since Ricoeur's book on Freud,[5] which makes it all the more noteworthy that the anti-materialist (anti-mechanist) interpretation of computer achievements has been developed both by Marxist and analytic philosophers, but not by phenomenologists.[6]

2. Two Aspects of the Model of Natural Language

An outstanding characteristic of natural languages is the fact that their mode of functioning is not independent of the matter or substance by which they are conveyed. 'Matter' and 'substance' are not to be taken metaphysically; they are shorthand terms for bundles of (micro-)structures which act as functional units, as vehicles of a function. In the case of language, one usually speaks of the 'sense' rather than the 'function' of an utterance.

Two simple examples shall serve as illustration. In natural languages, the two semantic properties most obviously dependent upon their respective matter are connotation and poetic ambiguity. In many cases, they are determined by the phonic matter (structure) of their respective language.

The German words *Alpdrücken* and *Alptraum* have a literal meaning comparable to that of the English word 'nightmare.' A kobold (an elf or a mare) threatens to smother the sleeper at night. The phonic association of the Old German word *Alb* ('elb') with the word *Alpen* ('alps') resulted in associating the feeling of being smothered with the weight of the Alps. The phonic association led not only to this interpretive shift but even to a change in spelling. The use of a *b* is felt to be archaic and today the word is virtually always written with a *p*. Both changes, semantic and graphic, could never occur in the corresponding English word 'nightmare' because of its different phonic structure.

For the sake of brevity, a pun, a piece of folk poetry, shall illustrate the dependence of poetic ambiguity on its phonic matter.

To be is to do.	Socrates
To do is to be.	Sartre
To be do be do.	Sinatra

The phonic parallelization of these three statements effects an ambiguity of Sinatra's "To be do be do" on the one hand and of the two philosophical maxims on the other. Through the phonic similarity of Sinatra's production with the two philosophical epigrams, one is led, for a brief moment, to believe that there must also be something profound about Sinatra's line and, for a second longer moment, to suspect that possibly the sayings ascribed to the two philosophers are basically not much more than "to be do be do." The univocity of the three lines, read in isolation, begins to crumble.

The double meaning of the three lines is given only in English. It depends on the phonic structure (alias, the phonic matter) of each of the three verbal strings. If the pun were to be translated into the languages of the two philosophers, it would lose its point.

In a presumably older, in any case rarer version of the pun, the second sentence is attributed to Marx. the displacement of Marx by the less familiar Sartre also appears to have been phonically, i.e. materially determined and certainly not ideologically. Unlike 'Marx', the sound of 'Sartre' is related to that of 'Socrates' and 'Sinatra' (initial-S, common vowel *a*, similar consonantal clusters *cr-t, rtr, tr*). The phonic substance in poetic contexts affects not only the meaning but even the reference! The pun is not at all an isolated case.

The second peculiarity of natural languages, their tendency to exploit pre-given structures plurifunctionally, is just as conspicuous in other natural systems whose success depends on progressive adaptation to their environment.

Swiss cheese, cited by Putnam in support of his opposing thesis of the independence of substance and function, can serve as an initial illustration. different kinds of cheese owe their distinctive character to different micro-organisms which activate the transformation process of the milk. The bacteria that create Swiss cheese not only produce its characteristic flavor but also, by generating carbon dioxide gas, give rise to its characteristic holes. Other bacteria or artificial means will never be able to produce a cheese with exactly the same nutritive and aromatic content (no less and no more), not to mention the holes which – as everybody knows – additionally fulfill an aesthetic function for connoisseurs and a propagandistic function for dealers.

The specific cluster of functional characteristics of Swiss cheese indicates which bacteria (lactobacillus helveticus, among others) were at work for someone who enjoys eating with his stomach, mouth, and eyes. These bacteria and no others are endowed with the appropriate plurifunctional structures. The human recipient, because of his specific material structure and sensibility, is not immune to a divergent chemical structure in an artificial product, even if it were to simulate all the effects of Swiss cheese. The divergent micro-structure of the artificial product is registered if not by sight at least by the gourmet's palate and the average consumer's stomach.

Every structural peculiarity of a food can become relevant, biologically and asthetically, and in fact constantly does so. What applies to foodstuffs also applies to natural languages. Every structural peculiarity of a language (both grammatical and phonic, visual and auditory) can become functionally relevant, communicatively as well as aesthetically, and in fact constantly does so.

Correspondingly, artificial foodstuffs betray themselves as do artificial linguistic theories, theories with no psychological or neurological reality. They are either too simple or too powerful or both at once. they lead to deficiencies (do not achieve what they should) and/or to side-effects (achieve more than they should). Swiss cheese can be used for many things that entirely different substances can also be used for, in principle, for example, as a computer component to simulate certain achievements of the brain. But only Swiss cheese can combine these functions, which it shares with other substances, simultaneously and exclusively with the aromatic and aesthetic effects that have made it famous. Each of its functions may be imitable in isolation, not, however, the specific cluster of its functional possibilities. Like every structure, it is equipped with a unique cluster of functional achievements.

It is not difficult to apply this point to the issue at hand. Computers, that is, models for the human brain, must be designed, whose performance depends not only on their primary functional organization, but also on their material structure, on the chemical-physical processes by which the primarily intended achievements are realized. According to the model of natural languages (and Swiss cheese), chemical-physical processes can have a side-effect (of an expressive kind in the case of communication systems, for example), independent of the primarily intended output.

The material and functional structures of linguistic utterances are more familiar to most philosophers than the refined structure and detailed function of Swiss cheese. Therefore a grammatical illustration shall serve to enlarge upon the thesis of the specific plurifunctionality of material structures.

The primary means of indicating subject and object is word order; the first noun designates the subject, the second the object, as demonstrated by a renowned example from the Grammaire de Port-Royal: *Le roi aime la reine* does not have the same meaning as *La reine aime le roi*. The difference is indicated by the change in word order alone. Not so in Latin: *Rex amat reginam*. Subject and object are indicated in the Latin sentence not only by word order but by the case-markers of the two nouns as well. Case-marking in this sentence is an additional redundant means of indicating subject and object.

An important insight into the significance of redundancy in natural systems is revealed in this simple illustration. Redundancies are typical not only of linguistic phenomena but of all bio-phenomena. Their function as interpreted by information theory lies in guaranteeing goal-oriented achievements. Redundancy compensates for interference. This may be its primary but it is certainly not its only function. A much more noteworthy function is that it enhances the feasibility of innovation and further evolution.

Because of their structure, case-markers can be used not only to indicate subject and object but also, through their agreement to indicate affiliations. *Magnam rex amat reginam*. No Latin speaker would affiliate the adjective *magnam* with the adjacent noun *rex*, but with the noun *reginam*, whose case agrees with the adjective. Furthermore, the indication of subject and object through case-markers permits the exploitation of word order for other functions, for topicalization and emphasis.

Thus, the case-marking system, understood to have been created to guarantee through redundancy the indication of subject and object, can also – thanks to its specific structure – assume a function that departs from its primary purpose of indicating subject and object. Word order and case-marking system may be considered functionally equivalent in terms of the one task of indicating subject and object; they are not, however, *omni*functionally equivalent (equivalent in all respects). The one means can perform tasks that the other cannot because its structure is different. The structures of natural systems are characterized by the fact that, as they develop, they are exploited in an increasingly plurifunctional fashion.

This can be formulated as a general law: there are no two (material) structures that are onmifunctionally equivalent. Let us return to an extralinguistic illustration to evaluate this insight. There are several means of getting from Tokyo to Osaka – by train, car, boat, plane, bicycle, etc. We shall restrict ourselves to train and car. These two are functionally equivalent in terms of the journey to Osaka but not in terms of other services. In the shinkansen, I can read, sleep, eat during the trip. In the car, on the other hand, I can listen as I choose to the news and to music (without earphones). I can also interrupt the journey anytime or combine it with a sidetrip somewhere. Every means introduced to execute a function permits the execution of specific additional functions. And natural systems are quick to exploit this functional potential. Dining cars, sleepers, and reading lamps are available in trains; automobiles are equipped with radios and cassette players. The specific cluster of activities at a person's disposal on a trip from Tokyo to Osaka overdetermines his method of transportation.

A well known illustration from the recent history of linguistics of the fact that existing structures, thanks to their potential plurifunctionality, assume additional functions for which they were not (at least in the view of some linguists) originally introduced, is the semantic relevance of surface structures. A restriction of semantic information to deep structures may be an economical ideal for the theoretical linguist; a natural language system will always be quick to exploit creatively the semantic potential of surface structures, which, of course, would not be denied by such a linguist either.

Unnatural speculations similar to those of mathematical linguists are also to be found in neurology. According to Dreyfus, the fact that neural pulse transmission is an all or nothing affair does not lead to the conclusion that its chemical-physical make-up implies a digital structure of the mediation of messages. A message can, in principle, be mediated by other characteristics of pulse transmission, by its frequency, for instance, and can thus be analogically structured. This argumentation is logically correct. But it is not functional argumentation (and therefore not biological, nor phenomenological either). An evolutionary, adaptive system, such as the brain, can be expected, sooner or later, to exploit a condition for the mediation of messages as economical as that of the digital structure of pulse transmission – together with the analogically exploitable characteristics of pulse transmission.

The progressive evolution of a natural system is due largely to the potential for plurifunctionality that characterizes every (material) structure. Plurifunctionality is founded on the fact that there is no such thing as an entity without properties. Different entities have different properties. They can thus be plurifunctionally exploited in different ways.

This also holds for redundant structures introduced primarily to safeguard the function of another structure. The redundant case-marking system with its feature of agreement permits an innovation that could never be achieved with word order.

3. Two Dogmas of Recent Philosophy of Mind

The philosophical weight of the two theses of the nonindependence of function and matter and the plurifunctionality of (material) structures is considerable. They invalidate the application of Duhem's thesis of the underdetermination of theories to linguistics and the bio-sciences (in linguistics, in the form of Quine's thesis of the indeterminacy of translation) on the one hand, and the popular defense of epiphenomenalism, on the other.

According to Duhem's thesis, the same empirical data can be explained by an infinite number of different theories. However, in human language, in fact in all artifacts whose constitution is steered by a code or a program, the situation is different. This is most evident in computer achievements. Input and output can be combined with each other in an infinite number of ways. The computer technologist is, however, in the fortunate position of being able to break open his black box, the computer, and ascertain code and program. The linguist's position is knottier. He must deal with two black boxes, both of which are only partially accessible: to the human mind he finds access through introspection, a frequently limited, unreliable, and correspondingly controversial means; to the brain through neurology, still in an incipient stage and correspondingly overestimated by outsiders.

The champions of the Duhem-Quine thesis maintain that even the most advanced neurology would be unable to eliminate indeterminacy. Indeterminacy applies, according to them, not only to linguistic output data, but also to the units of innate or acquired codes and programs. This is disputable, however, in view of the non-independence of matter and function and of the potential plurifunctionality of all structures. Different structures, codes and programs, categories and devices, as well as chemical-physical structures, are not omnifunctionally equivalent. Every structure developed to fulfill a certain function, be it in a language or in a brain, is plurifunctionally exploitable in a manner that is different from any other equivalent (with respect to this particular function) structure.

Every structure allows the exercise (and explanation) of all those specific functions that are possible with it and that will be realized by a natural system sooner or later which has acquired this structure. The real multiplicity of output data (functions) thus becomes the index of the actual underlying structures.

Linguistic structures are overdetermined through the functions actually fulfilled by a natural language. Neurological structures are overdetermined through the functions actually fulfilled by a brain. Every theory for the explanation of particualr linguistic or neural achievements is thereby not under- but overdetermined. Every alternative theory that recurs to other structures, i.e. structures with a differently exploitable plurifunctionality, inevitably proves to be not simple enough on the one hand, too powerful on the other. It is not simple enough inasmuch as it introduces several other strutures to explain functions which are fulfilled by one and the same structure thanks to its specific plurifunctionality. Since these other structures display a different cluster of functions corresponding to their different features, all alternative theories prove at the same time to be too powerful. They allow additional functions, which do not occur in the system in question and, because of its specific structure, would not be possible either. All of this ultimately means that the theory of a natural system such as that of natural language or a brain, whose categories coincide with the categories of the actual code and program in the black box, is also always the simplest complete and not overly powerful theory. Duhem's discovery of the underdetermination of physical theories represented a revolution in physical theory, but it is not pertinent to the sciences of natural (biological, neurological, linguistic) systems.

The thesis of the overdetermination of the functional structure of natural systems is of course an idealization. It holds only in principle. (In this respect, however, it is no different from Duhem's and Quine's theses, which – in their fashion – also hold only in principle and are of little practical importance.) The thesis of overdetermination presupposes a system that is endowed with the possibility of evolution, the possiblity of an increasingly better and progressively diversified adaptation to its environment, and that exploits this possibility. Complete determination is given only upon the exploitation of *all* possibilities. This ideal case is of purely theoretical interest. In view of the manifold factual constraints impoed upon both natural systems and scientific theory, one would be hard put to find a highly developed field of science in which alternative theories even come close to dealing as adequately with the same abundance of facts. In view of the principles of current scientific theory, a structure need not be exploited omnifunctionally, nor even multifunctionally; plurifunctional exploitation suffices to eliminate alternative theories as less simple and less coherent.[7]

The claim that a natural system with evolutional potential will inevitably exploit the plurifunctionality of its structures requires further elucidation. It is important to refute the dogma of the stable epiphenomenality of unavoidable side-effects in functional structures.

Epiphenomena are functionless side-effects of an organism's functionally valuable structures. It is not difficult to discover such unavoidable side-effects of adaptive evolution. But no consideration is to be found in the literature on epiphenomenalism of the liability of functionlessness, i.e. the so-called epiphenomenality of just these side-effects. It is claimed, for example, that the weight resulting from the polar bear's thick warm fur not only has no function, but must even be regarded as dysfunctional. This illustration smacks of scanty familiarity with biological dynamics. A natural system pressured to adapt will seek to exploit the functional potential residing in epiphenomenal and redundant structures.

Modern medicine has found that the food industry's extraction of all supposedly worthless and tasteless roughage from our food is not desirable after all since these seemingly epiphenomenal constituents have in the course of evolution long assumed manifold functions. They cultivate the growth of specific intestinal flora and guarantee a healthy, regular elimination of waste. The pressure receptors in the nerve plexus of the intestinal walls have long adjusted to a corresponding (pre-industrial) condition of fullness. It would be surprising if the weight of the polar bear's fur had not similarly affected the structure of muscles and bones, which may well be to the bear's advantage in more than one respect.

In addition to roughage, waste products are also considered prototypical epiphenomena. The human mind has been compared to such a product, to bile. Waste products reveal which function can be assumed by epiphenomena relatively quickly and easily. It is notably the information function. Hormones, for instance, seem to have sprung from waste products of cellular metabolism. In the course of evolution these wastes came to be used as signals. Similarly, many animals use the olfactory characteristics of their waste products for informatory purposes, just as railroad men – to cite Huxley's opening illustration of epiphenomenalism – use the whistle, a by-product of the excess steam escaping from the valve of an engine.

The speed with which a functionalization of epiphenomenal structures occurs must be empirically determined from system to system. Immense differences are to be found even in the information function, though it seems to be the easiest to effect. In natural languages it may arise in no time at all as demonstrated by the popular etymological exploitation of new foreign words. In other systems it may take millions of years. The eyes of our animal ancestors originally had an unconscious, non-visual, reflecting steering function. The perfection of this function resulted in a side-effect – the mirror image of the corresponding section of the environment on the eye. It took millions of years to be able to exploit the initially purely epiphenomenal image functionally, namely perceptually, as we do today. Not only redundant structures (which once merely functioned as a guarantee), and epiphenomenal structures (which were once functionless by-products of functional structures), but even irritating, dysfunctional by-products of functional structures, known in information theory as noise, are functionally exploited in natural systems. *Noise* is a typical term in the theory of artificial communications systems. Information theory denies any function to noise – just as it assigns a merely safeguarding function to redundancy. However, in natural communications noise (as technically defined) is an ephemeral phenomenon. It is as labile as epiphenomena are. In natural communications systems, noise is in fact very quick to assume an information function.

Telephone, radio, and records with their background noise as well as old movies that flicker on the screen are both good illustrations. Neither noise nor flicker have to be heard or seen very long to take on an expressive function. They serve to identify the sender as old-time, for example, and thus as having a certain flair and evoking a whole range of emotions. Even the background noise, varying according to the frequency of the broadcasting station and registered by the human ear below the level of consciousness, comes to have a familiar, almost comforting effect. Music and news on a station to whose underlying sounds the ear has become attuned are allegedly given a higher rating than comparable broadcasts on other stations. A Chaplin film that neither flickers nor jerks is like an antique piece of furniture that has lost its patina in restoration.

Language sciences have been blindly and unimaginatively oriented toward the technology of artificial communications systems far too long. 'Noise' is a central concept in the theory of technical communication systems. It is quite another story in the theory of natural languages. Language psychologists have repeatedly voiced the supposition that – apparently by way of evolution – man cannot suffer any meaninglessness. He will try to make sense out of a phenomenon that appears to make no sense and, since nothing occurs in isolation but always in an associative context, he will succeed.

The arguments discussed in this paper add fresh weight to two traditional suppositions of Philosophy of Mind that have commonly been taken for granted. (1) If one thinks in terms of biological analogies, then it would seem that the function a human mind is most likely to assume is an informational one. (2) If one thinks in terms of the analogy of natural language systems, then it would seem that mind – as a redundant process vis-à-vis brain processes – is (will be) beneficial (in a way that the brain alone could not be) to the creativity of mind-endowed animals, and this due to the specific plurifunctionality of its structure. But what are the neural and mental structures underlying the specifically human cluster of functional achievements? In the long race to answer these questions, both neurology and phenomenology are still at the starting line.

Notes

1. The creation of the first computer models was based on the introspection of the procedure in the planning and execution of corresponding human acts. See H. Schnelle, "Introspection and the Description of Language Use," in *A Festchrift for Native Speakers*, edited by F. Coulmas (The Hague: Mouton, 1981), 116ff., and also S. Watanabe, *Knowing and Guessing* (New York: Wiley, 1969), 387.

2. See E. Holenstein, *Roman Jakobson's Approach to Language*: *Phenomenological Structuralism* (Bloomington, Ind.: Indiana University Press, 1976), and "Von der Poetik und der Plurifunktionalität der Sprache," in Roman Jakobson, *Poetik* (Frankfurt: Suhrkamp, 1979), 7–60.

3. H. Putnam's rendition, *Philosophical Papers* 2 (Cambridge: Cambridge University Press, 1975), 392.

4. Ibid., 291.

5. *De l'interprétation – Essai sur Freud* (Paris: Seuil, 1965).

6. For the East German Marxist G. Klaus, *Philosophie in kybernetischer Sicht* (Berlin: Dietz, 1961), cybernetics and information theory confirm (holistic) dialectical materialism's critique of the (atomistic) mechanistic materialism.

7. See also the argumentations in Putnam, 337ff.; N. Chomsky, *Language and Responsibility* (New York: Pantheon, 1979), 166; Z.W. Pylyshyn, "Computation and Cognition," in *The Behavioral and Brain Sciences* 3 (1980), 123ff.

14. "The Whole Business of Seeing": Nature, World, and Paradigm in Kuhn's Account of Science[1]

Lenore Langsdorf and Harry P. Reeder

Thomas Kuhn recognizes that his discussion of paradigms in *The Structure of Scientific Revolutions* is a text which "can be nearly all things to all people" (1977, 293), but he suggests that his concept of the nature of a paradigm has been clarified during the years of discussion since that work's original publication in 1962.[2] It is not our purpose to review or reargue that extraordinary volume of discussion here. Rather, we want to argue that one central and oft-discussed issue – the extent to which a paradigm limits, controls, or determines seeing, saying, and theorizing – remains vague because of certain implicit and unexamined features in Kuhn's philosophical position.[3]

In the three sections of this paper, then, we propose that: (1) without an account of the extent to which paradigms limit and determine perception, there is no way to understand Kuhn's ability to give the account of science that he gives; (2) Kuhn's pervasive vagueness on this issue is necessitated by an uncritical committment to a theory of perception that requires two objects ("nature" and "world"), two processes ("looking" and "seeing") and two philosophical positions (naive realism and nominalism); and (3) the writings of Alfred Schutz provide an alternative philosophical foundation which enables us to appreciate both the limits of paradigms and the possibility of communicating across those limits.

I

Kuhn develops his theory of science largely through a study of the history of science. He claims to be able to observe this history with an encompassing, perspicacious glance, which enables the identification of "permanent attributes of science" (1977, 335; see also, 1970a, 250). Yet this would seem impossible, given his claim that there are "no external standards" by which to judge a paradigm-governed domain (p. 108; see also, 4, 7, 17).

Perhaps the most likely response for Kuhn to offer to this objection is that the scientist, but not the historian, is locked into paradigm-based ways of seeing. Thus, the historian of science can achieve a perspicacious view which is not available to the scientist. In his later work, however, Kuhn argues that not just scientific seeing, but *much* of our everyday seeing is also paradigm governed (pp. 121-29. See also, 1970a, 266-77; 1977, chap. 12). He does not tell us, however, what or how much seeing is *not* paradigm based, or how it relates to seeing which is so based. In other words, it must be asked: does any seeing transcend the specifications of the paradigmatic structure that governs it − and if so, how?

Without some account of how any view can escape paradigm governance, we cannot understand, for example, the very possibility of Kuhn's own endeavor. For when we apply Kuhn's theory to the theory of scientific revolutions, the question arises: if paradigms place the sort of blinders Kuhn describes on any investigator − historian, average citizen, or scientist − how is it that Kuhn himself can transcend his discipline's paradigmatic structure, so as to present a picture of the history of science that is not restricted by (and to) that structure? Furthermore, how can he claim an accurate and encompassing view of other histories, as well as particular research problems, such that he can identify, compare, and evaluate them objectively − that is, without influence from his own paradigmatic structure? It seems to us that Kuhn, in practice, claims to see what his theory forbids him to see. Thus, we need an account of how he can transcend his theory − and that requires inquiring into the limits of what paradigms do, rather than what the word means, or how Kuhn did (or should) use the term.[4]

A second area in which we need a clearer account of the limits of paradigm governance involves the possiblity of correcting or compensating for our limited views through linguistic communication. Kuhn stresses the limits paradigm governance places on adherents of different paradigms: "languages cut up the world in different ways, and we have no access to a neutral sub-linguistic means of reporting" (1970a, 268). Nonetheless, he goes on to claim that "the signs used in the two languages are identical, or nearly so . . . *most* of them function in the *same* way in both languages" (1970a, 269). But, if a language cuts up the world in one way, and a second language cuts it up in another way, and a translation manual involves a theory or paradigm, how can Kuhn claim that signs in two languages are "nearly" identical in function? According to his own view, there could be at best only similarity of function and thus only partial communication between the two languages. So long as Kuhn denies access to a neutral, sub-linguistic sphere, he has no warrent for assuming that "most" signs "function in the same way."

The account of child language acquisition that he gives in support of these problematic remarks is nominalistic.[5] We grow up "learning language and nature together by ostension"; this process utilizes

> a learned ability to group objects and situations into similarity classes which are primitive in the sense that the grouping is done without an answer to the question, "similar with respect to what?" (1970a, 274).

Since "the similarity relations change" in every scientific revolution (1970a, 275), Kuhn's nominalism leads him to a relativism that he seems anxious to avoid.[6] The question as to whether he is a relativist should be discussed in terms of the duality of objects, processes, and philosophical positions already mentioned. As is shown in the next section, Kuhn adopts a form of naive realism by proposing that although our "sensations" (the result of neural processing) differ under the governance of different paradigms and cause us to "see" different "worlds," we all "look at" the same "nature" which affects us by way of "stimuli" that "are, under pain of solipsism, the same" (1970a, 276; see also, 1977, 308). In regard to the transient multiplicity of "worlds" seen from different paradigms, then, Kuhn is a nominalist with a theory of science that is a form of conventionalism, and may indeed lead to relativism. But in regard to "nature," Kuhn is a naive realist.

Naive realism is certainly a common, and even a natural, assumption for scientists to make.[7] It may well be a nonpernicious assumption, for it serves as a vague stimulus to empirical testing. However, the philosopher of science can neither allow this assumption to remain unchallenged, nor adopt it in regard to his own subject matter. Especially in this case, where the realism is added to a relativism in order to avoid solipsism, the basis for its assumption must be identified and evaluated. We find the basis for Kuhn's ontology of realism in an implicit dichotomy within his theory of perception. Let us, then, turn to his theory of perception.

II

In the postscript to the *Structure of Scientific Revolutions*, Kuhn tells us that one goal of that work is the rejection of a particular notion of perception:

> What I have been opposing in this book is therefore the attempt, tradi-
> tional since Descartes but not before, to analyze perception as an inter-
> pretive process, as an unconscious version of what we do after we have
> perceived (p. 195).

In opposition to that tradition, Kuhn proposes a strict separation of the two processes: "In the metaphorical no less than in the literal use of 'seeing', interpretation begins where perception ends" (p. 198). As support for this alternative, he develops (in the body of the book) an analysis of perception as comprising two distinct processes − looking and seeing − and involving two theoretical entities: stimuli and sensations.

Although this analysis has received some attention in the many articles, discussions, and responses called forth by Kuhn's work, that attention has been directed to its involvement in the incommensurability doctrine. In the course of his remarks (especially, those about translation) in the postscript (1970b), as well as at other times (1970a, 1974, and 1977), Kuhn has modified that doctrine almost to the extent where it could be possible to speak of retraction. However, very little has been said about the theory of perception which gives rise to that doctrine.

In this section this theory of perception is extracted from Kuhn's general account of the nature of discovery. It is then argued that the theory does not yield an analysis of perception that opposes the traditional epistemological paradigm as "initiated by Descartes" (p. 121). Instead, it is found that the lack of any account of the extent of paradigm governance forces Kuhn into a positivistic variant of the Cartesian doctrine.[8] This variant presents even more difficulties than the original, and actually necessitates the strong incommensurability thesis which he no longer supports (and perhaps never intended).

Kuhn finds that the specialized character of science depends on a basic "assumption that the scientific community knows what the world is like" and assumes "firm" (although usually unarticulated) "answers to questions like . . . : What are the fundamental entities of which the universe is composed?" (pp. 4–5). In the post-Cartesian era, Kuhn (as historian of science) finds a "nest of commitments . . . both metaphysical and methodological" that are implied by those basic assumptions (p.

41). Commitments at a "higher level" require differentiation and specialization:

> The scientist must, for example, be concerned to *understand* the *world* and to extend the precision and scope with which it has been ordered. That commitment must, in turn, lead him to *scrutinize* . . . some aspect of *nature* in great empirical detail (p. 42).

Scrutiny involves (at the very least), perception. In order that the scientist "investigate some part of nature in detail and depth" (p. 24), he must know *where* to look for, and *how* to recognize the presence of, the entities and details assumed proper to his field.

Kuhn's theory of paradigms, especially when conjoined with his remarks on the training of scientists and the schools or communities into which they are inducted, provides a sociological account of how *he* knows where to look. The adequacy of that account is not what concerns us here. Regardless of the authority that tells us where to investigate and what to look for, the *"how* to recognize" issue remains. It is in order to answer this question that Kuhn appeals to a philosopher.[9]

In order to account for the "identification of a paradigm" by "direct inspection" – "a process that is often aided by, but does not depend upon the formulation of rules and assumptions" – Kuhn turns to the later work of Wittgenstein (p. 44). When "confronted with a previously unobserved activity" (or object) we can identify and name it as for example, a chair, a game, or a paradigm-governed research problem

> because what we are seeing bears a close "family resemblance" to a number of activities that we have previously learned to call by that name. For Wittgenstein, in short, games, and chairs, and leaves are "natural families," each constituted by a network of . . . resemblances. The existence of such a network sufficiently accounts for our success in identifying the corresponding object or activity (p. 45).

Kuhn thus appeals to Wittgenstein in order to understand the identification of objects or acts – whether these be everyday entities, such as chairs, or theoretical entities, such as paradigms.

In this appeal, Kuhn borrows two fundamental Wittgensteinean distinctions. The first is an exclusive focus on "what we are seeing": that is, on perception, in contrast to conception, thinking, or interpretation. Wittgenstein admonishes us:

> Don't say: There *must* be something common, or they would not be called "games" – but *look* and *see* whether there is anything common at all . . . To repeat: don't think, but look! (1958, 31).[10]

This distinction is crucial to Wittgenstein's claim that his own work is descriptive, rather than theoretical, and aims at a portrayal of the world, rather than an explanation. In order to carry out that endeavor, he must limit himself to, for example, reporting a series of conventions that can be seen (apprehended) in the *use* of a word, rather than thinking of (conceiving) a meaning shared by these uses. Kuhn's endeavor is quite different from Wittgenstein's, however, he goes beyond mere description in order to avoid solipsism by making crucial conceptual assumptions about stimuli and nature.[11]

The second feature adopted from Wittgenstein is the notion of "natural families" constituted by a network of "family resemblances." Kuhn stresses that the "possibility of immediate recognition of the members of natural families depends upon the existence, after neural processing, or empty perceptual space between the families to be discriminated" (1974, p. 197). This stipulation suggests the direction of Kuhn's later research, which would provide a computer model of the process which results in identification of "natural families" (pp. 192, 197; see also 1974, 472–82). In this way Kuhn would satisfy a lack which he finds in his philosophical basis: "Wittgenstein . . . says almost nothing about the sort of world necessary to support the naming procedure he outlines" (1974, p. 45). In order to remedy this situation, Kuhn adopts a naive-realistic ontology which Wittgentein rejected.

From these partially Wittgensteinean foundations Kuhn builds a theory of perception that accounts for both "immediate recognition" of "natural" characteristics, and paradigm-governed knowledge of the entities displaying those characteristics. In order to do so, he must divide the "look and see" prescription. The result is a theory of perception and knowledge in which we all *look* at the same "nature" but *see* "different things," or even, a "different world" (pp. 111–12, 117, 118, 120). The differences between what we *look at* and what we *see* are accounted for by differences in paradigmatic orientation.[12] We can now consider this account more closely, before comparing it to the post-Cartesian view that Kuhn would replace.

The very presence of what we see is paradoxical at its inception. Although the scientist (within a mature, puzzle-solving discipline) does not "aim at novelties of fact or theory," both are "repeatedly uncovered" in a process which

> commences with the awareness of anomaly, i.e. with the recognition that nature has somehow *violated* the paradigm-induced expectations . . . it closes only when the paradigm theory has been adjusted so that the anomalous has become the expected . . . until the scientist has learned

to *see* nature in a different way . . . the new fact is not quite a scientific fact at all (p. 52).

The process Kuhn posits here in one in which mere *looking* discloses "*that* something is" present, although we do not see "*what* it is" until we theoretically understand its characteristics, that is, have identified what we see *as* a particular something (p. 55). The phenomenon is then a "fact."

A structure of activity and passivity is thereby posited. Nature is initially active; it confronts us with unexpected phenomena that we passively receive. In the terminology of his later work (as used in the postscript) nature provides "stimuli," although we have no direct knowledge of their existence:

> But people do not *see* stimuli . . . they *have* sensations, and we are under no compulsion to suppose that the sensations of our two viewers are the same. . . . Much neural processing takes place between the *receipt* of a stimulus and the *awareness* of a sensation. . . . We posit the *existence* of stimuli to explain our perceptions of the world. . . . But our world is populated . . . not by stimuli but by the objects of our sensations (pp. 192–93).

As we noted earlier, this and other "posits" amount to an assumption of naive realism which is at odds with Kuhn's nominalistic account of perception and conception within a paradigmatic structure.

Kuhn holds that we do attain some knowledge of nature by means of these stimuli:

> we must speak of the experience and knowledge of nature embedded in the stimulus-to-sensation route. Perhaps "knowledge" is the wrong word . . . we have no direct access to what it is we know, no rules or generalizations with which to express this knowledge (p. 196).

Direct access and rule-governed knowledge commence at the level of sensations which we "have." Since the "processing" that occurs prior to our having these products (sensations) is not one in which we take an active part, Kuhn borrows Michael Polanyi's phrase, "tacit knowledge" as the name for this "mode of knowing that is less systematic or less analyzable than knowledge embedded in rules, laws, or criteria of identification" (p. 192; see also, pp. 191, 44).[13] Tacit knowledge of stimuli, then, occurs at an elementary level in which we passively experience nature.

This question of the origins of knowledge is crucial for the differences Kuhn stresses between his account of perception and that of the post-Cartesian tradition, and so his comment on what does occur, and how, in "neural processing," must be considered carefully. He notes that "past experience is embodied in the neural apparatus that transforms stimuli to sensations" (p. 195), and that this "embedded" or "embodied" experience makes a difference in the way that a man "processes the stimuli which reach him" (p. 197). However, this is merely a "conditioned processing" (p. 193), not a "deliberative process by which we choose among alternatives" (p. 194).

The consequences of this passivity are indicated most forcefully in a response by Kuhn to a remark by Dudley Shapere:

> We have no recourse to stimuli as given, but are always – by the time we can *see* or talk to do science – already initiated into a data world that the community has divided in a certain way . . . and initiates are stuck with it. . . . There is no way to get outside it – back to stimuli – and . . . compare it with all the ways in which the world might have been divided (1974, 509).

A strong sense of essential passivity – indeed, even captivity – is portrayed in remarks such as this. (Being "stuck with" one's initiation raises the question discussed in Section 1: how does any investigator, including Kuhn, become "unstuck" so as to see the environment in a new way?)

Further reflection on this situation suggests that Kuhn's dualism of objects, processes and philosophical positions, does *not* extend to a corresponding duality in the investigator's attitude. In other words: it is not the case that we are "passive" in regard to "nature," but "active" in regard to the "world." For at the most elementary level "nature" *provides* unknowable (or at best, "tacitly knowable") stimuli – posited as the same for all who receive them, in order to "avoid both individual and social solipsism" (p. 193). At a higher level, the "group" – "whether an entire culture or a specialists' sub-community" (p. 193) – *provides* recognizable sensations. Sameness is once again posited.

> To the extent . . . that individuals belong to the same group and thus share education, language, experience, and culture, we have good reason to support that their sensations are the same . . . [They] *learn to see* the same things when confronted with the same stimuli . . . by being shown examples of situations that their predecessors in the group have already learned to see as like . . . and as different (pp. 193–94).

Rather than a difference between activity and passivity, then, we have only a difference in the supplier of the requisite programming.

A schematic summary of the systematic dualism we find in Kuhn's theory of perception may be helpful at this point:

looking (posited)	*seeing*
that x exists	what x is like
perceiving	perceiving as
nature: active	world: active
perceiver: acted upon by nature	perceiver: acted upon by world
a) stimuli	a) sensations
b) phenomena (objects without recognition)	b) facts (recognition of things)
c) tacit knowledge of nature)	c) rule-governed knowledge of world

When his theory of perception is presented in this schematic fashion, the basis for the thesis, which may well be the most controversial of Kuhn's claims, becomes evident.

There are "several senses," he holds, "in which we may want to say that after a revolution scientists work in a different world" (p. 135). Although this claim has provoked considerable debate, and despite its causal relationship to the "incommensurability" and "conversion" theses (with their associated charges of irrationality, subjectivism, and relativism) Kuhn has repeatedly defended it — while acknowledging that the analysis given for its support is less than adequate:

> In a sense that I am unable to explicate further, the proponents of competing paradigms practice their trades in different worlds. . . . Two groups of scientists *see* different things when they look from the same point in the same direction. . . . Both are *looking at* the world, and what they look at has not changed. But in some areas they *see* different things (p. 150).

The schematic summary enables us to see that this thesis is a *result* of the looking-seeing and stimuli-sensations dualisms. Kuhn's inability to explicate this thesis, we believe, results from the implicit and unexplicated character of this dual structure in his analysis.[14]

A second area of difficulty arising from the same implicit duality concerns Kuhn's ambiguity about our access to "nature." On the one hand, he explicitly and repeatedly denies the availability, and perhaps even the possibility, of a "neutral observation language" which would reflect and facilitate access to and knowledge of nature (pp. 125–27, 129, 145–46, 201). Yet at several points he implies that we do have some mode of access to (and thus knowledge, in more than the "tacit" sense, of) nature: the decision to accept or reject a paradigm "involves the comparison of both paradigms with nature" (p. 77); the "awareness of anomaly," with which discovery begins, is a "recognition that nature has somehow violated the paradigm-induced expectations" (pp. 52–53; see also p. 127); "doing problems is learning consequential things about nature" as well as learning to "interrelate symbols and attach them to nature" (pp. 188–89; see also, p. 190–91); it is so "hard to make nature fit a paradigm" that even after accepting Dalton's theory, chemists "had still to beat nature into line" (p. 135).

These characterizations of nature suggest that (contrary to Kuhn's response to Shapere) we *can* "get outside of" the "data world" into which we have been "initiated": we are not just "stuck with it," but have *some* recourse to an external standard – nature itself – from which to judge competing paradigms. Without such recourse, scientists could never recognize anomalies as such. However, Kuhn's dominant line of thought denies any possibility of stepping out of our historical-cultural situation and performing such a reflective analysis. Even translating between situations (by analogy with linguistic translation) is problematic: "For most people translation is a threatening process, and it is entirely foreign to normal science" (p. 203; see also, pp. 199–203; and 1970 55–57, 266–70). The scientist lacks any "external standard" by which to evaluate "alternative perceptual possibilities"; he "can have no recourse above or beyond what he *sees* with his eyes and instruments" (p. 114). Thus (as Kuhn recognizes) his own analogy between gestalt shifts and paradigm changes falters: only in the former case is there "an external authority, the experimenter" to assure the subject that "regardless of what he *saw*, he was *looking at*" the same phenomena (p. 114; Kuhn's emphasis).

Despite these difficulties in explicating the "nature" and "world" concepts, Kuhn's implicit theory of perception is recognizable: we *look* at objects in nature; we *see* things in a world. Before offering an explication of the sense in which it *is* appropriate to say that "the proponents of competing paradigms practice . . . in different *worlds*" (p. 150), it will be helpful to compare this theory with the post-Cartesian "attempt . . . to analyze *perception* as an *interpretive* process, as an unconscious version of what we do after we have perceived" (p. 195). In rejecting that attempt, Kuhn notes, he is opposing an entrenched paradigm:

> Many readers will surely want to say that what changes with a paradigm
> is only the scientist's *interpretation* of observations that are themselves

fixed once and for all by the nature of the environment and of the perceptual apparatus. . . . This very usual view of what occurs when scientists
change their minds . . . is an essential part of a philosophical paradigm
initiated by Descartes. . . . That has served both science and philosophy
well. . . . Today research . . . suggest[s] that the traditional paradigm is
somehow askew (pp. 120–21).

Kuhn's alternative demands a strict separation of perception and
interpretation:

In the metaphorical no less than in the literal use of 'seeing,' interpretation begins where perception ends. The two processes are not the same,
and what perception leaves for interpretation to complete depends
drastically on the nature and amount of prior experience and training
(p. 198).

Perception (which includes both "looking" and "seeing") seems to be
"involuntary, a process over which we have no control"; therefore,

we may not properly conceive it as something we manage by applying
rules and criteria. To speak of it in those terms implies that we have access
to alternatives, that we might, for example, have disobeyed a rule, or
misapplied a criterion, or experimented with some other way of seeing.
Those . . . are just the sorts of things we cannot do . . . until *after* we have
had a *sensation*, perceived something. . . . Then we may engage in interpretation, a deliberative process by which we choose among alternatives
as we do not in perception itself. . . . We try, that is, to interpret sensations already at hand, to analyze what is for us the given (pp. 194–95).

It is the nature of this "given," then–rather than its strict separation from
interpretation – which provides the crucial difference between the
traditional post-Cartesian view, which Kuhn rejects, and his proposed
alternative.

Both accounts are based on a notion of "immediate experience" that
is "given" to the perceiving, thinking individual. For the traditional
theory, this "given" would correlate to Kuhn's "stimuli." However, Kuhn's
"given" is "sensation," and thus is radically different from the "raw data"
or "brute experience" that is traditionally associated with "immediate
experience" (p. 125). For the "epistemological viewpoint that has most
often guided Western philosophy for three centuries," there is "sensory
experience [that is] fixed and neutral," in contrast to "theories [that are]
simply man-made interpretations of given data" (p. 126). Kuhn retains
this conception of theory (in contrast to paradigm) as a separable
interpretation of the perceptual "given."[15] But he rejects the correlated

---

traditional notion of perception as yielding a domain of "stable" experience: "the immediate content of Galileo's experience with falling stones was not what Aristotle's had been," since "immediate experience" *only* delivers "the perceptual features that a paradigm so highlights that they surrender their regularities almost upon inspection" (p. 125; see also, p. 124).

At the start of this paper we suggested that Kuhn's theory of perception is a positivistic variation of the traditional post-Cartesian theory, rather than a genuine alternative. That characterization can now be elaborated and defended, for it refers to these retained and altered aspects of Kuhn's analysis of perception and interpretation. Unlike a traditional positivism,[16] Kuhn's variation turns out to be pessimistic about the very possibility of science. For traditional positivism, while recognizing the "theory-laden" nature of much observation, considered that to be a corrigible state of affairs. In principle, observation and theory – Kuhn's perception and intererpretation – were held to be separable. Since theoretical terms were to be interpretable in observational terms, and the latter were tied to direct empirical evidence amenable to experimental confirmation or disconfirmation, theoretical disciplines could attain empirical knowledge which, when systematically organized and accumulated, comprised a science.

This process is truncated by Kuhn's introduction of an immediate given that is *already*, without the perceiver's aid or interference, preselected to fit a paradigm (rather than neutral) and mutable in accord with paradigm shifts and scientific revolutions (rather than stable). In effect, the barriers to knowledge previously attributed to the involvement of a perceiver, or dictates of a theory, are still present, but in a far more pernicious form: as determined by a paradigm.

Kuhn's stated purpose (in 1970b) was to refute a traditional paradigm that "analyzed perception as an interpretive process, as an unconscious version of what we do after we have perceived" (p. 195). We have argued that Kuhn establishes separation between perception and interpretation only by importing into perception, by way of its determination by a paradigm, at least some of the features associated with interpretation by the traditional theory.[17]

If Kuhn is correct in his proposal that *all* perception (seeing, as well as mere looking) is an accomplishment in which a paradigm functions as a "time-tested and group-licensed way of seeing" (p. 189), it *cannot* be the case that perceivers (including historians and scientists) "simply see" rather than "see as" (p. 85).[18] Instead, his account of perception is one in which interpretation (as pervasively and unavoidably provided by a paradigm) is even more entrenched within perception than in the post-Cartesian paradigm that Kuhn would replace.

III

Our criticism of Kuhn's account of science has focused on two problematic issues: whether paradigms totally, or only partially, determine an observer's experience; and whether perception and interpretation are, even in principle, separable. We argued that Kuhn set out to give an affirmative answer to the latter question, but failed to do so. Furthermore, the pervasiveness of divergent interpretations embedded in different paradigms dictates his position on the former issue: a paradigmatic structure determines both everyday and systematic (that is, scientific) observation, quite without the observer's assent or even awareness.

The determinative power of paradigmatic structures in Kuhn's theory gives rise to the problem discussed in the first section of this paper: how can Kuhn, as social scientist, claim the perspicacious glance that his project – the identification, analysis, and comparison of prior paradigms – requires? In other words: how can he account for the trans-paradigmatic standpoint from which he writes? We find that Kuhn implicitly limits the power of paradigms to determine what he himself observes about science. In effect: Kuhn claims a vantage point of "nature," beyond the strictures of a predetermined "world," and from which he can identify and describe the *real* nature of observation – without offering any explication of this freedom. What is needed here is an understanding of how paradigms could *partially* determine perception. Without such an understanding, we stressed, readers cannot assess Kuhn's own project, which purports to transcend its own paradigmatic frame.

In this section, we propose that Alfred Schutz's investigations of everyday experience (the context of acts that forms the life-world), and the social scientist's role and practice as investigator of that experience, provides a philosophical basis for articulating the nature of paradigms, as well as their function within perception and interpretation. Schutz's analysis thus enables us to understand how it is that Kuhn – and any other observer – is "initiated into a data world," but is not thereby "stuck with it"; is not powerless to "compare it with all the ways in which the world might have been divided" (1974, 509; quoted earlier in context).[19]

Schutz's basic interest in the methodology of the social sciences led to extensive research into the nature of social action and, in particular, into the process by which meanings are constituted by actors in everyday social life. Much in Schutz's work provides a phenomenological confirmation of Kuhn's observations concerning the radically different accounts of situations which are apt to be forthcoming from scientists with diverse orientations. However, there are also important differences in their projects. First, Schutz follows Husserl's practice in seeking to understand the nature of any specialized experience – such as scientific research – in terms of its genesis in the life-world of everyday experience. Kuhn stresses the discontinuity of scientific and prescientific knowing, as well as the discontinuities among areas within the scientific enterprise. (His discussions of education as an initiation process and conversion from one paradigm to another support these discontinuities.)

Secondly, Schutz's concept of meaning incorporates several Husserlian elements, such as, intentionality; lived experience; passive and attentional layers of constitution; and retention, reflection, and protention as essential structures of temporality. These elements of phenomenological analysis are used to explicate the relationship between an experiencing subject and those observations and interpretations that generate that subject's experience. However, Schutz reorients Husserl's theory from a basis in perceptual experience to an equally pervasive basis in human action – and especially, social action. The basic unit (so to speak) in Schutz's account is an actor whose interpretive structures are expressed in his actions; the resultant meaningful action is accessible to phenomenological description. Therefore Schutz has no need to posit a division of perception into a looking directed at an *objective* nature, in contrast to a *seeing* which is *subjective*, that is, which interprets data in accordance with a paradigm in order to constitute a world.

The two issues in Kuhn's account that we have criticized can be restated as questions correlated to these differences between their projects. We can then suggest how Schutz offers a philosophical basis for resolving these problems in Kuhn's theory. 1) Is there any limit to the determinative effect of paradigms on perceiving and interpreting, so that we can account for the limited transparadigmatic communication to which Kuhn admits, as well as the perspicacious view required for his own analysis? 2) If there is a difference between perception and interpretation, can be elucidate it without depending on posits (for example, stimuli in contrast to sensations) and a correlated ontology – neither of which are supported by any kind of evidence?

Schutz's account of social action and the constitution of intepretive structures speaks to both questions. He finds that individual actors do indeed construct their environments (Kuhn's "worlds") on the basis of patterns for action that are provided by their communities. The life-world (a persisting context of mostly taken-for-granted activity) is pre-structured for an individual who acts and thinks in accordance with the prevalent and prior interpretations forming that structure. Usually, this occurs without any reflection on the nature and extent of the determination offered (or perhaps, required) by the structure.

Any action or cognition, however, *can* be reflectively analyzed in terms of its socially provided structure. Correlatively, the actor can reflect on his own being, and that of other actors, as both *users* of this "stock of knowledge" and *products* of such usage. Schutz's analysis, then, is both *reflectively* directed on the environment and *reflexively* directed on the actor's role in promulgating and integrating features of that environment. The two directions are unified as functions of the investigator (sociologist, historian, or philosopher) who provides an initial example of the ideal type under investigation, the social actor.

Thus far, Schutz's account of the prestructuring of an environment is quite compatible with Kuhn's account of the paradigmatic determination of a world. There are certain distinctive features of Schutz's inquiry: a focus on actions and interpretive structures rather than on perception, and a consistent correlation of the reflective (object- or world-directed) and reflexive (subject- or actor-directed) dimensions. These could be understood as simply a more explicit treatment of the sociological, psychological, and philosophical themes that are at least suggested in Kuhn's account. That this is not the case becomes apparent when we continue comparing the accounts, and consider the complex of issues leading to, and surrounding, Kuhn's incommensurability thesis. In this connection, we find that Schutz's bipolar account shows how multiple, partial, and even contradictory interpretations of the environment are necessary for identifying and understanding one's own environment as well as those of others. In contrast, Kuhn's account presents this multiplicity as a discontinuous series of worlds that permit only partial (at best) transparadigmatic communication.

The crucial structural feature that divides Schutz from Kuhn here is the reflexive aspect of Schutz's analysis. The actor recognizes not only his own place within a community, which develops and sustains certain interpretive schemes. He also recognizes that his community is finite. It is, so to speak, juxtaposed to other communities, both past and present, in which the actions of members – especially, their linguistic activities (including texts) – also display a communal structure. Implicit to a membership in this community, then is the status of *outsider* in another community. Indeed, understanding the nature of one such structure includes a recognition that there are others.

This reflexive analysis also reveals that differences of view exist *within* a community. If for no other reason than the need to accomplish certain tasks, members typically enter into mediation procedures in order to resolve these differences. Schutz finds a basic and rarely explicated principle at work in such procedures: an assumed *reciprocity of perspectives*. Each actor assumes that if the other were in his situation, he would understand the situation in the way that actor does. This assumption is displayed in an obvious (but highly instructive) way when a mere spatial exchange is needed; for example, when one actor explains or demonstrates a mechanical process while speaking in the first person, and then exchanges places with his listener – who proceeds, quite naturally, to do again what the first speaker has done.

Most differences of view within a community require more extensive mediation than the simple exchange of actor's positions. However, this elementary example provides a model for understanding communication within a community as involving assumed *conceptual* reciprocity of perspectives in addition to, or perhaps instead of, mere spatial reciprocity. An actor is, necessarily, an outsider in relation to other groups within his community. But, equally necessarily, he can overcome that status by using a variety of techniques that rest on an assumed reciprocity of perspectives. The same type of situation can be recognized and surmounted (in principle, at least) in regard to other communities with radically different patterns for action and interpretation. We have here a basic structure for understanding both the possibility of recognizing divergent paradigms (and other anomalies) that appear within paradigm-governed contexts, and the possibility of trans-paradigmatic communication.

In order to use Schutz's work in this way, we must recognize two basic philosophical positions which support the reflexive and reflective dimensions of his bipolar analysis, and are not shared by Kuhn. We noted that Schutz considers human beings as actors, rather than as observers. In accord with that basic orientation, he stresses the role of these actors in recognizing and choosing to apply the patterns that determine their environments – including their scientific establishments – and themselves. Schutz's reflexive dimension, then, incorporates a philosophical conviction: the investigator is understood as an *active participant in* the constitution of his investigation. "Choosing among projects of action" is a major theme in his research.[20]

Although Schutz did not write on the history of science explicitly, we would argue that his research supports this conclusion by Joseph Agassi:

> the history of science is the history of the *choice* of central problems, and of the various schools of thought which attempted to answer those problems. But inductivism tells us that science begins . . . with observations of hard and fast facts. Inductivism cannot attribute intellectual interests

to *free* choices, which are *based on* preconveived *ideas*, but only to extra-intellectual factors – usually of a socio-economic character (1963, 27; emphasis added).[21]

For Kuhn, in contrast, the scientist is a passive observer *acted on* by both nature and the world, and thus theoretically unable to make the "free choices . . . based on preconceived ideas" that are cited by both Schutz and Agassi as intrinsic to scientific inquiry.[22]

The reflective dimension of Schutz's bipolar analysis also incorporates a philosophical orientation quite opposed to Kuhn's ontology. Schutz's focus, following Husserl, is on the conceptual and interpretive structures constituted in interaction with the physical and social environment. These are objective by virtue of the reciprocity of perspectives discussed earlier. Thus, Schutz locates objectivity in a sphere accessible to the investigator, rather than (as does Kuhn) in a posited, but inaccessible, nature that provides stimuli. Within that objective sphere, he investigates both sameness and difference in multiple "finite provinces of meaning" in terms of the genesis and maintenance of interpretive structures.

This approach does not imply or require either realism (to account for the sameness of nature) or conventionalism (as a response to the difference in worlds). Furthermore, the understanding of paradigms as conceptual and interpretative structures constitutive of finite provinces of meaning, which in turn provide the "preconceived ideas" on which intellectual interests – including Kuhn's – are based, offers a way to understand the very possibility of Kuhn's own project. He is indeed based in a structure that determines his view. But he is not "stuck with it," insofar as his recognition of other views allows *him* to determine – that is, choose – an alternative, transcending standpoint that permits a perspicacious view of the history of science.

We would stress that we are not advocating Schutz's phenomenological method for the analysis of social phenomena – including scientific revolutions – as a way of refuting Kuhn's account, but as an appropriate means for subjecting its presuppositions and claims to investigation. The result, we believe, can only be a clarified and more useful understanding of science.[23]

Notes

1. The title is adopted from Wittgenstein (1975, 212):

Do I really see something different each time, or do I only interpret what I see in a different way? I am inclined to say the former. But why? – To interpret is to think, to do something; seeing is a state. We find certain things about seeing puzzling, because we do not find the whole business of seeing puzzling enough.

2. Quotations in this paper are from Kuhn (1970b), and all emphases are our additions, unless otherwise noted.

3. We are not concerned with vagueness in the use of the term, *paradigm*; that is, ambiguity of meaning is not the issue here. As Masterman (1970, 61–66) pointed out, and Kuhn (1970a, 234, 271–73) acknowledged, linguistic vagueness is indeed a problem in Kuhn's presentation. (Scheffler [1967, 89] and Shapere [1964, 385–86] also note this problem.) What we are addressing here, however, is vagueness in the thing itself: that is, the extent to which these conceptual entities (paradigms) govern everyday as well as scientific experience. The problem of section 1 arises from epistemic and ontological, rather than linguistic, vagueness.

4. Two specific aspects of this question of Kuhn's ability to do what his theory implies cannot be done (or can only be done with great difficulty – whereas Kuhn reports no difficulty) are thoroughly discussed by two other critics, and so we have not dealt with them in detail. On the question of whether identification of paradigms can occur by "direct inspection" (p. 44) see Shapere (1964). On Kuhn's comparison of both paradigms and conclusions reached within paradigmatic structures, despite his denial of the possibility of those paradigm--transcending meanings or conclusions which would be needed for such comparison, see Scheffler (1967, 52–53, 82–86).

5. This nominalism extends from language into perception itself; see pp. 125ff; Kuhn (1977), p. 17 and chapter 12.

6. The question of whether Kuhn is a relativist has been discussed at length in the still growing literature concerned with his theory. As Stegmüller (1976) correctly points out:

> Whether or not Kuhn himself embraces something like an "epistemological relativism" is an irrelevant question as long as this position does not find its way into his historical analysis. What could be a *real cause for concern* is the *circumstance that epistemological relativism appears to follow from* his statements about scientific revolutions (p. vii; author's emphasis; see also pp. 149, 157).

To many critics, this latter circumstance is present in Kuhn's work.

Gary Gutting's anthology provides a convenient sampling of judgment on the issue. In his introduction, Gutting indicates that Kuhn is a relativist, although not a skeptic (1980, 11, 18). Dudley Shapere implies that Kuhn is "indulgently relativistic," in the manner characterized by Stegmüller, giving "real cause for concern." For Shapere argues that Kuhn, "carried away by the logic of his notion, holds a relativisim that "is a *logical* outgrowth of conceptual confusions" (1980, 36, 37–38; author's emphasis).

Although Alan Musgrave concludes that "Kuhn is far from relativism" (1980, 48; see also 49, other contributors attribute varying degrees of relativism to his theory. Wolfgang Stegmüller discerns a "grain of truth" in the "charge of relativism" – perhaps because lack of an "adequate concept of scientific progress" leaves Kuhn caught between "the Scylla of technological metaphysics and the Charybdis of relativisim" (1980, 86–87). However, Stegmüller finds this form of relativisim to be "defensible" (1980, 89). (For an indication of the likely nature of this defense, see Stegmüller's discussion (1977, II;13ff.) of the paradigm as a perspective) M. D. King finds relativism in Kuhn only in relation to the rules for doing science (1980, 105), whereas John C. Greene says that "Kuhn seems to favor a loose, relativistic concept of science" (1980, 298). David Hollinger notes positive aspects of the theory's "perspectivism," on which Kuhn "exercises an important control" which "prevents it from turning into the more complete relativism" (1980, 212–13). This evaluation is allied with one which sees relativism in some, but not all, of Kuhn's work. Ian Barbour, for example, notes that "truth is entirely relative" in "Kuhn's earlier work" (1980, 236; see also p. 231, where he cites Shapere's view [1971, 708] that Kuhn's later writings are "as relativistic, as antirationalistic as ever"). Mark Blaug, however, finds that although

> Kuhn does his best, of course, to defend himself against the charge of relativism . . . a wholly convincing defense would reduce his account of "scientific revolutions" to a nonsense (1980, 142).

Although we would agree with this last assessment, special importance must be placed on Kuhn's own conclusion: "I do not myself feel that I am a relativist" (1970a, 264–65). That remark returns us to the crucial distinction in Stegmüller's remark, quoted at the start of this footnote. The relevant question is not whether Kuhn "feels" that he is a relativist, but whether his theory necessitates, logically, an "epistemological relativism." We agree with Blaug's and Shapere's conclusion: it does. Indeed, we would borrow Popper's phrase: we find that Kuhn gives a "logic of historical relativism" (1970, 55–57).

7. Joseph Agassi, in the context of commenting on French conventionalist theories (especially, that of Pierre Duhem), offers an intriguing thesis on the "historical roots of this realism . . . and its corollary radicalism" (that is, rejection of continuity among successive theories). Says Agassi concerning Duhem,

> it is due to the overconfidence in mathematics as the language of Nature shown by some Renaissance scientists, [and to] . . . naivete in others; what is common to overconfidence and to naivete, to realism and to radicalism, is – intellectually speaking – the lack of imagination (1981, 292).

8. In referring to Kuhn's theory of perception as positivistic, we are aware that the term may well be too broad to be informative, and that commentators (including Kuhn himself) generally consider his work to be part of an antipositivistic "new philosophy of science." (See, for example, Kuhn [1977, 267], Shapere [1964, 389–90], and Doppelt [1978, 33].) The reasons for proposing that Kuhn's theory of perception is a variant, rather than alternative, to the post-Cartesian paradigm, as presumed by, for example, logical empiricism, are discussed toward the end of this essay.

The label is used, also, in order to suggest a thesis which is only mentioned briefly late in the paper. Kuhn's argument is against the (traditional positivist) notion of the cumulation of scientific knowledge; but he fails to notice the ties that *do* bind successive paradigms – including those that link his own conception to its predecessor. Shapere (1966, 68) identifies this failure to find a "middle ground", between accumulation vs. relativism and meaning-invariance vs. context-dependence, as "the place where Kuhn and Feyerabend took a wrong turn." See also notes 6 and 15.

9. Kuhn does "borrow . . . a useful phrase," "tacit knowledge," from another philosopher: Michael Polanyi (see also note 13). Elsewhere (for example, pp. 80, 87, 207) he refers to philosophers and philosophy only briefly and somewhat disparagingly.

10. Wittgenstein's own introduction of family resemblances as immediately (nonconceptually) recognized features occurs later in the same passage:

we see a complicated network of similarities overlapping and criss-crossing: sometimes overall similarities, sometimes similarities of detail. . . . I can think of no better expression to characterize these similarities than "family resemblances" (1958, 32).

11. We do mean to imply that Wittgenstein's work cannot provide the philosophical basis Kuhn seeks there. The themes which divide Kuhn and Wittgenstein are:

1. Kuhn requires an ontology; Wittgenstein has no such interest.

2. Kuhn seeks a way out of the incommensurability of paradigms; Wittgenstein accepts a multiplicity of language games.

3. Kuhn uses the notion of "natural kinds" to support a realism; Wittgenstein does not draw that conclusion, and even insists that his descriptions are not to be taken as theoretical.

4. Kuhn concludes that only "conversion" can bridge the discontinuities between paradigm-governed "worlds"; Wittgenstein relies on ordinary language as the ultimate arbiter of scientific language(s). This last point indicates an area of convergence between Wittgenstein's inquiries into "forms of life" and Schutz's (following Husserl's) investiga-

tions of the "life-world" as composed of multiple "finite provinces of meaning." See also Stegmüller (1976, 170–80) for a discussion of the relationship between paradigms and games, and Popper (1970, 53) for a note on the relationship between puzzles and problems.

12. Most of the emphases added to quotations in this paper are for the purpose of stressing the looking-seeing and nature-world dichotomies.

13. Kuhn acknowledges the similarity of Polanyi's concept to the learning by doing, "rather than rule-acquired, character of paradigms (pp. 44, 190–91). However, he does not explore or adopt any other features of Polanyi's work, or indicate that Polanyi offers any solutions to puzzles in Kuhn's own work. His general orientation to Polanyi's tradition is suggested by this remark: "I am not . . . a mystic or a man who finds that notions like intuition, *Verstehen*, or empathy are useful to philosophy of science in their present form" (1974, 510–11).

In contrast to what appears to us a rather limited borrowing, however, Agassi emphasizes a closeness between Kuhn and Polanyi – even referring to Kuhn's views as "by and large Polanyite" (1981, 182), to a "Polanyi-Kuhn Theory" (1981, 280, 499), and to Kuhn as "Polanyi's most distinguished disciple" (1981, 97).

14. Kuhn's usage is surprisingly, although not completely, consistent in regard to all three dualities, despite his lack of explicit acknowledgement of the dual structure in his account. For examples of divergence from the general usage, see page 110, where paradigms are "constitutive of nature," and page 150, where "two groups of scientists . . . are looking at the world, and what they look at has not changed.

15. This correlation between theory and interpretation depends on Kuhn's differentiation between theory and paradigm. The "priority of paradigms" and correlated derivative status of theories and rules is established in (1970b), and is closely tied, to one of Kuhn's crucial insights: the priority of learning from practice and examples, rather than by ingestion of formulated rules. However, this differentiation is one of those threatened by his too-broad usage of the label *paradigm*. As Masterman (1970) notes, many critics are mislead, and "assume without question . . . that a paradigm is a 'basic' theory'" (p. 61; see also, pp. 66–67). Despite some unfortunate locutions – for example, "To be accepted as paradigm, a theory must seem better than its competitors" . . . (p. 17; see also 1974, 500), the nature of the differentiation is clearly stated: the paradigm is "prior to the various . . . theories that may be abstracted from it" (p. 11).

16. Rather than the logical positism or empiricism associated with the Vienna Circle and related movements earlier in this century, we are thinking here of their origins in Comte and, especially, of Comte's precriptions for a "social physics" or "sociology" that would achieve the scientific status of already advanced sciences, such as astronomy. "Positive" thus had the sense (among others) of "optimistic" about the expansion of science. See also, note 8.

17. The stress on *"all* perception" is occasioned by Kuhn's later research into the nature of perception in general (as reported in greatest detail in 1974, 472–82). Our "ordinary" perception, he concludes, is just as much governed by paradigms as is our "scientific" perception. The degree of paradigm overlap, and thus the degree of commensurability, between these two worlds (and their sub-sets) is problematic. This topic has been of enduring interest in many fields; for example, in linguistics, the Sapir-Whorf hypothesis; in philosophy, Wittgenstein's "language-games" and Alfred Schutz's "finite provinces of meaning"; in cultural criticism, C. P. Snow's "two cultures."

18. See Wittgenstein (1958, 197): "'Seeing as . . . ' is not part of perception. And for that reason it is like seeing and again not like." (On "seeing" vs. "interpretation," see note one). Hanson argues, contrary to Wittgenstein, that "the logic of 'seeing as' seems to illuminate the *general* perceptual case" (1958, 19; our emphasis).

19. The following sketch of several themes in Schutz's phenomenological sociology is necessarily brief, and does not make any attempt to provide a synthesis of his work. Also, it presumes the reliance on Husserl, as well as Weber, that Schutz demonstrates throughout his work and frequently explains and summarizes. Although Schutz's methodology is elaborated throughout his work, the essay entitled "Common Sense and Scientific Interpretation of Human Action" (1962, 3–47) is particularly relevant for our criticism of Kuhn. For a concise and perceptive account of Schutz's relationship to mainstream sociology, see Thomason (1982, especially chaps. 2 and 3).

20. It is also the title of one of his papers (see 1962, 67–96).

21. We do not mean to imply that Kuhn is an inductivist. Within Agassi's (1963, v) tripartite classification – inductive, conventionalist, and critical – Kuhn would seem to be a conventionalist since he denies that there are "hard and fast facts," which science cannot begin without. However, Kuhn does not retain the indebtedness (of one thinker on a predecessor) thesis that Agassi (1963, 30) identifies as characteristic of conventionalist views. To do so would commit him to some form of progress in science, or at least, to rational change. On his rejection of that thesis, see note 22.
We would argue that phenomenological evidence, including that developed by Schutz, supports the critical view, according to which "scientific theories explain known facts and are refutable by new facts" (Agassi 1963, v). This view is most closely associated with Karl Popper. In a recent paper, we argue that Popper has moved closer to an Husserlian view in at least one central feature of his critical philosophy: the efficacy of essential structures (see Langsdorf and Reeder 1983).

22. With reference to the problems discussed in the first section of this paper: this theoretical inability to choose is refuted by Kuhn's actual choice of a

divergent view of the history and philosophy of science. This criticism of Kuhn can thus be restated by focusing on the choice issue: Kuhn neglects a reflexive analysis of his own project; thus he cannot give any account of the actual choices involved in rejecting dominent paradigms in his own field, or those similarly involved in the "revolutions" he describes (see 1970a, 262).

The "two rationality gaps" identified in Stegmüller's (1976, vii–viii, 135–70; see esp. pp. 166, 262–63) critique of Kuhn would be narrowed, if not closed, by applying the results of research on "choosing among projects" which shows that rational (free) choice, rather that irrational factors (for example, conversion or socioeconomic pressures) is a prevalent basis for scientists' changing convictions.

The broader sense in which Schutz's research provides a rational account of actions that Kuhn characterizes as irrational is suggested in this observation by Agassi:

> Popper's answer to Kuhn's question: How does science develop without public knowledge of its rules? is:. . . . In the West most modern scholars know enough about criticism to keep things moving. . . . Discrepancies in Popper's view can be smoothed out by putting greater emphasis on the social character of science (1966, 353).

See also Jarvie (1972, 133ff.) for a discussion of the sociology of knowledge as proposing alternate approaches to understanding rationality. Thomason (1982, 31, 38–39, 91) stresses that Schutz's research elucidates the very *possibility* of this "social character of science." It is because Schutz provides an account of the preconditions of scientific rationality in everyday situations where we "know enough . . . to keep things moving" that we find his work to be an invaluable means for subjecting Kuhn's (and Popper's) claims to criticism. See also notes 13 and 19.

23. An earlier version of this paper was read at the 1981 meeting of the Society for Phenomenology and Existential Research. We would like to thank Ted Kiesel for his comments on that paper.

References

Agassi, J. 1963 *Towards An Historiography of Science* (*History and Theory*, Beiheft 2). The Hague: Mouton.

_____. 1966 [Review of SSR] *Journal of the History of Philosophy* 4; 351–54.

_____ 1981. Science and Society. Dordrecht: Reidel Publishers.

Barbour, I. 1980 "Paradigms in Science and Religion." In Gutting 1980, 223–45.

Blaug, M. 1980 "Kuhn's vs. Lakatos, or Paradigms vs. Research Programmes in the History of Economics." In Gutting, 1980, 137–59.

Doppelt, G. 1978 "Kuhn Epistemological Relativism: An Interpretation and Defense." *Inquiry* 21; 33–86.

Feyerabend, P. 1965a. "On The Meaning of Scientific Terms." *Journal of Philosophy*62; 266–74.

_____. 1965b. "Problems of Empiricism." In *Beyond the Edge of Certainty*, edited by R. Colodny, 145–260. Englewood Cliffs, N.J.: Prentice-Hall.

Greene, J. C. 1980. "The Kuhnian Paradigm and the Darwinian Revolution in Natural History." In Gutting, 1980, 298–320.

Gutting, G., ed. 1980. *Paradigms and Revolutions*. Notre Dame: University of Notre Dame Press.

Hanson, N. R. 1958. *Patterns of Discovery*. Cambridge: Cambridge University Press.

Hollinger, D. 1980. "T. S. Kuhn's Theory of Science and Its Implications for History." In Gutting, 1980, 195–222.

Jarvie, I. C. 1972. *Concepts and Society*. London: Routledge and Kegan Paul.

King, M. D. 1980. "Reason, Tradition and the Progressiveness of Science." In Gutting, 1980, 97–116.

Kuhn, Thomas S. 1970a. "Reflections on My Critics." In Lakatos and Musgrave, 1970, 221–78.

_____ 1970b. *The Structure of Scientific Revolutions*, 2nd ed. Chicago: University of Chicago Press.

_____ 1974. "Second Thoughts on Paradigms." In *The Structure of Scientific Theories*, edited by P. Suppe, 459–82. Urbana: University of Illinois Press.

_____ 1977. *The Essential Tension*. Chicago: University of Chicago Press.

Lakatos, I., and A. Musgrave, 1970. *Criticism and the Growth of Knowledge*. Cambridge: Cambridge University Press.

Langsdorf, L., and H. Reeder, 1983. "A Phenomenological Critique of Popper's World 3." Paper delivered to the Fifteenth Annual Meeting of the Husserl Circle, Emory University.

Masterman, M. 1970. "The Nature of a Paradigm." In Lakatos and Musgrave, 1970, 59–89.

Musgrave, A. 1980. "Kuhn's Second Thoughts." In Gutting, 1980, 39–53.

Popper, K. 1970. "Normal Science and Its Dangers." In Lakatos and Musgrave, 1970, 51–58.

Scheffler, I. 1967. *Science and Subjectivity.* New York: Bobbs-Merrill.

Schutz, A. 1962, 1964, 1966. *Collected Papers,* vols. I, II, and III. The Hague: Nijhoff.

Shapere, D. 1964. "The Structure of Scientific Revolutions." *The Philosophical Review* 73; 383–93; reprinted in Gutting, 1980, 28–38.

_____. 1966. "Meaning and Scientific Change." In *Mind and Cosmos,* edited by R. Colodny, 41–84. Pittsburg: University of Pittsburg Press.

_____. 1971. "The Paradigm Concept." *Science* 172; 706–9.

Stegmüller, W. 1976. *The Structure and Dynamics of Theories.* New York: Springer-Verlag.

_____. 1977. *Collected Papers on Epistemology, Philosophy of Science and History of Philosophy,* 2 vols. Dordrecht: Reidel.

_____. 1980. "Accidental ('Non-Substantial') Theory Change and Theory Dislodgment." In Gutting, 1980, 75–93.

Thomason, B. 1982. *Making Sense of Reification.* Atlantic Highlands, N.J.: Humanities Press.

Wittgenstein, L. 1958. *Philosophical Investigations,* 3rd ed. New York: Macmillan.

15. Science and the Theoretical "Discovery" of the Present-at-Hand

Joseph Rouse

The title of my paper, "Science and the Theoretical 'Discovery' of the Present-at-Hand," is drawn from several passages in *Being and Time* in which Heidegger claims that scientific knowledge is the "discovery" or "grasping" of things present-at-hand.[1] My aim, however, is to challenge this claim. I will propose not only that science does not discover things present-at-hand, but that there is no genuine phenomenon corresponding to presence-at-hand. *Being and Time* can thus be read as the final development of the ontology of presence-at-hand: Heidegger still mistakenly reserves a place for things present-at-hand in his interpretation of what it means to be, but he also provides the basis for finally abolishing that place.

My argument against there being anything present-at-hand is based on Heidegger's own investigations; to which there are four parts. I will first show that the claim that science discovers the present-at-hand conflicts with Heidegger's other claims about science in *Being and Time*. Then I will argue that the conflict can be resolved by exhibiting and correcting a crucial misunderstanding of scientific research which the claim about presence-at-hand embodies. The third part of my argument will be to show that Heidegger himself came to realize this error, and that his later reflections on science and technology represent an attempt to correct it. Finally, I will argue that Heidegger's original misinterpretation of science reflects an important characteristic of science: it is a significant error whose reinterpretation can advance our understanding.

Let us begin by examining what Heidegger actually says about science in *Being and Time*. His discussion can be organized around four principal themes. He insists first of all that, "as ways in which man behaves, sciences have the manner of being which this being – man himself – possesses," and argues that this requires an "existential conception of science" (BT, H357). Such an existential conception would examine science primarily as the activity of research rather than just looking at the logical structure of the *results* of that research. Heidegger presumably would not have us ignore the knowledge which results from research, but he would expect us to consider its basis in *Dasein*'s being-in-the-world. One would expect that this existential interpretation of science, when fully worked out, would be based on the existential analytic of *Dasein* and its temporal interpretation.

The second theme of Heidegger's early philosophy of science is that science is based on a prior understanding of being, the clarification of which "must run ahead of the positive sciences" (BT, H10). Heiegger remarks that,

> Basic concepts determine the way in which we get an understanding beforehand of the area of subject-matter underlying all the objects a science takes as a theme, and all positive investigation is guided by this understanding. (BT, H10).

The attempt to lay out in advance what is thus understood "signifies nothing else than an interpretation of those beings with regard to their basic state of being" (BT, H10). Heidegger claims that science's

> real progress comes not so much from collecting results and storing them away in "manuals" as from inquiring into the ways in which each particular area is basically constituted . . . The real "movement" of the sciences takes place when their basic concepts undergo a more or less radical revision which is transparent to itself (BT, H9).

Heidegger does not, however, examine in any detail what the ontological status of the basic concepts of the sciences is, or what the implications are of such revisions in their basic concepts. As we shall see, this leads him into difficulties in his account of science.

The third theme is the claim I have already identified as the target of all my criticism, namely, that the ontological significance of theoretical science lies in its discovery of beings present-at-hand. When discussing the ideal of scientific knowledge, for example, Heidegger speaks of the "legitimate task of grasping the present-at-hand in its essential unintelligibility" (BT, H324). What is present-at-hand is characterized by this unintelligible brute factuality because it has been decontextualized, deprived of the references to the world of practical activity within which things have a place and make sense. A thing present-at-hand would not belong anywhere or with anything else. What it is is completely defined by its "properties," and is quite unaffected by its relationship to anything else. Heidegger regards this decontextualizing discovery as

> a distinctive kind of making-present. This making present is distinguished from the Present of circumspection in that − above all − the kind of discovering which belongs to the science in question awaits solely the discoveredness of the present-at-hand (BT, H353

Thus Heidegger insists in his discussion of Descartes (BT, H95–96) that the Cartesian ontology of the world as "constant presence-at-hand" is one which mathematics and mathematical physics are "exceptionally well-suited to grasp.

This connection between science and the present-at-hand leads Heidegger to the final theme of his remarks on science. The theoretical discovery of the present-at-hand is not self-sufficient; it ontologically presupposes the unthematized disclosure of the world through practical, circumspective concern.

> If knowing is to be possible as a way of determining the nature of the present-at-hand by observing it, then there must be a *deficiency* in our having-to-do with the world concernfully. When concern holds back from any kind of producing, manipulating, and the like, . . . the *perception* of the present-at-hand is consummated (BT, H61).

Theoretical disclosure of the present-at-hand thus has its origins in a holding back from practical manipulation, tarrying, and considering a situation with our involvement in it partially suspended. Heidegger argues that the existential and ontological origin of theoretical knowing lies in the moment of truth when things fail to function in our ordinary, everyday activities. Such disfunction forces us to draw back and bring explicitly into our concern the equipmental context which had functioned more transparently. But such reflection lasts only briefly, for our tendency is to be reabsorbed in a new circumspective task: inspecting to see what went wrong, repairing, replacing, or removing the source of the problem, and so forth. Such activity is ontologically equivalent to any other sort of circumspective absorption in a practical task. However, Heidegger seems to think that the practice of inspecting the repairing can gradually disentangle itself from its referential context and grasp the things before it as merely present-at-hand:

Why is it that what we are talking about – the heavy hammer – shows itself differently when our way of talking is thus modified? Not because we are keeping our distance from manipulation, nor because we are just looking *away* from the equipmental character of this entity, but rather because we are looking *at* the ready-to-hand thing which we encounter, and looking at it "in a new way" as something present-at-hand (BT, H361).

But Heidegger never does indicate what makes for this sudden leap to a new way of looking at things. This omission is significant. Heidegger does not account for the transition to a decontextualized viewing of the present-at-hand, because he cannot; it does not occur. Theoretical science does not decontextualize things from the world in which they are ready-to-hand. Science puts out of play some of our ordinary concerns with things, to be sure, but only in order to manipulate them in a new way, whose ontological character is no different from that of everyday practical concern. Science, we shall argue, discovers not the present-at-hand, but new ways (that is, new contexts) in which things around us can be ready-to-hand. This claim will thus compel us to modify the fourth theme of Heidegger's analysis, as well as to abandon the third. The generation of theoretical discovery out of the breakdown of nontheoretical concerns is not the ontological history of the discovery of a new way of being, presence-at-hand, but at best an ontic account of how one sort of practical concern leads to another. The story Heidegger tells may well be substantially correct, and may even have been essential to the development of anything like science in its modern form, but it does not have the ontological significance he claims for it. Remember that the basis for these claims will be twofold. First, I will argue that the interpretation of theoretical science as a discovery of beings present-at-hand is inconsistent with Heidegger's more fundamental claim that science is a mode of *Dasein's* existence whose basic concepts belong to an understanding of what it is to be. I will then show how Heidegger's initial failure to recognize this is a plausible misunderstanding which is itself rooted in the phenomenon of scientific research, and which reflects an important characteristic of scientific practice.

Let us turn to the first part of the argument. Heidegger accepts that science itself requires some practical involvement with the world, but suggests that such involvement is of limited scope. To illustrate his claim that "theoretical research is not without a praxis of its own" (BT, H358), he cites the technical design and setup of experiments, the preparation of microscope slides, and archaeological excavation. Clearly Heidegger realizes that these examples are limited to what we might call the praxis of observation, for he goes on to say;

But even in the "most abstract" way of working out problems and estab-
lishing what has been obtained, one manipulates equipment for writing,
for example (BT, H358).

What is conspicuously absent in his choice of examples is the claim
that we "manipulate" equipment for setting up and working out the problems themselves, or for applying, extending, or correcting our theories.
Heidegger allows that theoretical activity has circumspective concern
associated with it, but not that it itself is a form of circumspective
concern.

But why should we claim that theorizing itself is a mode of practice, comprised of circumspective concern for a context of equipment
ready-to-hand? We must first realize that the characteristics of things
which are significant for scientific research are not simply there for
anyone to see if they were able to decontextualize an object and merely
look at it. Scientifically interesting aspects of the thing, often very subtle and esoteric ones, stand out as significant only against a background
of the current goals and practices of scientists working within a given
field. Only those properties which can be worked with in interesting
ways, and which are accessible both to current observational technique
and to theoretical description, are scientifically significant. It is easy
to see that Heidegger has not taken serious enough the practical difficulty of determining *which* supposedly present-at-hand properties of
things will be scientifically useful. Consider the key passage in division 2 when he actually addresses the question of the ontological genesis
of theoretical behavior out of circumspective concern. Speaking of the
decontextualizing of the assertion that the hammer is heavy, he says;

> When this kind of talk is so understood, it is no longer spoken within
> the horizon of waiting and retaining an equipmental totality and its
> involvement-relationships. What is said has been drawn from looking at
> what is suitable for an entity with "mass." We have now sighted something
> that is suitable for the hammer, not as a tool, but as a corporeal thing
> subject to the law of gravity (BT, H361).

The idea seems to be that "mass" gets selected as a significant property
because the practical heaviness of the hammer had already been sighted
circumspectively. But this will not do. For one thing, very few scientific concepts have obvious practical correlates, in the way mass and
weight are related in ordinary practice. What, for example, is the circumspective source for the discovery of the nuclear magnetic resonance
spectrograph of an organic compound? But more importantly, even mass
does not become scientifically significant because of its relationship

to our practical experience of heavy objects, but because of its relationship to other theoretical concepts such as acceleration, force, inertia, and momentum, as they were developed in application to specific scientific problems. The origin of the modern scientific conception of mass, for example, can be usefully traced to the flying arrow problem posed in the fourteenth century by Marchia and Buridan. Against their concern to interpret all species of change within a given Aristotelian explanatory schema, the motions of arrows and other projectiles stood out conspicuously. Efforts to accommodate projectile motion to the Aristotelian schema were never fully satisfactory, and, as in other cases when equipment fails to function effectively, this problem's reference to a context of involvements became more explicitly indicated. Such making explicit allows one to reorient oneself toward the task of repairing one's equipment, replacing it, or, failing either, restructuring the task at hand. In this case, of course, the context of involvements which was sighted was a theoretical one: the task at hand was to explain certain phenomena in terms of certain others, using a basic explanatory framework within which each of these phenomena had its place. The ability to see a hammer as a mass (that is, a resistance to acceleration) within a gravitational field is a circumspective ability which gradually arose over several centuries through a reinterpretation of the task of explaining motion in a unified way. This shifting interpretation was a response to the persistent recalcitrance of the flying arrow problem, among others (not the least of which was that of the motion of the planets once astronomical considerations motivated the move to Copernicanism). The efforts to solve these problems arose from a prior practical understanding of how to construct theoretical explanations of motion, based on a tradition of such explanations. The result was a new understanding of motion, which to be sure reflected a new understanding of what it is to be. But this new understanding cannot be interpreted ontologically as a discovery of the present-at-hand, since no such thing was discovered.

To be sure, the history of the circumspective discovery of mass is grossly oversimplified in the account I have just given, but a more subtle historical study would not change the basic philosophical point. For that matter, such an analysis could be made in *any* case where what Heidegger called "a crisis" in the basic concepts of a science existed. Such crises reflect the breakdown of practical scientific research. Scientists often encounter the phenomena of conspicuousness, obtrusiveness, and obstinacy in the course of their work. Problems for which the anticipated fairly straightforward solutions remain recalcitrant; others, admittedly more difficult, seem to pose insurmountable obstacles. When such problems persist and cannot be ignored, the efforts to get around the difficulty eventually make significant changes in scientific practice. Conceptual change in science typically results from the attempt to lay out what was alredy intimated to the application of its conceptual precursors.

The analysis I have been giving is, I think, implicit in Heidegger's own realization that science cannot be understood by taking the retrospective analysis of its results as its primary manifestation. Science always runs ahead of itself. It is well-known that scientists have been able to tolerate severe conflict between their theories and the available empirical evidence so long as they could foresee promising possibilities for research to reduce the discrepancies (or to solve other problems while successfully ignoring the discrepancies). As long as there is a sufficiently shared sense of what needs to be done in a field of research, how one might go about doing it, and what would count as having done it, science can proceed despite widespread empirical anomaly or conceptual obscurity. But when this shared understanding begins to break down, so that what would count as significant research itself becomes unclear, *then* science confronts a crisis in its most fundamental concepts. That is, a conceptual crisis is primarily a breakdown in the coherence of its research practices. It is the inability to immerse oneself in ongoing research which leads to a crisis of confidence among researchers, and such a mood often foreshadows a fundamental change in scientific practice.

What we see emerging in this analysis is the claim that science is an example of *Dasein*'s everyday concernful absorption in the world. The scientific researcher is confronted with a task whose significance arises from the context of referrals to which it belongs. Researchers have at their disposal a variety of equipment (instruments, problem formulations and solutions, theoreteical concepts, mathematical techniques, and the like) whose use is regulated and made possible by everyone's concern to conform to accepted techniques and standards. Indeed, the research task itself is singled out as significant by the same sorts of social concerns, which Heidegger has described as the *Abständigkeit* of *Dasein*'s subjection to *das Man*. The particular task belongs to a larger "in-order-to-for-the-sake-of" structure of science and its particular subfields, which, in turn, belong to the world as the clearing opened by the whole of *Dasein*'s concerns. As those familiar with *Being and Time* will have already inferred from my earlier remarks, our belonging within this clearing takes the form of interpretation based on a prior projective understanding and thrown submission, which have already been discursively articulated. This schematic outline of how science reflects the basic structures of Heidegger's existential analytic can, of course, be spelled out in some detail, but I have already done this elsewhere.[3]

The question which remains, however, is why did Heidegger himself fail to make this connection fully, and insist on claiming that science was the theoretical discovery of the present-at-hand? One answer, correct as far as it goes, is that Heidegger did realize this very soon, and that the result was his reinterpretation of science in "The Age of the World-Picture" and his essays on technology. In the former essay, Heidegger describes the historical transformation of science into the activity of ongoing research. What is characteristic of such research is that it investigates by experiment rather than observation.

> To set up an experiment means to represent or conceive the conditions under which a specific series of motions can be made susceptible of being followed in its necessary progression, i.e., of being controlled in advance by calculation.[4]

The decontextualization of things in order to encounter them in "the way they look" (BT, H61) has no place here, and with it has vanished the notion of the notion of presence-at-hand. Instead, Heidegger insists,

> The research worker necessarily presses forward of himself into the sphere characteristic of the technologist in the essential sense. Only in this way is he capable of acting effectively, and only thus, after the manner of his age, is he real.[5]

Thus the seventeenth century revolution in physics is interpreted in "The Question Concerning Technology" as the initial display of an "ordering attitude and behavior" which "pursues and entraps nature as a calculable coherence of forces."[6] Heidegger no longer employs the same terminology as in *Being and Time*. Instead of "presence-at-hand" (*Vorhandenheit*) and "readiness-to-hand" (*Zuhandenheit*), he uses the terms *Gegenstand* (object) and *Bestand* (standing-reserve). But the important point is that he insists that the interpretation of things as autonomous objects (*Gegenstände*) is a misunderstanding which conceals their belonging to the essence of technology.[7] We can represent things as being present-at-hand, but in doing so we fail to see them for what they are.

The question remains, however, of why this was not apparent even in the writing of *Being and Time*, where the basis for it was already developed. One might suggest that Heidegger, in his concern to challenge the traditional primacy philosophy granted to theory over practice, could not yet see his way clear to challenge the very distinction between theory and practice. But there is a more fundamental point, one which Heidegger makes but fails to apply to science, which explains how the contextual readiness-to-hand of scientific theories might be obscured. When equipment functions normally, it recedes from our awareness in order to let the work be produced stand out. Thus, we need not think about the pen with which we write, and can focus on what is to be said. We overlook the microscope as we look through it to see the cell. As Don Ihde has pointed out in the case of observational practice,[8] our instruments thus promote a realist illusion. The withdrawal of the instrument from any thematic awareness encourages us to confuse the object as worked on using the instrument with the object as it *really* is apart from its disclosure in practice. When Ihde's point is expanded to apply to the entirety of our scientific equipment, including our basic concepts and the techniques for applying them to particular cases, we can see the basis for the illusion of the presence-at-hand of things disclosed by theoretical research. As long as science functions well, it will *seem* to reveal things in a totally decontextualized way, as they *really* are.

This illusion has an equally mistaken correlate in the instrumentation which often accompanies a loss of confidence in the adequacy of our theoretical vocabulary and practices. The interpretation of scientific theories as mere instruments or calculating devices conceals a closet realism, the belief that *some* description of the world is ontologically privileged even though our scientific theories are not. Instrumentalism merely claims that scientific theory cannot be (or at least cannot be known to be) that final truth about the world. Heidegger himself avoided the extreme forms of both of these errors, because he never forgot that even the discovery of the present-at-hand would presuppose the prior disclosure of the worldhood of the world. He only failed to realize that this dependence must undermine the very possibility of encountering the present-at-hand at all.

I have suggested that the denial that things present-at-hand are ever manifest was important for the development of Heidegger's own thinking, and that within the philosophy of science it undercuts the debate between realists and instrumentalists. But there are other implications for the philosophy of science, some of which deserve mention even though they cannot be argued for here. Efforts to develop a calculus of confirmation, whether hypothetico-deductive, Bayesian, or otherwise inductive, seem doomed to fail if this analysis is correct. Heidegger has already argued that the referential context constitutive of the significance of anything ready-to-hand cannot be described as a formal system of relationships (BT, H83–88). This would mean that what counts as confirmation in science cannot be ahistorical or even abstracted from the practices of a particular scientific community. Theories of confirmation attempt to define confirmation in terms of a relationship between assertions, the thing asserted about, and in some cases the subjective probability assessments of those knowledgeable in the field. But such relationships presuppose their placement in a larger context of relationships which cannot be either explicitly formulated or abstracted from their place in that actual historical situation. This was the point of Heidegger's discovery of the worldhood of the world and its relationship to the things and activities disclosed within it. This can be seen in another way if one realizes that the breakdown of the theory/practice distinction leaves us with no viable philosophical distinction between epistemological and moral justification. If Heidegger is right, there cannot be a universal prescriptive account in either case.

This is a more difficult point to see, but I think the various attempts to use ontological criteria to distinguish the social or biological sciences from the physical sciences also seem destined to break down. There may be good moral, pragmatic, or scientific reasons for not treating human beings or other living things as ready-to-hand for theoretical calculation and control, but it cannot be due to an ontological difference between persons and things.[9] Heidegger's later writings do not provide us with transcendental limits on the possibilities of scientific investigation. Whether or not it is the destiny of human beings to be totally subjected to the essence of technology cannot be determined in advance (it cannot be calculated!). Finally, the appeal to science's quest for a truth independent of all cultural contexts has often been used to dismiss any political or cultural critique of science. But this argument cannot be adequate, if neither scientific claims nor their validation can be decontextualized. If science is to have a privileged place among the practices of our culture, this can only be adequately defended by appealing to considerations internal to that culture and its understanding of what it means to be.

Notes

1. Martin Heidegger, *Being and Time*, translated by E. MacQuarrie and J. Robinson (New York: Harper & Row, 1962). Notes refer to the original German pagination, given in the margin of the translation; all future references to this work will be in the text, as (BT, H__).

2. Joseph Rouse, "Kuhn, Heidegger, and Scientific Realism," *Man and World* 14; 3 (October 1981), 269–90.

3. Martin Heidegger, "The Age of the World-Picture," translated in Martin Heidegger, *The Question Concerning Technology* (New York: Harper & Row, 1977), 121.

4. Ibid., 125.

5. Martin Heidegger, "The Question Concerning Technology," in *The Question Concerning Technology*, tr. David Krell, *op. cit.*, 21.

6. Ibid., 17.

7. Don Ihde, *Technics and Praxis* (Dordrecht: D. Reidel, 1979), chaps. 1–4.

8. A detailed argument for this claim is developed by Mark Okrent, "Hermeneutics, Transcendental Philosophy, and Social Science" *The Review of Metaphysics*, forthcoming.

16. Phenomenology and Economic Science

Kenneth W. Stikkers

One way to understand phenomenology as a unified movement, despite numerous variations within it, is to see it as a radical response to the crisis of Western civilization, a civilization whose earmark has been its boasted sciences. What lies at the heart of this crisis, Edmund Husserl observed, is scientism – the hypostatization of scientific reason in *naturalism* and *objectivism*. Such objectivating reason is forgetful of subjectivity, human *spirit*, the thing that makes anything like science possible. Scientism is reason that has disengaged itself from the flow of concrete human experience out of which it originated, and in its veins of thought "no real blood flows." Detached from its life-world roots, scientism condemns itself to collapse into antireason and barbarism.

What the rise of scientism means is that the various natural and social sciences, servants of mankind in their initial conception, have become increasingly responsive to, and, since evaluated according to their own abstract principles of objective measurability, are decreasingly responsive to, the vitally felt, subjective interests of concrete persons. For example, a modern physician might well claim, without any sense of contradiction, that his operation was a success although his patient died (for example, the case of artificial-heart recipient, Barney Clarke) – "success" here being defined as conformity to certain rationally predetermined surgical procedures rather than promotion of the patient's own subjective feeling of health. Similarly, throughout the modern age, we see abstract, objectively measurable requirements of bureaucracies and technologies, built on scientism, taking priority over the felt, subjective needs of concrete persons, whom such bureaucracies and technologies are, in principle, supposed to serve.

We witness the rise of scientism most clearly in the development of modern economics; among the social sciences economics is the most removed from its life-world origins. Increasingly within the domain of modern economy persons feel that they must choke down their own value preferences in homage to the abstract requirements of increased profits, industrial efficiency, and gross national product. Economists, who judge policies successful even though poverty and human stress increase, are in danger of becoming like the physician previously described. Perhaps no science exerts more influence today than economics, but it is the one about which phenomenologists have remained most silent. They have described at great length the rise and nature of modern technologism but have said almost nothing about the economism that seems to steer it.

It is my intention here to briefly identify three specific places where economy's detachment from the life-world shows itself and where phenomenology can help recover economic science's forgotten roots:

1. the notion of scarcity

2. the uprooting of the marketplace

3. the transvalution of economy values.

Scarcity

Virtually every contemporary textbook on economics includes in its definition of that discipline the notion of scarcity. Economics is generally defined as the science of the production and distribution of goods and services in the light of *scarcity* of resources: scarcity is what makes production and distribution of goods and services a problem for economists because, it is assumed, human wants are unlimited.

Now it is interesting to note that while modern Western economy bemoans the scarcity of objects for consumption, the niggardliness of nature, communal life-style people, such as tribal peoples partake much more regularly in rituals of thanksgiving and celebrate the bountifulness of nature, even though, by all objective measures, the latter should be much more acutely aware of the earth's presumed scarcity. But communal life-style people, living close to the land and constantly aware of the ever-turning circles of nature, are more profoundly aware of another sort of scarcity: the relative scarcity, the *finitude*, of human life.

Indeed, relative to the vast contents of this universe, it is our existence that is scarce. It is our own being-unto-death that makes all things seem scarce and precious and bestows on the world anything like value – economic or otherwise. Economic scarcity is but one manifestation of human finitude. Were we not creatures of such finitude, then all possible objects of desire would be attainable, and the world would cease to be a realm of values. We can well grasp this point by imagining ourselves with only a few moments left to live. In such a situation the world would appear quite differently than it does in our everydayness, when we take it for granted. The trees, the sky, the air we breathe, the very earth we walk on – everything would take on a heightened sense of meaning. In the direct face of our own death everything appears precious and attains, what playwright Thornton Wilder termed, "a value above all price." But this imagined situation is not so different from that in which we find ourselves now or at any other moment of our lives. For death hovers over every instant of our lives, and in its shadow all things glow with value before us. Seeing the riches of the earth clearly within the context of one's own mortality, who would be foolish enough to put price tags on them?

The notion of economic scarcity is thus an anthropomorphizing of nature, an attempt to disburden our finitude onto the world. Correspondingly, to say, as economists tend to say, that human desires are unlimited and insatiable, is to confess secretly one's inability to confront, let alone accept, one's own finitude, one's own death. Indeed, as sociologist Phillip Aries has shown,[1] accompanying the growth of modern economy has been Western man's increasing tendency to deny his mortality, for death poisons our material pleasures and mocks all our ambitions for power and wealth as vain and futile. The more a society is obsessed with unlimited economic growth and consumption of goods, the more death appears as a violent intrusion on one's liberty to consume and the more scarce appear the goods of the world. On the other hand, the more deeply a society accepts death as a natural part of life – that is, the more it accepts death as a natural part of life – that is, the more it accepts human finitude – the less interested it will be in endless economic growth and accumulation of goods: the more bountiful the world appears, and the more generosity guides human behavior.

Yes, scarcity is a fact of life, but it is not an objective quality of nature, as economics commonly imply. Rather, the experience of scarcity is generated by human desires, and these desires in turn stem from human finitude. Were finitude not a fact of our existence, we would desire nothing and consequently have no experience of scarcity.

The notion of economic scarcity thus works to conceal our finitude from us, and in accepting it as the basis for our economic science, we spin from it a web of economic constructs that threaten the enmesh

us in self-deception. We begin to imagine that we are immortal, that
we could endlessly consume, if only nature would provide, and indeed
that meaning in life stems from such consumption, which feeds our
presumedly infinite thirsts.

The Uprooting of the Marketplace

Modern economy's divorce from its life-world roots is most apparent
in its notion of the marketplace. The marketplace has spread enormously in recent history. In ancient Greece it was limited to a parti-
cular, identifiable location, $\eta\ \alpha\gamma o\varrho\alpha$: recall, for instance, that Aristotle
gives "in the market" as an example of the category of location, $\pi o\nu$.[2]
And until this century, the term connoted primarily a village or street
market. But what economists commonly call the marketplace today,
appears to us as an *unlimited, nonlocalizable* matrix, generated by
calculative, commercial thinking. As such, it closely parallels the "absolute space" described by Newtonian physics.[3] This matrix of commer-
ciality seems to engulf the entire universe: virtually everything in the
modern world appears enveloped by the realm of business transactions
and converted into a commodity. Everything is for sale and has a price
in this expanded marketplace. In short, the localized marketplace of
the life-world community or village has spread and been transformed
into the unbounded market *space* of calculative commercialism.

As we walk through modern department stores and supermarkets,
the gaudy packagings and rationally calculated exchange values displayed on the price tags, *conceal* from us the *felt* values of life that
ultimately make anything like trading, bargaining, or speculating possible: they offer scarcely a hint of their primal source, the earth. By
contrast, the market of the village *discloses* the values of life, the values
of the earth: soil, fruit, crafts, rain, sun and sea are gathered and held
together in its transactions. The primordial marketplace celebrates the
life values that have been harvested from the bounty of the earth, but
which modern commercialism takes for granted.

As a gathering place, the market is properly identified by Socrates
as the place for philosophic dialogue, which gathers together ($\lambda\epsilon\gamma\epsilon\iota\nu$)
in $\lambda o\gamma os$ the One, which is also $\tau o\alpha\gamma\alpha\theta o\nu$, from out of $\tau o\ \pi\alpha\nu\pi\alpha$, belonging to the earth. The market is the dwelling place of $\lambda o\gamma os$. By my
participation in, my being in, the market, the market belongs to me.
That is, through the din of idle gossip ($\delta o\chi\alpha$), the life values gathered
in the marketplace speak to me from out of the silent depths of the
earth. The goods of the earth announce to me their worth, addressing

my *felt* vital interests and competing with one another to fulfill my vital intentionalities; they *possess me*, before I bid, not bid, bargain or pay. As Manfred Frings writes, "Being-in the market I be-hear (gehoren) the unconcealing Logos" of life values.[4]

In the modern market, the earth is parceled out and sold as real estate – as one more commodity among many. But in life's communal market, the earth itself cannot be subject to buying and selling, for who can possess what is the ground from which all of life's values spring? One makes the earth and her fruits one's own not by possession (that is, power) but through investment of one's sweat, toil, and blood – ownership in the fundamental sense (as all labor theories of value recognize).

What its severance from the earth means, is that modern market *space* knows no bound ($\pi\epsilon\varrho\alpha s$) (as is frequently claimed in the current "limits of growth" debate): it contains in its conception no principle of balance or proportion ($\alpha\varrho\mu o\nu\iota\alpha$), necessary for a harmonious and peaceful world and life. It approaches the Anaximanderan α-$\pi\epsilon\iota\varrho o\nu$. Consequently the modern market's matrix of valuation, lacking any humility before higher values of life and spirit, freely and arrogantly asserts its measure of being over all realms of human experience, bringing about a profound perversion in the process of economic valuation.

The Transvaluation of Economy Values

Martin Heidegger has shown quite thoroughly how the disclosedness of *Dasein* as crashing-unto-death, makes possible our capacity to *care* about being, to bestow value on anything – persons and all the creatures of the earth, and it confers on us the privileged ontological position of "shepherds of being."[5] Now, as we have suggested above, the calculative thinking of modern economic science attempts to disburden us of our finitude, our being-onto-death, and casts it upon the world through the notion of scarcity. Moreover, the modern market and its matrix of values are no longer ontologically connected to the earth or bounded. Thus we might well expect that in the modern economy care becomes lost: we become forgetful of our privileged status, and all valuation emanating from disclosure of that status becomes inauthenticated and distorted. Indeed, in the modern marketplace we witness a profound transvaluation and perversion of values. Disembodied from their life-world origins and rootedness in care, the abstracted, quantifiable values of economy have spread without limit and have asserted their own autonomy and right to cast final judgement on all matters. As economist E. F. Schumacher states, "Call a thing immoral or ugly, soul-destroying or a degradation of man, a peril to the peace of the world or to the well-being of future generations, as long as you have not shown it to be uneconomic you have not really questioned its right to exist, grow, and prosper."[6]

In his essays *Ressentiment*[7] and "Der Bourgeois,"[8] Max Scheler well describes the social history of this transvaluation of economy values. The latter grew, he tells us, out of the profound *ressentiment* of the rising bourgeoisie, since the thirteenth century, while under the domination of the old aristocracy. Suddenly,

> this *ressentiment* exploded and its values spread and were victorious. As the merchants and representatives of industry came to dominate, especially in the Western countries, *their* judgments, tastes, and inclinations became the selective determinants of cultural production, even in its intellectual and spiritual aspects. Their symbols and conceptions of the ultimate nature of things . . . came to replace the older religious symbols, and everywhere *their* type of valuation became the criterion of "morality" as such. . . .
>
> [T]he merchants' and the industrialists' professional values, the qualities that enable this particular type of man to succeed and do business, are set up as *generally valid* (indeed the "highest") *moral values.*

What are those values? Scheler continues:

> Cleverness, quick adaptability, a calculating mind, a desire for "security" and for unhampered transactions in all directions (and the qualities that are fit to bring about these conditions), a sense for the "calculability" of all circumstances, a disposition for steadiness in work and industriousness, economy and accuracy in concluding and observing agreements: these are the cardinal virtues now.[9]

In short, bourgeois morality elevated the values of industrialism above the values of life: life is made accountable to productivity, efficiency, economy. This transvaluation of values Scheler denounced as "decadence.[10] "[T]he *most profound* perversion of the hierarchy of values," he declared, "is the subordination of life values to values of usefulness, which gains force as modern morality develops. Since the victory of the industrial and commercial spirit . . . this priciple has been penetrating ever more deeply, affecting the most concrete value judgments."[11] What this means is that

> now life itself – the sheer *existence* of an individual, a race, a nation – must be justified by its *usefulness* for a *wider* community. It is not enough

if this life in itself contains higher values than usefulness can represent – its existence must be "earned." The right to live and exist, which the older preindustrial morality included among the "natural rights," is denied both in theory and in practice.[12]

Indeed, in the modern marketplace one must *earn a living* and this means serving the abstract goals of increased corporate profits and gross national product, regardless of whether such activity is life enhancing or life destroying. Life ceases to exist for its own sake or for *spiritual values of the person* but must make itself economically accountable.

This reversal of the values of life and usefulness has profound implications for modern man's self-understanding. Karl Marx already well described how in the modern market economy persons are reduced to the commodity "labor," and workers' complaints about being treated like commodities, like machines, are all too familiar to us. But in the more advanced stages of the "industrial ethos," people begin to think of *themselves* in such terms: throughout today's society we hear people talking about "selling themselves" in the labor market, packaging themselves in whatever manner is necessary to make a sale. Recently posted on a university's bulletin boards were advertisements proclaiming, *"Your Future Depends On How You Market Yourself."* Moreover, in an age that values machines over life, people will increasingly see themselves as well-oiled machines and adopt mechanistic views of life, in order to preserve their sense of self-worth. As Scheler writes,

> "life" itself is no longer an original phenomenon, but merely a complex of mechanical and mental processes. The mechanistic view of life sees the living being itself as a "machine," its "organization" as a sum of useful tools which differ only in degree from artificially produced tools. If this were true, then naturally life could have no independent *value* apart from the combined utility values of these "organs."[13]

Persons value themselves as economically productive machines.

But economy's primordial rootedness in communal life values, rather than in values of usefulness, is shown in its original meaning as οιχο-νομιχ namely, care of the human home, that home being the living earth, generally with the constellation of one's familial relations at its heart. The well-being of the family is the original measure of economy.

Increasingly, though, as Scheler demonstrates, economy has become the measure of life in general and of the family in particular. The well-being of a family is judged not by the vitality of its interpersonal relations and the depth of its members' love for one another, but according to its economic viability and wealth. Family positions are reduced to economic functions and judged by commercial standards. A "good husband" and "good father" is a "good provider"; a "good wife" and "good mother" is a good consumer, a "smart shopper"; and children are viewed as commodities or investments.[14] Originally, economy was seen as family rooted, but certain social theories, for example those of Karl Marx, describe the family as primarily an economic institution and certainly not as an abode of personal love.

More broadly, economy, as a value rooted in family, is a value of conservation rather than one of thriftiness, as it is commonly thought today. Out of a heart-felt reverence for the earth, communal life people economize her fruits. The most revered members of the tribe are those displaying the least need for material goods: such individuals exhibit the highest degree of vital fitness. Thus, even today among various tribes of North American Indians, generosity remains the highest virtue: through acts of generosity one celebrates one's vitality and health.[15] In the preindustrial West, Werner Sombart has pointed out, economy was valued as expressive of vital fitness among the poor and for them alone. It denoted one's ability to make do with one's lot in life. Within Christianity, by contrast, economy was attached to the ideal of "voluntary poverty" and the virtue of sacrifice. Sombart writes, "That was the new, unheard of thing: that one had the means and *still* economized! *The idea of economy appeared in the world*! Economy not by necessity, but by choice – not as a need, but as a virtue."[16] One economized perhaps out of care and reverence for the earth and her creatures (for example, St. Francis) but certainly not as a celebration of life values. Rather, one economized primarily for self-redemption, self-liberation of one's soul from the earth.

The above notions of the value of economy are in sharp contrast to the modern notion of it as "thrift" – a bastardized version of the communal life and Christian notions. What are economized are not fruits of the earth, the life that blossoms forth from the earth, but the hypostatized units of exchange, such as, money.[17] One is said to economize when one gets the most for one's money – even when that means increased consumption and waste of the earth's goods (say, when one shifts to cheaper markets). Moreover, as the value of money, the economizing of abstract exchange units, increases, the felt-values for the earth and its life decrease. Schumacher describes the matter this way: "economic thinking . . . takes the sacredness out of life, because there can be nothing sacred in something that has a price. Not surprisingly, therefore, if economic thinking pervades the whole of society, even simple non-economic values like beauty, health, or cleanliness can survive only if they prove to be economic – that is, profitable.[18] Thus modern market economy presents itself as a strange contradiction: it most loudly bemoans the scarcity of nature's goods, as we previously observed, but then exhausts and wastes those goods at unprecedented levels. This contradiction is possible because modern economy, divorced from its life-world origins and communal-life values, measures itself according to its own abstract, rationally constructed criteria – which it takes for objective reality – and not according to vital feelings of well-being.

Not only the value of economy itself but also numerous related values become transvaluated in the modern market. Let us mention just three.

1) Self-control. "Originally," Scheler tells us, *self-control* meant primarily the sovereignty of the spiritual person over the chaos of sensuous impulses." It meant the "will to dominate one's appetites" through "humility before and in God . . . regardless of whether the consequences are good or bad from the viewpoint of personal utility. But now self-control becomes a *mere means* of financial success and for prevailing over one's competitors."[19] It has ceased to be a positive spiritual value in its own right but is ascribed a mere instrumental function.

2) Liberty. Originally liberty was a religiously based notion that described one's ability to act in accord with one's (moral) *conscience*, free from physical, social, or political constraints. Liberty was valued not for its own sake but as necessary for moral behavior and responsibility.[20] But modern market economy has detached liberty from these religious, ethical roots: liberty has become a right of self-interest, the freedom to maximize consumption in the market place without any necessary regard for one's social responsibility or for the common good. Indeed, such concern would be a liability to one's competitive position, claim certain modern economists (for example, Milton Friedman[21]).

3) Trust. In the economies of communal-life people, the basic psychological disposition tends to be one of mutual trust and understanding, coupled with a sense of generosity. But in the modern market economy, trust tends to become a liability. Trust suggests a shortage of good business sense and a lack of shrewdness: it makes one more vulnerable to one's competitors. Distrust has emerged as the new value of the modern market place, and a huge legal system has evolved to mediate business transactions based on it. We require that everything be put into writing. Contracts are rooted in distrust, and they are insulting to the integrity of communal-life persons, for whom one's word

is sufficient.[22] (The latter is still the case among Japanese businessmen for whom recourse to a court of law is a sign of one's personal inability to resolve disputes peacefully and a mark against one's honor.)

In this paper I have merely touched on what I perceive as a vast, largely unexplored area for phenomenological analysis: the forgotten life-world roots of economic science. This science, perhaps more than any other, exhibits the crisis of Western civilization, to which phenomenologists point, a crisis rooted in the naturalizing of spiritual consciousness and which engenders a loss of *felt* meaning for the life of Western man. I have merely suggested three places where economy's disembodiment from the life-world exhibits itself and where phenomenology can redisclose those forgotten roots. 1) Phenomenology helps us to reroot the economic concept of scarcity in human finitude: scarcity is made possible by our ontological status as beings-unto-death rather than in the stinginess of nature. 2) A phenomenological analysis reminds us that prior to becoming an infinite matrix of commercial transactions, unanchored to the earth at any particular location, the marketplace is primordially a *place* of gathering and celebration of life values, a place where the life values of the earth speak to us, address our felt, vital interests prior to any rational calculations of maximum utility. And 3) phenomenology discloses our fundamental ontological disposition to the world as one of care. Such a disposition is foundational for all acts of valuation, including those whereby rationally calculated prices are attached to the goods of the earth. Where an economy's values become divorced from this fundamental disposition, they become perverted, hollow, and empty: life is made into something useful; the organism begins to serve the machine.

In at least these three ways phenomenology can make a momentous contribution to the rehumanization of our contemporary world – a contribution to the revitalization and respiritualization of a world that has become increasingly dead and impersonal under the intellectual tyranny of the icy laws of objective scientism. Economy has been a prime instance of this scientism. By the above remarks I mean to imply no specific economic policies, nor do I mean to suggest that we return to some medieval economy. Rather, I wish to arouse certain human sensitivities that have been chiefly dormant in modern economic thought and life; I wish to recover that fundamental human experience of the world that makes something like economy and economic science possible. Moreover, insofar as phenomenology's response to the crisis of modern science has been to retrieve, from underneath the sedimented layers of objectivating thinking, our primordial relationship to the world, the project which I have only suggested here, falls clearly within the larger project that phenomenology has set for itself. Phenomenology calls economy out of the sterile world of bloodless hypostatization, and invites it to return to the communal-life world where it was born but from which it has been, in the twentieth century, mostly absent.

Notes

1. *Western Attitudes Toward Death from the Middle Ages to the Present*, trans. Patricia M. Ranum (Baltimore: Johns Hopkins University Press, 1974).

2. *Categories* 4, 2^a: 1-2; 9, 11_b: 10-14.

3. Sir Isaac Newton, *Mathematical Principles of Natural Philosophy*, 3rd ed. (1726), Scholium. See also, John Locke, *Essay Concerning Human Understanding* (1690) II, 13, 23.

4. "Insight-Logos-Love" (Lonergan-Heidegger-Scheler), *Philosophy Today* 14 (Summer 1970); 110.

5. James M. Demske, *Being, Man, and Death: A Key to Heidegger* (Lexington: University Press of Kentucky, 1970), 136.

6. E. F. Schumacher, *Small Is Beautiful: Economics as If People Mattered* (New York: Harper & Row, 1973), 42.

7. "Das Ressentiment im Aufbau der Moralen" (1915), in *Vom Umsturz der Werte: Abhandlungen und Aufsatze*, 4th ed., edited by Maria Scheler, vol. 3 of *Gesammelte Werke* (Bern: Francke, 1955), 33-147; *Ressentiment*, translated by William Holdheim, ed. Lewis A. Coser (New York: Free Press of Glencoe, 1961).

8. (1913/14), in *Vom Umsturz der Werte*, 343-61.

9. *Vom Umsturz der Werte*, 131-32; *Ressentiment*, 155-56.

10. *Vom Umsturz der Werte*, 147; *Ressentiment*, 174.

11. *Vom Umsturz der Werte*, 131 *Ressentiment*, 154-55.

12. *Vom Umsturz der Werte*, 134; *Ressentiment*, 158.

13. *Vom Umsturz der Werte*, 135; *Ressentiment*, 160.

14. Edward Albee beautifully satirized the treatment of children as commodities and investments in his play *The American Dream*. And Thorstein Veblen well described the bourgeois wife as a tool of her husband's "conspicuous leisure" and "conspicuous consumption." *The Theory of the Leisure Class: An Economic Study of Institutions* (1899; New York: New American Library, 1953), 68-69.

15. Ella C. Deloria, *Speaking of Indians* (Vermillion: Dakota Press, 1979), 45-48, 77-87.

16. *Der Bourgeois* (Munich and Leipzig: Duncker & Humblot, 1913), 139; *The Quintescence of Capitalism: A Study of the History and Psychology of the Modern Business Man*, trans. M. Epstein (New York: H. Fertig, 1967), 106.

17. I take Georg Simmel, *The Philosophy of Money*, trans. Tom Bottomore and David Frisby (London: Routledge & Kegan Paul, 1978), to be the most penetrating description of the genesis of money out of communal-life relations and the transformation of those relations brought about by its hypostatization.

18. Schumacher, *op. cite.* 45.

19. Scheler, *Vom Umsturz der Werte*, 133; *Ressentiment*, 156–57.

20. Jonathan Edwards, *Freedom of the Will* (1754), pt. I, sec. V.

21. "The Social Responsibility of Business Is to Increase Its Profits," *New York Times Magazine* (September 13, 1970), reprinted in Thomas Donaldson and Patricia H. Werhane (eds.), *Ethical Issues in Business: A Philosophical Approach* (Englewood Cliffs, N.J.: Prentice-Hall, 1979), 191–97.

22. Ferdinand Tonnies, *Community and Society (Gemeinschaft und Gesellschaft)* (1887), translated by Charles P. Loomis (New York: Harper & Row, 1963), 49, 65, 240–42; Scheler, *Der Formalismus in der Ethik und die materielle Wertethik: Neuer Versuch der Grundlegung eines ethischen Personalismus*, 5th ed., ed. Manfred Frings, vol. 2 of *Gesammelte Werke* (1980), 518; *Formalism in Ethics and Non-Formal Ethics of Values: A New Attempt toward the Foundation of an Ethical Personalism*, trans. Manfred S. Frings and Roger L. Funk (Evanston: Northwestern University Press, 1973), 529.

Part V.
Phenomenology
and the Social

17. Hannah Arendt's Critical Appropriation of Heidegger's Thought as Political Philosophy

Mildred Bakan

As moderns we look to the work of a political thinker hoping for some guidance as to what we might do to improve our difficult times. If we approach the work of Hannah Arendt in this frame of mind, we are apt to be disappointed. She writes about the interplay of thought and action in all of her work, but her basic answer to the question: What are we called on to do? seems to be that the question is itself misguided. If our political sphere of life were not distorted, we could work out what to do among ourselves through a discourse in relationship to our situation. The distortion of our political life renders us impotent. Neither does she show us how we might recover a relevant political life. But she does seek to remind us of what a political life is.

However, according to Arendt, remembrance of this sort is no trivial matter. Though it is not only out of remembrance that we act, remembrance is deeply influential; and though instances of fulfilled (or true) political life may be rare, and short lived at that, their remembrance keeps the possibility of their occurrence alive in darker times.

Arendt's assessment of her aim as a political thinker follows Heidegger's way of thinking. Yet in the course of her work, I think it is not too much to say – though it may strike one as an exaggeration at first – she maintains a dialogue with two important and very different thinkers. One of them is Heidegger, who, she herself suggests, introduced her to what thinking is.[1] The other is Marx, whose thought seems to preoccupy her with nagging persistency. On her desk in her New

York City home she kept three photographs: one of her mother, the other of her husband, Heinrich Blücher, to whom *Origins of Totalitarianism* is dedicated. The third photograph is of Heidegger.[2] Her mother was an active socialist and an admirer of Rosa Luxemburg, the legendary Marxist revolutionary. Her husband participated with Rosa Luxemburg in the Spartacist revolt in Germany in 1918–1919 and in the foundation of the German Communist Party.

In the opening essay of *Between Past and Future*, titled "Tradition and the Modern Age"[3] she cites Marx as having formulated the essential shift of our times: the massive increase of the productivity of labor. Indeed she accords him the status of being one of the three greatest thinkers of our time, the other two being Kierkegaard and Nietzsche. She goes on to explicate the central thought of both Kierkegaard and Nietzsche in terms of Marx's analysis of the corruption of use value by exchange value in capitalist society – a point to which she often returns in her analysis of the modern cultural crisis.[4]

Her concrete issues are drawn from her own experience of our times, especially in the context of the rise of Hitler in Germany; but the parameters of her thought reflect the influence of Marx. That she shared something of Marx's vision of a communal society is indicated by her own claim that Marx was influenced, as she was, by the Greek experience of political life.[5] In the same essay, "Tradition and the Modern Age," she characterizes the Western political tradition as beginning with Plato and ending with Marx – no mean praise.[6] Nevertheless she found Marx, whom she on occasion describes as the single greatest historically minded thinker of our times,[7] seriously wanting. Marx's thought poses for her an abstract intellectual problem. On the other hand, Heidegger's thought poses the concretely acute intellectual dilemma of her life.

Heidegger was a thinker in the best sense of the word. How could he then, like so many other German intellectuals, be taken in by National Socialism to the point of fascination?[8] It is pertinent to note here that in her later life she judged Eichmann's criminality to be due to the absence of thought, that banality which I take to be further explicated by the description of the experience of *das Man* in *Being and Time*. According to Arendt, Marx still sought to understand what was going on in the Western world in terms of the concepts and ideals of the Western tradition, though that tradition was losing its relevance to our experience.[9] Heidegger, however, recognized, as did the young thinkers of her own generation (those coming of age after World War I) who were drawn to him, as she was, that the tradition was dead and must be overcome.[10] And it is in this intellectual climate that Heidegger's lectures were so exciting. He gave no answers, but he was thinking in a fresh way, as though no one had thought before, bringing classic texts alive with relevance to the present. If, she writes, assessing his importance as a thinker on the occasion of his eightieth birthday, we are all reading this way today, it was Heidegger who did it first.[11] The very advent in our times of totalitarianism, which, according to Arendt, cannot be understood in terms of our traditional modes of political thought at all, is itself a manifestation of a breakdown of that tradition, the lost authority of old religious institutions and indeed of all standards external to our experience.[12] Totalitarianism, as such, is a totally unprecedented phenomenon and hence requires understanding in a wholly unprecedented way – without any preconceptions whatsoever. Therefore we must indeed think as no one thought before. We must reread the thinkers of the Western tradition as if no one had ever read them before. And that is the way Heidegger was reading the great philosophers of our philosophical tradition when, as a student, she met him, well before the rise of Hitler.

Though she rarely used the word phenomenology, we clearly recognize in her thought a phenomenological aim: to distinguish and describe what she herself calls the phenomena of political life. If in making these distinctions she takes note of language and its etymological roots, as Heidegger does, to regain their meaning in their original experiential context, it is to grasp the relevant differentiated nuances of our own political experiences. Attention to the etymological roots of language, by taking account of original texts, in turn both requires and facilitates the suspension of received notions, allowing us to apprehend what is going on, the reality of our world. Indeed, received notions are suspended – and must be suspended – because we cannot understand our experience.

Her concept of understanding, as reaching "the things themselves" free of prejudice, and her concern with the essence of political phenomena show her to be a Husserlian of sorts. I say "of sorts" because her political phenomenology is not marked by an epistemological interest. Her approach to the phenomena themselves is that of Heidegger not Husserl. The meaning of phenomena is found, beheld, by the thinking mind. Somehow the phenomena speak out of themselves. And it is the crisis itself – the emptiness of the tradition (Heidegger's stance) – that renders any other approach but a phenomenology inappropriate.

But Arendt never lays down a methodology. Her basic *interest* is in the realities of experience. So she frequently draws on examples, the unique instances, to extract the lessons of experience as their essence. Nevertheless, she insists that her thought is only tentative, an invitation to others to join her in thinking.[13] For true thinking, like birth itself, always marks a new beginning, as Socrates, whom she takes as the ideal example of a thinker, understood.[14] Instead of the *epoché*, she emphasizes the role of the political position of the newcomer, as an outsider seeking a place in the world with others.[15] This political position, like thought itself, demands a new beginning. It is the concrete inadequacy of received notions that sends us back to our past, to find fragments which illuminate the reality of our times in a critical light, allowing us to understand what is going on without yielding to events. In an essay on Walter Benjamin, comnmenting on the affinity of his thought to Heidegger's own later work, she describes Benjamin's thought − like Heidegger's − as a poetic thinking which rips fragments − "pearls and corals," she calls them − out of classic texts to speak to us in the present as world essences.[16] On occasion she used the phrase "pearl fishing" to describe her own work. The recovered pearls and corals allow us to recover a present, which to begin with, we do not have, with appropriate critical illumination. She deepens the historical approach of both Heidegger and Husserl by acknowledging the role of alienation from the world as a political matter. Nevertheless, she takes as her aim understanding without prejudice, free of preconception.

What we find in her work is, in effect, a hermeneutical phenomenology of political life which takes into account historical events and records and the classic texts, placed in the context of their time so as to reveal their critical relevance for the presnt. Political life is always rendered comprehensible as experience, as human experience, which itself, at its core, is concerned with meaning − and indeed the meaning of a life as a whole in the face of death (and birth) and the inevitable ruin of time. She never uses the word *Dasein* but, as we shall see, her analysis of political life finds its foundation in the web of human relationships among persons taken as in effect *Dasein*, Being-in-the-world. But if for Heidegger, *Dasein* is *Mitsein*; for Arendt *Mitsein* is *Dasein*. Human experience is primordially with others. The Husserlian reduction to my own experience is itself set within the Western tradition as a deeply problematic feature of that tradition. According to Arendt, the philosophical experience as solitary thought is to be understood in Plato's terms as a dialogue with oneself − a two-in-one − in which the self I talk to takes the place of others.

Furthermore, Being-with-others is itself bifurcated. She follows the Greeks in their distinction between the *Bios Ananke* and the *Bios Politikos*. Indeed this distinction, developed in *The Human Condition*,[17] became central to her thought. For the distinction is the setting of our experience of freedom which takes place only in the context of the *Bios Politikos*. Thus she makes the seemingly bizarre claim that the family, as belonging to nature and necessity, the *Bios Ananke*, is not a political phenomenon at all. Furthermore she seems to extend the *Bios Ananke*, the life lived out of necessity, to include whatever is done habitually, thoughtlessly, out of convention.[18] Thus political life seems, for Arendt, to take on the role of the clearing that Heidegger maintained has not been thought, for it is only in the context of political life, a life lived with others as equals, that we are irreducibly unique persons capable of authentic – and free – action and speech.

Clearly this understanding of political life involves an important rethinking of the thought of both Marx and Heidegger. For on this basis, democracy, as acknowledging pluralism, the essential plurality of human beings in their uniqueness, is in the truth in a way that tyranny, despotism, and simple collectivity are not, though in the end, according to Arendt, a democratic political life is a matter of preference. To elaborate this concept of the political, Arendt returns to Kant's work to develop a stunning interpretation of his concept of judgement as a thinking that is relevant to action; that is, a political thinking.

II

According to Arendt, the political sphere of life clears a space,[19] a world which allows us to appear to each other in terms of our words and actions, showing who we are: that is, as unique persons. The same world also allows the things we make to endure for others to see. Art works are preeminently worldly in this sense, but objects made for use are also worldly. This world, which is generated spatially in terms of the things we make, is our common world. As our common world, it is the world of which it is relevant to say that we are at home in it or not; it is meaningful to us or it is not. As shared, we can talk about this world with each other in the political space cleared which in turn preserves, and is preserved by, the remembrance of the words and deeds of others who participate in the keeping of this space. Thus history itself has its locus in the political sphere. Just this political sphere is, properly speaking, the realm of practice (*praxis*), involving judgment. Even art is a matter of *techné* requiring craft and distance from oneself.

Arendt's conception of political life singles out 1) the special relationship of our self-identity in terms of discourse and action with others to *praxis* and 2) the special relationship of *praxis* to the constitution of our world itself. She maintains the special dimension of human life, which she isolates as the political has not, as such, been thought of in our tradition, though it was exemplified in the Greek *polis*. As other paradigmatic examples of political interrelationships, she takes the Paris commune, the Russian soviets, and the New England town meeting.[20] She provides a vision of a participatory democracy, organized at its base in terms of decentralized councils which elect representatives to higher councils forming a hierarchy, such that authority finds its justification from below. Power is to rest with the base – the people – through ongoing respect for plurality by seeking consensus within the council structure through discussion. According to Arendt, participation in these councils allows an authentic political elite to emerge. She is, on the one hand, critical of the party systems characteristic of liberal democracies and, on the other hand, of the typical organization of Communist parties.[21]

Marx, however, takes as his model for *praxis*, she claims, *homo faber*,[22] the fabricator of things to which means-end considerations are relevant. Furthermore, Marx fails to distinguish work from labor. Labor, as our basic metabolic interchange with nature (a concept developed by Marx), is in fact an endless, repetitive, ongoing necessity. But fabricated things which are not consumed but used – and art works (as well as other fabricated works constituting our culture, such as written history, philosophy, and literature) – endure to make a world as labor cannot. And indeed, for Marx, as for Hegel, labor and work are not distinct. Useful objects are taken to be fabricated through the willfull transformation of nature. Both Marx and Hegel set human labor in the context of world making.[23] Housekeeping comes to mind as an excellent example of labor in Arendt's sense. Also perhaps food growing. Her model is drawn on the basis of the Greek separation of the public from the private. In Greek political life, whose sole concern was the affairs of the public world, only the male head of the household participated in the assembly. The women's task was the management of the household, which lay outside the public world altogether. But as ongoing and repetitive labor, the individuality of making that even art and craft allow, cannot appear. In her critical assessment of Marx, she seems to identify labor, rather than work, as the economic sphere. Yet she acknowledges Marx's acuity in having recognized the importance of the extraordinary productivity of labor in our times.[24] Out of this perspective, she characterizes a consumer society as one in which all things are treated as food to be used up and not preserved.[25] She herself renders Marx's confusion of labor and work understandable. She points out that Marx, recognizing the ubiquity of exchange value in capitalist society, understood all values had become exchangeable and relative, mere commodities, and so foresaw the "devaluation of all values."[26] And she draws on this conception of the deformation of use value to characterize the

bourgeois life against which both the intellectual elite and the mob —
her terms — united under Hitler to found a new order.[27] But, however,
acute Marx may be in his analysis of capitalist society, he mistakenly
treats the political sphere as though it too can be made like an object
for use — or for that matter an art work. Like Hegel, he conceives of
men as making their own history.[28] Herein lies the basic defect of Marx's
thought, a defect overcome among Marxists only by Rosa Luxemburg,
whom Arendt continued to admire. Indeed she claimed that Rosa Luxemburg was no longer a Marxist.[29] But that is a highly questionable
interpretation.

On the other hand, Heidegger's criticism of technological thought,
which amounts to a criticism of the model of man as fabricator, is not
sufficient to overcome Marx's deficiency. In his "Letter on Humanism,"[30]
Heidegger describes Marx as having uncovered an essential dimension
of history and adds, that the reply to Marx has not yet been made. Certainly this indicates that he, Heidegger, is at least interested in such
a reply. Indeed, we find Heidegger already concerned with the theme
of work, if not labor, in *Being and Time*, in the context of his explication
of the "hermeneutic-as." In his later work, Heidegger seeks to rethink
the nature of work as an involvement with nature (consider his essay
"Building, Dwelling, Thinking"[31]) which does not dominate nature, as
Marx envisions, but lives rather in continuity, responsively with nature,
clearing a human space as a world. Such work remains in thanksgiving remembrance of the gift of the earth. But on reading Arendt, one
wonders whether "Building, Dwelling, Thinking" is not more aptly
appropriated to the building of a city than a bridge. Clearing a human
space such that the works, deeds, and speech of men may show and
be remembered is, for Arendt, a political act. Arendt simply dismisses
Heidegger's interpretation of work as basically too rural, preindustrial,
in inspiration to be relevant to our modern world.[32]

In the posthumously published interview in *Der Spiegel*, Heidegger takes issue with democracy, in particular, as a political way of life.
That is the single current issue with respect to which he does take a
stand, and a negative one at that. Yet *Being and Time* does not as such
rule out democratic political organization. Each of us as a human being
is capable of authenticity, of recovering ourselves as thinkers and, at
least in a certain sense, as actors. That the point is on Arendt's mind
is shown by a comment she made at a conference on her work a few
years ago: "every human being has a need to think . . . while he is living. And he does it constantly."[33] Why not then a plurality of perspectives? Nowhere, however, does Heidegger discuss how such a plurality
might be resolved. *Dasein* is *Mitsein* in terms of a unified disclosure

or understanding of Being. Gadamer develops this implicit possibility inherent in Heidegger's thought in terms of a fusion of horizons involving dialogue, but only through participation in a language game which moves within a shared foreconception of Being.[34] Arendt singles out the plurality of perspectives as crucial for the political sphere.[35] But it is not a shared foreconception of Being that allows dialogue; it is rather a shared common world, as her experience of German anti-Semitism so forcefully demonstrated. However culturally well assimilated, the German Jew was still excluded from the German world. Indeed, according to Arendt, it is through dialogue involving multiple perspectives of the appearing world that a shared common world emerges.

III

It is out of deep concern for this issue that she elaborates the political relevance of Kant's concept of judgment delineated in the *Critique of Judgment* in connection with taste in art. She credits Kant with the discovery of a faculty of judgment, distinct from the faculties of thinking and willing. Judgment related us to each other communally by developing the universal out of particulars without rules. In the *Critique of Judgment* Kant points out that in judging a work of art we take into account the appearance of the work to others. These others constitute a community of taste in which one participates by judging the work of art for oneself. For in such judgment we evaluate the work of art as a contemplative spectator out of, according to Kant, a disinterested interest that amounts to (or allows) an enlarged mentality, implicitly taking the possible experience (judgment) of others into account.

Disinterested interest is not without interest. But the interest is not private. The distinction here is between, let us say, behaving out of individual particularized desire and acting or judging in relation to others as others.[36] It is pertinent to note in this connection that Kant distinguishes the categorical imperative from behavior motivated by desire, the latter being simply natural. *This* distinction, when put in the context of Arendt's thought, is clearly analogous to the Greek distinction between the *Bios Politikos* and the *Bios Ananke*, which Arendt draws on as crucial to political life. But Arendt takes issue with the categorical imperative as a principle informing our communal relations with others. Instead she turns to the concept of judgment, as developed by Kant in connection with art, for the conceptual basis of that sort of thought that draws us into a culturally specific community of others who share a common world.[37]

Arendt also finds Kant the source of the important distinction between thought and cognition which, like judgment, she claims Kant left undeveloped.[38] Thought apprehends what is absent and so is capable of remembrance which she describes, like Heidegger, as the most primordial form of thought. Judgment, it should be noted, is impossible without a relationship to absent others. Thought, she says, seeks meaning and, as such, does not, like cognition push to the attainment of knowledge. Thought, questioning, can undo the frozen habituality in the use of words, arousing perplexity on the one hand, and, on the other, recovering the experiential context of empty concepts; that is, their authentic meaning. Of course, it is thought in this sense which preoccupies Heidegger in his thinking about thinking. This distinction, which frees thinking from knowledge, is crucial for Arendt's own thinking. The recovery of full – or authentic – meaning illuminates worldly experience. The illumination may be the mark of truth but it is the illumination that Arendt stresses and that remains both deeply personal and worldly. Such thinking aims at no overt worldly consequences. Yet we have a need to think simply to apprehend the meaning of our lives by connecting our disparate worldly experiences. Whereas, following Kant, cognition is restricted to knowledge of real objects, the apprehension of meaning allows personal reconciliation with reality, relevant to a poetic yes-saying, even-perhaps, precisely-as critical.

In her later work, following *Eichmann in Jerusalem*, she is absorbed with the question of the relevance of this sort of thinking for political life. She writes of a need to think rather than a need to know. Thinking interrupts routine not merely to achieve understanding of what one is doing in the context of what is really going on. Thinking is for its own sake. Nevertheless, thinking questions orientation, lifting it out of the habitual. Above all, thought can simply remain with perplexity, and so *allow* judgment of the concretely particular without preconceptions.

Thinking founded on remembered experience is both solitary and withdrawn from our common world. Thought, as solitary, can, however, also remain rooted in our common sense, which Arendt describes simply as a mental organ for discerning the real, a concept of Aristotelian origin, with which Kant's concept of judgment, in relation to a community of taste, has strong affinities. Common sense orients us with respect to the common world we experience, and though science develops out of common sense, according to Arendt, common sense has also crucial political relevance.[39] The Western tradition with its emphasis on prediction, calculability, and deduction has destroyed the intellectual respectability of common sense. It is important to note that according to Arendt, totalitarianism itself thrives on the destruction of common sense by using terror to destroy the possibility of communal relations.[40] That thinking which withdraws from our appearing world, by introducing perplexity, allows us to see our common world anew, free of conventional prejudice. But judging is a kind of thinking which assesses – evaluates – what appears in our common world. Judging, though solitary, nevertheless takes account of the standpoint of others who share our common world, maintaining, in just this sense, a disinterested interest – the attitude of a worldly spectator. A judgment, according to Arendt, amounts to an opinion calling for discussion with others with the aim of achieving agreement or consensus, not concerning the truth as such, but such questions as action (clearly involving decisions), taste (preference – implicitly decisions as to how the world is to appear), and also the significance (meaning) of past history and present events. Discussion informed by judgment reaches agreement by persuasion not proof, but judgment itself is a thinking *oriented* toward possible agreement. Throughout, thinking as judging remains in touch with the common world in terms of an enlarged mentality by keeping in mind the standpoint of others with respect to that world.[41]

The common world we share is a life world, a world of appearance. It is in that world that we appear to each other. In locating the relevance of the experienced common world for human social and political life, we find a point at which Marxism and phenomenology intersect. Arendt herself explicitly credits Marx with the insight that, following the Industrial Revolution, accepted modes of thought had become irrelevant to the experiential context of human affairs.[42] Indeed, she hails Marx as having been the first major thinker to criticize philosophy for withdrawing from the worldly concerns of politics. But neither Marx nor Heidegger develop the singular relevance of our lived-world as such to the political sphere in Arendt's sense, as a world in which we relate to each other, not just simply empathetically, but in terms of the standpoint of others taken as both unique and equal. It is into this common world that we act, about this common world that we engage in discourse in our political life and it is to the affairs of this common world that judgment is relevant.

Our common world is not identical with nature; it is of human origin, but not humanly *made*. To be made is to be fabricated with an end in mind. Artists are interested in the endurance of this common world as guaranteeing the appearance of their work to others. But Arendt identifies the care of the world as a place which preserves and allows the appearance of all fabricated works (including written philosophy and history and, also, works of art!) as a *political* activity.

Artists, she insists, like others interested in fabricated works, are susceptible to domination by means-end calculation. Yet artworks are most
unlike objects made simply for use. Artworks are made simply to appear
– to embody the intangible – and, as such, to endure forever. Artworks
are thus exemplary with respect to the role of works as *cultural*.[43] Cultural works endow our common world with continuity beyond our lives,
as do all fabricated works (including written philosophy and history)
that embody testimony – remembrance – of who we are. And, according to Arendt, it is the endurance of this common world beyond our
individual life span that lends point to human life itself. But only par-
ticipants in political life for its own sake can judge things without regard
to utility or function, out of the right love of the common world, as
a world which allows us to relate freely to each other as both unique
and communally sharing that world – belonging together. As humanly
originated, our common world is a communal world, intrinsically shared
as a way of being at home in the universe, in reality.

Whereas for Heidegger the world as that for the sake of which we
work is disclosed as Being in terms of the sending of *Sein, Seinsgeschick;*[44]
for Arendt, this world is humanly originated and is political in essence,
if not wholly in origin. Heidegger emphasizes in connection with
Dasein's world, the keeping of Being, with language as the house of
Being and Being itself as sending, claiming us as humans to the care
of Being through the care of the world. For Arendt, however, the common world is crucially a sphere that allows and preserves human
freedom in terms of the power to act in concert and to speak to each
other showing who we are. Thus the care of the common world is care
of a world in which we are – or can be – in the fullest sense, persons
in relation to each other, the sphere in which Hegelian mutual recognition can take place – a political concern.

But the demand for public mutual recognition is the ethical presupposition of Marx's thought as well. Arendt often seems to reduce Marx
to an economic historian, but Marx was, as she well knew, a political
economist who took the alienated social relations of capitalism to be
inseparable from the usurpation of use value by exchange value. Arendt
was introduced to the thought of Marx, Lenin, and Trotsky by her husband Heinrich Blücher, and, in fact, developed a concept of *praxis* in
terms of political action from his experience – or tales of his experience
– of the left revolt in Germany led by Rosa Luxemburg,[45] whom, as
I pointed out earlier, Arendt continued to admire. Rosa Luxemburg
stressed the spontaneity of revolutionary action, that it is in the course
of the revolutionary situation that relevant political action is developed.
A revolution cannot be planned by blueprint. Of course Marxists, in

general, call for political action to effect social change. But Rosa Luxemburg was sharply critical of Lenin's concept of a Communist party as a small revolutionary elite. She claimed that revolutionary action cannot be effectively guided by any small group. Revolution must emerge from the spontaneous involvement of large numbers of people in rebellious action. And, according to Arendt, it is in the very context of revolutionary practice that we experience the unique joy of the freedom of true political life.[46] Thus revolutionary practice itself teaches us who we are. Moreover, she maintains, it is just in the political sphere that we show who we are in *spontaneous* speech and deed. We cannot know who we are in terms of any fixed essence, any fixed nature, unlike our knowledge of tables and chairs, things in the world. We can always be surprised by others, and even by ourselves.[47] But, it is interesting to note, Arendt describes spontaneity as an act of *unified will* in the course of her discussion of Augustine in *The Life of the Mind*.[48] Arendt is seeking to isolate willing as a dimension of *praxis* that is not tied to instrumentally productive interest. Rosa Luxemburg, she writes, knew that a *deformed* revolution was more to be feared than a defeated one.[49]

This defines the thrust of her analysis of the *Vita Activa*, the subject matter of *The Human Condition* and the title of the book in its German translation. Our active life is analyzed as consisting of three distinguishable aspects: labor, work, and *praxis* in terms of speech and deed, the last alone being purely political. It is important to note that Arendt distinguishes labor and work from praxis as, in effect, instrumental. But labor, work, and praxis are essential factors of Marx's own thought, however interwined. Indeed, Arendt herself describes Marx as confirming that "man's humanity consists of his productive and active force, which in its most elementary aspect he calls labor power."[50] Thus Arendt retains Marx's activist orientation and, indeed, radicalizes it in terms of a singularly human compacity to originate which is our freedom to begin our life with others anew, and indeed to revolt and found a new political order. Now Heidegger, to overcome the tradition, seeks to overcome willing itself as the will to will, the will to power, particularly in his later work through the exploration of the implications of *Gelassenheit* – letting be – allowing thinking as thanking. In *Being and Time*, authentic willing is restricted to *individual* resoluteness which, in the face of the inevitability of one's death, is open to one's situation in everyday life. *Dasein* as authentic is self-accepting as thrown possibility. Arendt however, insists on taking the will as an uniquely human faculty which is not restricted to the free will (the *liberum arbitrium* of Christian thought as the choice among possibilities) central to the experience of sinning – the individual inability to do what is apprehended as good. The will as a faculty is rather tied to acting as a real power to bring forth something new – a power to do, she says, in the Greek sense of a unity of I will and I can: the discovery of the Greeks, as she points out again and again, in the course of their own political life, though we owe the discovery of the will as self-moving to Christianty. This power to act surpasses every attempt to understand the human being solely in terms of strict necessity. The will as wholly self-moving acts out of preference – or love – not knowledge.[51]

To account for the deficiency of philosophy with respect to the understanding of the will in the context of the power to originate, she claims that philosophers as thinkers have an occupational deformation with respect to the comprehension of freedom as the power to act – Heidegger no less than Plato. The truth, even as the disclosure of Being, *aletheia* – as opposed to opinion – *compels* rather than persuades precisely because truth is not a matter of opinion. Truth leaves nothing further to discuss. Kant alone, she writes, among the great philosophers, escapes the fascination of tyranny.[52] As I have pointed out, Arendt's expansion of the *Bios Ananke* to whatever is done routinely, habitually, thoughtlessly, out of convention calls to mind Heidegger's description of *das Man* as nobody. So, for Arendt, the power to originate entails also the power to break routine by recovering oneself, to "stop and think,"[53] in some way to be able to take thought with regard to what one is doing. Such thought is not aimed at reaching an absolute grounding, which she would take to be mistaken, but it can achieve distance from one's particular impulses, to judge what is done *in relation* to absent others. Thinking of this sort can inform action – indeed willing – without being simply predictive with respect to consequences. Thinking and acting in relation to others *taken* as equals by taking account of their possible standpoints with respect to a shared world – a matter of politics informed by judgment – takes the place, with respect to ethical relations with others, of Kant's categorical imperative and of Heidegger's individual resolute authenticity open to its fate.[54]

In judging, Arendt suggests, we are – or can be – inspired by the example of individuals or persons who show their character in terms of what they say or do.[55] Correlatively, in acting we set an example. The implication is that in the political sphere the achievement of consequences is less important than our relations to each other. In fact we cannot count on consequences in the political sphere at all. She praises the student movement of the sixties in so far as it is morally inspired, pointing out that though Marxists are also morally inspired, theoretically they deny the relevance of moral considerations.[56] The consequences of acting as intrinsically unpredictable, for acting takes place in a world shared by others, in relation to others, at the mercy of the response of others who are themselves free to originate. But if we cannot count on the consequences of political action, we can hope to be remembered.

The human sphere is thus a sphere of unpredictability unlike the natural sphere. Accordingly, history, the remembrance of this human sphere, is to be understood as narrative, and the understanding of human affairs as essentially a matter of weaving a coherent meaningful story, suggestive of *Geschicte*, a term Heidegger uses as well with respect to historicality, glossing *Geschichte* as *Geschick*. But for Arendt this narrative is about actors who could have done otherwise. Narrative remembrance, seeking reconciliation with reality, is prone to interpret what has happened as destiny.[57] Historical narrative, keeping alive the memory of who the actors were and what they did, keeps alive thereby the possibility of true political life.[58]

Remembrance and action seem to pull in opposite directions. When we act, we bring into reality – being – what has never been before, something new, unheralded. In that sense, to act is to initiate. But when we remember we keep present what has been before. As humans our condition is essentially marked by natality and mortality, birth and death. Unlike the merely biological birth and death of animals, our birth and death, our appearance into the world and disappearance from the world, haunt our lives demanding that we give meaning to our sojourn on earth. Knowing that we will disappear, we long for remembrance. The dead, Arendt said on the occasion of the funeral memorial for Jaspers, *need* to be remembered.[59] And being born, we need a place in the world and must, indeed, as newcomers, originate *act* to claim that place which – as political – will preserve our words and deeds so that we may be remembered. And, it is important to note that, according to Arendt, to act effectively – that is, with power – we must act in concert honoring plurality.

The common world itself arises out of the multiple perspectives of a plurality of actors. Since we need a common world to be a self, to lead meaningful lives which have some point and direction, even to be able to act at all – that is, to be persons – it is the political dimension of the world which seems to ground the fabricated world as well. The common world thus, as a world of which we have different perspectives, allowing us to lead meaningful unique lives, is a world with regard to which a dialogue about *opinion* is relevant. As in the case of taste, the distinction between subjective and objective in the sense of Galileo is rendered moot. The common world is an appearing world of singularly human importance, always relative to others who must address us and whom we must address with respect to its appearance to persuade each other if we are to be a community. And, according to Arendt, this sort of persuasion is what the Greeks took to be "the typically political form of people talking with one another."[60]

But the common world is also a real world. Common sense is a *mental* organ for discerning real things. On occasion Arendt writes of the right to have rights by virtue of being a member of community that, as a polity, makes its home on some piece of the earth.[61] She finds the Enlightenment concept of the abstract rights of man factically empty. Reduced to themselves as their individual human nature, people are worldless.[62] This understanding of political life clearly draws on Heidegger's understanding of *Dasein* as dwelling in the world, but, it is important to note, Heidegger's conception meshed with Arendt's own experience as a Jewish outcast. Enlightenment thinking, she claimed in an early work on Rahel Varnegen, robs one of one's self as unique.[63] One presumes to be introspectively objective about one's inner life as one is objective about reality. Thus it is the assimilating Jew who thinks of himself in terms of the Enlightenment. Hannah Arendt's growing awareness of herself as Jewish drew from Heidegger's own critique of Enlightment thought as ignoring specific community – *Volk* – identity, grounded in shared history, shared language, shared home. She herself lived her developing understanding of political life by becoming involved in her younger years in Zionist efforts to establish a Jewish homeland.[64] And despite her serious differences with specific Zionist policies – indeed the very concept of a religious state – she always regarded herself as a member of Israel's loyal opposition.[65] Through her political writing, such as her *Eichmann in Jerusalem* and her earlier *Origins of Totalitarianism* (and in many shorter essays throughout her life), she continued to engage in political life relevant to Zionism and Jewishness, despite her self-understanding as a thinker rather than as an actor. Inviting discussion, her writing on these matters engaged that lively debate about policy and judgment – discourse – that she took to be especially political.

From a political perspective, Marx's thinking unversalizes to the point of losing communal differences rooted in shared language and history. Indeed labor, work, and *praxis*, though parameters of Marx's thought, can be taken as different aspects of human dwelling. Marxist universalization theoretically loses the uniqueness of individual persons in history's progress and thereby also loses, theoretically, the political power to act that resides in community limited by a shared common world. Labor, work, and *praxis* are glossed over by Arendt as ways of active dwelling in the world relevant to human identity.[66]

IV

Has Arendt then achieved an answer to Marx? Let me approach this question via a detour. In an interesting comment on Heidegger in volume two of the *Life of the Mind*, "Willing," she speaks with admiration of his conception of appearance as coming from Being and returning to Being.[67] I take that as related to a paradoxical comment in her essay "Heidegger on his 80th birthday" to the effect that thinking is nature's way of preserving the past.[68] For Arendt, thinking as remembrance keeps alive what is worth remembering of a human being. Does Arendt think of thinking as remembrance as the Being that keeps appearance? For Heidegger, of course, the Being which keeps appearance, letting appearance be, is not simply thinking. It is Being that calls thinking to its task, the keeping of Being. There is a sense in which Arendt keeps thinking in the human world more distant from nature's extent beyond thought than Heidegger cares to, but then Arendt takes as part of the ideology of National Socialism that the process of nature is the ultimate truth of Being.[69]

Arendt's thought is, in many respects, sketchy and only exploratory. As we know, she died before the completion of the third part of *The Life of the Mind*, which was to have been on the all important topic of judgment. Others have pointed out that her skill lay in making important distinctions, not in bringing them into relation. Indeed, I think she thought it far more important to keep the tension of distinctions in mind than to blur them. With respect to some matters, often by virtue of her insistance on the sharpness of her distinctions, she is distressingly conservative. Political life, she writes, has nothing to do with the preservation of life for the world cares nothing for that.[70] In the world we are called on to become persons only as distinct from nature and therefore ready to die. The common world outlasts our merely mortal lives. So the meaning – the point – of our lives derives from this common world rather than the reverse. She held herself to this interpretation of what is humanly important. When she became ill, she refused to give up her habit of smoking, insisting she would not live for health alone.[71] In the common world, our shared human world, our life is, at its best, heroic. On the one hand, acting (as free) shows who you are; on the other hand, acting (as free) cares nothing for life. In rejecting the Platonic bifurcation of reality from appearance she generates another bifurcation, the human world and nature. This bifurcation reaches into her criticism of Marx.

Work, as well as speech and action, involves initiative and a sense of the future. As such, work, in conjunction with the political sphere, opens us to the world though in different ways.[72] Work, including art, as an *activity* opens us to things as real in the context of our transforming effort. Moreover, human labor certainly occurs in the context of preserving a world as our home. If we set human labor, as I think we must, in the context of work as world-building without losing the differeniation of the products produced, then we can speak generally of work (with the exception of perhaps art and other fabricated cultural objects), as Marx and Hegel do, as our thought informed metabolic interchange with nature which nevertheless grounds our separation from nature as it opens a world for human dwelling. By failing to recognize the significance of work in this sense, the basis of a structural analysis of our mode of dwelling in nature, which amounts to economics, is lost and with that, the relevance to our political life of a crucial human concern.

If, now, we think of work as an essential dimension of the world opening in the way that I have suggested, then the political sphere, as the sphere in which acting and thinking in concert take place, emerges as the unthought presupposition of Marx himself, albeit in conflict with some aspects of what has often been called the scientific side of his thought. But it is important to note that labor, precisely as the metabolic interchange with nature, which Arendt accepts, invites – indeed demands – scientific analysis.

Nor can I accept Arendt's assessment of knowledge as violating freedom. We can only know out of freedom, the absence of coercion, as Kant himself pointed out.[73] It is the loss of subjectivity – the relevance of awareness and thought for knowledge – that is the problem. Arendt in effect turns Marx's thought on itself in such a way as to provoke precisely the sort of thinking she admired, both with respect to her own work and that of Marx.

Notes

1. Hannah Arendt, "Martin Heidegger at Eighty" (referred to below as HE), translated by Albert Hofstadter, reprinted in Michael Murray (ed.), *Heidegger and Modern Philosophy* (New Haven; Yale University Press, 1978), 297.

2. Elizabeth Young-Bruehl, *Hannah Arendt: For Love of the World* (referred to below as HA) (New Haven; Yale University Press, 1982), xx.

3. Hannah Arendt, "Tradition and the Modern Age" (referred to below as TMA) in *Between Past and Future* (New York; Penguin, 1977), 32.

4. Ibid., 32–33. See also "The Crisis in Culture" (referred to below as CC), in Arendt, *Between Past and Future*, 204.

5. Arendt, TMA, 19–20. Arendt adds that Marx mistakenly looked forward to the disappearance of all government. That I take to be a misinterpretation of Marx's prediction of the ultimate disappearance of the state. Marx did not claim that *self-government* would disappear! Indeed, Arendt herself believe the modern nation-state to be outmoded. For her vision of the form of ideal government, see this paper; p. 000.

6. Ibid., 17.

7. Arendt, "The Crisis of History" (referred to below as CH) in *Between Past and Future*, 81.

8. Young-Bruehl, HA, 69.

9. Hannah Arendt, TMA, 21ff.

10. Hannah Arendt, HE, 295.

11. Ibid.

12. Hannah Arendt, *The Origins of Totalitarianism* (New York: Harcourt Brace Jovanovich, 1973), viii.

13. Melvyn A. Hill, *Hannah Arendt: The Recovery of the Public World* (referred to below as RPW) (New York; St. Martin's Press, 1979), 338.

14. Hannah Arendt, *The Life of the Mind* (referred to below as LM) (New York; Harcourt Brace Jovanovich, 1978), vol. 1,, 167ff.

15. Hannah Arendt, "The Crisis in Education" (referred to below as CE), in *Between Past and Future*, 185–86, 192–93.

16. Hannah Arendt, "Walter Benjamin 1892–1940," in *Men in Dark Times*, (New York; Harcourt Brace Jovanovich, 1968), 203ff.

17. Hannah Arendt, *The Human Condition* (referred to below as HC) (Garden City, N.Y.; Doubleday, 1959), 25, 29–112.

18. Arendt, LM, vol. 2, pp. 30, 32.

19. Arendt, HC, 155, 175; also see CC, 215ff.

20. Hannah Arendt, "Thoughts on Politics and Revolution" (referred to below as PR), in *Crises of the Republic* "Thoughts on Politics and Revolution" (referred to below as PR) (New York; Harcourt Brace Jovanovich, 1972), 231.

21. Ibid., 201ff.

22. For an explication of Marx's views on labor, work, and *praxis* see, in general, Hannah Arendt, *The Human Condition*, and also, TMA, CC, and CH.

23. For an explication of the relationship between Hegel's and Marx's views on the relationship of labor and work to world making see Mildred Bakan, "Hannah Arendt's Concepts of Labour and Work" in Hill, RPW.

24. Arendt, HC, 92. See also note 3.

25. Arendt, CC, 207. Also Arendt, HC, 113ff.

26. Arendt, TMA, 32-33.

27. Arendt, *The Origins of Totalitarianism*, 326ff.

28. Arendt, CH, 57. Arendt finds the modern root of this conception of history in Vico who maintained that we can understand only what we make and so can only understand our history. Vico is thus the herald of our modern age which celebrates fabrication, and more generally productivity, to the point of usurping the description of political life.

29. Arendt, "Rosa Luxemburg, 1871-1919," in *Men in Dark Times*, 51.

30. Martin Heidegger, "Letter on Humanism," translation reprinted in William Barrett and Henry Aiken (eds.), *Philosophy in the 20th Century*, vol. 111 (New York; Random House, 1962).

31. "Building, Dwelling, Thinking" in *Poetry, Thought and Language*, edited and translated by Albert Hofstadter (New York; Harper & Row, 1975).

32. Young-Bruehl, HA, 220. Arendt, in the important essay, "The Crisis of Culture" in *Between Past and Future*, claims the concept of culture originates in the Roman understanding of agriculture as "cultivating and tending nature until it becomes fit for human habitation." She adds "it indicates an attitude of loving care and stands in sharp contrast to all efforts to subject nature to the domination of man." (CC 211-12). These lines, it seems to me, obviously refer to Heidegger's thought about work. In *The Life of the Mind*, she restricts Heidegger's thanking thinking to a *poetic* "yes-saying," which has remained from the time of the Greeks important to poetry and the arts (LM, vol. 2, pp. 185-86, also p. 92). In short, yes-saying is irrelevant to work. See however, Arendt, HC, 92ff., where labor is linked to the blessing of life as a whole! ·

33. Hill, RPW, 303. In her essay, *Existence Philosophy* ([referred to below as EP] *Partisan Review* 8:1, [Winter 1946], 34-36), which she would not allow to be published with her other essays in book form, Arendt takes authenticity (in Heidegger's sense) as grounding contemplation, philosophical questioning, as the "exceptional existential possibility of human reality . . . a reformulation of Aristotle's *Bios Theoretikos*, of the contemplative life as the highest possibility for man." She adds that, for Heidegger, the recovery of oneself as authentic amounts to the recovery of oneself as Being-at-issue with no allowance for real freedom and power. (Arendt, EP, 48). Later, in the same essay, she notes that Heidegger's authenticity amounts to a wholly isolated self whose "essential character . . . is absolute egoism, its radical separation from all its fellows" (ibid., 50). She adds: "If it is not part of the concept of man that he inhabits the world

with his fellows, then there remains only a mechanical reconcilation [some naturalistic superstition] by which the atomized self is given a substratum essentially discordant with its own concept. This can only serve to organize the selves engaged in willing themselves into an over-self, in order to make a transition from the fundamental guilt, grasped through resoluteness, to action" (ibid., 51).

Of course Heidegger insisted in *Being and Time* that *Dasein* is *Mitsein*, emphasizing a shared language, shared home, and shared foreconception of Being. Arendt ignores this aspect of Heidegger's thought and focuses instead on Heidegger's isolation of authentic individuality. That she shifted her overall assessment of Heidegger's thought is evident from the essay "Heidegger on the Occasion of his Eightieth Birthday" (Arendt, HE). A revised attitude is evident also in *The Life of the Mind*. In the context of the chapter "Warfare between thought and common sense (Arendt, LM, 88), she writes "what for common sense is the obvious withdrawal of the mind from the world appears in the mind's own perspective as a 'withdrawal of Being' or 'oblivion of Being' – *Seinsentzug* and *Seinsvergessenheit* (Heidegger). And it is true, everyday life, the life of the "they" is spent in a world in which all that is "visible" to the mind is totally absent. In her later work she integrates Heidegger's thinking about thinking in her description of thinking, both as withdrawal from the appearing world and as withdrawal from action.

34. Hans-Georg Gadamer, *Truth and Method*, trans Garrett Barden and John Cumming (New York; Seabury Press, 1975), part III.

35. Arendt, HC, 53.

36. Arendt, LM, vol. 2, pp. 257–58.

37. Arendt, CC, 219ff.

38. Arendt, LM, vol. 1, 13ff., 53ff.

39. Arendt, CC, 221.

40. Arendt, "Ideology and Terror," in *The Origins of Totalitarianism*, 464ff.

41. Arendt, CC, 219ff.

42. Arendt, TMA, 3ff.

43. In the essay, "The Crisis of Culture" (*Between Past and Future*), Arendt points out that the Greeks took the love of beautiful things as an activity which should be guided by "the right love of beauty," taste, to which of course, Kant's analysis of judgment is relevant (CC, 213ff.).

44. Letting-be, as explicated by Heidegger, is sometimes interpreted as a relation to others which, in effect, allows mutual recognition. But Arendt interprets letting-be, (I think properly) as that opening to Being that allows its thinking (Arendt, LM, 178). She praises Heidegger for having thought through the end of metaphysics by thinking through thinking as a silent repose which as *Gelassenheit*, lets being be (Arendt, HE, 303). Such thinking, according to

Heidegger, makes way for (is receptive to) the sending of Sein, and Arendt points out, can happen only by withdrawing from worldly affairs. The thinker thinks Being in solitary withdrawal from the world. But the mutuality of recognition is marked by *plurality* in the context of *worldly experience.*

In *The Life of the Mind* (vol. 2), Arendt takes note of the "Greek notion that all appearances, in as much as they appear, demand recognition and praise." She adds: "This notion was a kind of philosophical justification of poetry and arts . . . [W]orld alienation, which preceeded the rise of Stoic and Christian thought succeeded in obliterating it from our tradition of philosophy – though never entirely from the reflection of the poets" (Arendt, LM, vol. 2, p. 92). She later points out in her discussion of Heidegger's thought, that Heidegger's thinking that is also thanking, thereby overcoming the will to will, has affinities to this poetic "yes-saying." But this thinking thanking remains "obedience" to the call of Being as its thinking, and, as such, is not acting in the world at all (Arendt, LM, vol. 2, pp. 182, 185–87). See also notes 32, 33.

45. Young-Bruehl, HA, 128.

46. Arendt, "Preface," in *Between Past and Future*, 3–15.

47. Arendt, CC, 223. Also Arendt, HC, 157ff.

48. Arendt, LM, vol. 2, pp. 101ff., 110.

49. Arendt, "Rosa Luxemburg, 1871–1919," in *Men in Dark Times*, 53.

50. Arendt, TMA, 35.

51. Arendt, LM, vol. 2, pp. 130ff.

52. Arendt, CC, 222–23. Also, Arendt, HE, 303.

53. Arendt, LM, vol. 1, p. 4.

54. I should indicate my uncertainty at this point. Is it only *thinking* in relation to others as equals – judging – that takes the place of "Kant's categorical imperative and of Heidegger's resolute authenticity open to its fate?" Since judging is a kind of thinking, the intimate relation of judging and acting puts in question Arendt's distinction between thinking and acting. Arendt sought to keep thinking *disinterested*, or *capable of disinterest*. Action is always *interested*. Yet judgment *can* inform action! And judgment certainly informs opinion, which *is political*. On the other hand, opinion calls for discourse and discourse relevant to decision belongs with action to the political sphere. On the other hand, thinking for Arendt, like authenticity, for Heidegger, is marked by withdrawal from worldly action. In the case of judgment thinking withdraws from *idiosyncratic* interest rather than the world as a *concern*. Yet Arendt herself suggests a categorical imperative for action, which unites the spectator as judge, and the actor! (Arendt, LM, vol. 2, p. 271).

In discussing Kant's concept of the idea of mankind Arendt notes that acting informed by judgment serves to realize the community of man to which, as persons, we ideally belong. This implies, Arendt adds, a categorical imperative for acting itself: act on the principle through which the idea of mankind, the principle informing judgment, "can be actualized into a general law." She is quoted as having said, in her lectures on Kant's *Critique of Judgment*, "it is by virtue of this idea of mankind present in every single man that men are human and they can be called civilized or humane to the extent that this idea becomes the principle of their actions as well as their judgments. It is at this point that actor and spectator became united; the maxim of the actor and the maxim, the standard, according to which the spectator judges the spectacle of the world become one" (Arendt, LM, vol. 2, pp. 271ff). I take Arendt to be speaking here for herself as well as describing Kant's thought. However, the idea of humanity as an ideal community of man seems to lose the specificity of concrete community. No doubt she wants to keep both in tension (see this paper, p. 000).

Judgment, oriented to decision and decision informed by judgment, are unified, it seems to me, from the standpoint of action, or not at all. For according to Arendt, judgment itself cannot tell us how to act. Yet, with respect to acting in a particular situation, judgment as a thinking that takes account of the standpoint of others is relevant. Judgment in this context is close to, if not part of, political speech. The question of the relationship of such judgment to action resolves then into the question of the relationship of speech to action, about which Arendt says very little.

It has been pointed out to me by David McNally of York University that Adam Smith defines virtue as the unity of the standpoints of the actor and spectator! It is suggestive to note in this connection that Arendt takes virtue to be performative.

55. Arendt, LM, vol. 2, p. 272.

56. Arendt, *Crisis of the Republic*, 125.

57. Arendt, "Isak Dinesen, 1885–1963, in *Men in Dark Times*, 104. Also Arendt, LM, 30.

58. Arendt, "Truth and Poflitics," in *Between Past and Future*, 238, 261ff.

59. Young-Bruehl, HA, 423.

60. Arendt, CC, 222. It is illuminating to note, in this connection, what Heidegger writes of the relation of rhetoric and persuasion in *Being and Time*:

Aristotle investigates πAΦη (affects) in the second book of his *Rhetoric*. Contrary to the traditional orientation, according to which rhetoric is conceived as the kind of thing we "learn at school," this work of Aristotle must be taken as the first systematic hermeneutics of the everydayness of Being with one another. Publicness, as the kind of Being which belongs to the "they" not only has in general its own way of having a mood, but needs moods and "makes" them for itself. It is into such a mood, and out of such a mood that the orator speaks. He must understand the possibilities of moods in order to rouse them and guide them a right." (Martin

Heidegger, *Being and Time*, trans. John Macquarrie and Edward Robinson, [New York; Harper and Row, 1962]; 178].

Clearly, for Heidegger, rhetoric "persuades" by achieving politically crucial attuning of the mood of "they" to the orator as leader. Persuasion tilts to rhetoric as propaganda rather than to discussion.

61. Ron H. Feldman [ed.], *The Jew as Pariah* [New York; Grove Press, 1978], 26–27. I am especially indebted to Melvyn Hill for alerting me to the importance of this book, and indeed, more generally, to the importance of Arendt's own experience as a Jew to the development of her political thought.

62. Ibid., 286–87. It is interesting to note in this connection that Arendt ties private property to home as dwelling rather than labor or work. *In The Human Condition* Arendt draws on the Greek conception of the private household as the basis of participation in the *polis* to develop a concept of private property as a piece of the earth which, as one's place, protects privacy and political equality. She distinguishes wealth which "has grown to such proportions that it is almost unmanageable by private ownership" from private property "in the sense of a tangible, worldly place of one's own" [Arendt, HC, 62].

63. Ibid., 33ff.

64. Ibid. Also, Young-Bruehl, HA, 105ff., 138, 139, 173ff., 226ff. See also the essay, "The Jew as Pariah: A Hidden Tradition," in Feldman, *The Jew as Pariah*, especially p. 90.

65. Young-Bruehl, HA, 232–361.

66. Yet Arendt avails herself of the economic dimension of our life to explain important events – partially. So she relates Hitler's rise to power to widespread unemployment and inflation – with a single sentence [Arendt, *The Origins of Totalitarianism*, 265]. Human conduct involves an element of chance, even luck, certainly contingency. It is as though real contingency allows human freedom. How that unemployment is taken is a matter of conduct and so a political question with respect to which we, acting in concert, can be original by taking thought, interrupting the economic process, to allow discourse about what is going on. But it is difficult to see how we can act in concert at all effectively without some prediction of consequences. It might be replied that the crucial question politically concerns the ends in view and it is with respect to these that we must reach a consensus by taking each other into account rather than behaving on the basis of private desire. But the ultimate end of political life is to preserve the political sphere, for political life turns on itself as an end in itself.

67. Arendt, LM, vol. 2, pp. 189ff.

68. Arendt, HE, 300.

69. Arendt, *The Origins of Totalitarianism*, viii, 314, 460ff.

70. Arendt, CE, 186.

71. Young-Bruehl, HA, 447.

72. Arendt points out in *The Human Condition* that the "things" of the common world are "between those who have it in common. The world, like every in-between-relates and separates men at the same time." But Arendt does not take the *activity* of *making things* as crucial to our experience of a world (Arendt, HC, 48).

73. Arendt is well aware of this point! "For Kant," she points out in *The Life of the Mind*, "sheer spontaneity, which he often called 'absolute spontaneity' exists only in thinking. Kant's will is delegated by reason to be its executive organ in all matters of conduct (Arendt, LM, vol. 2, p. 149). Indeed, according to Arendt thinking itself is restricted to after thoughts (Arendt, LM, vol. 2, p. 37)! Given that conception of thought, thought and action are necessarily opposed as the dependence on what is or has been (thinking) and the creation of what has never been (willing)! Since judging is intimately related to acting, problems arise in connection with the conception of judging as thinking. With respect to the relation of *knowing* and willing, she cites Karl Jaspers: "not knowing is the root of having to will" (Arendt, LM, vol. 2, p. 22).

18. Husserl on Reason and Justification in Ethics

Gary E. Overvold

A discussion of Husserl's views on ethics presents special difficulties for both presenter and audience. Contrary to the economy of reference possible with familiar positions (for example, with Mill or Kant), with Husserl no prior acquaintance can be presumed. Reasonbly, then, exposition would have to precede criticism. Yet, I do not want merely to report on some exotica retrieved from the Husserl Archives for at least for my interests, what's intriguing about Husserl's views on eithics is their exhibiting of the complications of claiming rational knowledge in ethics and, of course, *that* issue is not peculiar to Husserl. The time constraints of this colloquium spare us one solution, so conciseness, not completeness, must guide. Let me adopt as a strategy, then, a two phase presentation. I will begin with an all too brief summary of Husserl's general views on ethics and then try to develop them somewhat more fully by engaging them in a conversation on some topics in the epistemology of ethical knowledge.

The most telling motif in Husserl's ethics is an analogue to formal logic. There is both a formal and a material (contentful) ethic where the former designates the collection of purely general (that is, context-free laws of value, and the latter, the structures of specific values. For those familiar with the stages of Husserl's philosophical development, it is instructive to note that the bulk of his writing on ethics occurred between 1902 and 1910, that is, after the publication of the *Logical Investigations* but before the publication of *Ideas I*. His idealism is decipherable in the manuscripts, though, as would be expected, relatively little discussion of the transcendental ego and its constitutive activity is found. We have , then, what has sometimes (misleadingly) been called the Platonic phase his thought. This is evidenced in the manuscripts by repeated reference to values as ideal objectives. Let me make this more apparent by next turning to the epistemological question of justification.

Ethical judgments need justification both as ethical and as judgments. The task of providing warrants to render defensible specific moral judgments is incumbent on anyone who wishes his particular claims to be heard sympathetically by his fellows and, ideally, even by himself. Among the uses of theoretical work in ethics is the providing of presumably adequate and defensible schema on which can be grounded rules or principles which in turn can be used, sometimes as the needed warrants, and sometimes as the basis from which such warrants can be derived.

Husserl's phenomenology is not known for its concern with ethics. His own view of his own phenomenology saw it as a discipline *sui generis*, a new kind of first philosophy. Those who judge such matters in the broader sweep of history might be inclined to see greater similarity than Husserl did of his work to other ambitious schemes for providing foundational grounding for human knowledge. That is, they may see Husserl as like many other modern philosophers in being principally an epistemologist.

But Husserl's work on the nature and condition of knowing does include some reflections on ethics. Such material is largely confined to unpublished manuscripts, notably a series of lecture notes for courses given at Göttingen and Freiburg between 1902 and 1924.

The manuscripts are fairly extensive (this is not surprising for, at least in writing, Husserl was not a man of few words – witness the 45,000 plus pages *un*published manuscripts in shorthand in the Husserl Archives). The manuscripts on ethics range over a fair number of topics germane to issues in ethics understood broadly, (including anthropology, formal ontology, pure psychology; and they are, in the fashion too characteristic of Husserl, largely programmatic. That is, there is a frustrating absence of specific, worked out investigations of particular ethical issues; instead there is an abundance of briefly sketched grand schemes and a familiar insistence on the need for future rigorous examination.

In this paper I will not pursue the grander schemes – or at least not do so thematically. I shall engage Husserl in conversation on the narrower issue of how he saw justification for ethical claims. In this project I am chiefly interested in one aspect of the epistemology of ethics, and thus less interested in the content of ethics, that is, any discussion of what might be good or bad, or even how we might sensibly talk about what might be good or bad. In order to consider Husserl's views on justification, I will need to involve in outline his more inclusive project for a general phenomenology of ethics and his taxonomy of the parts of the overall structure of human experience of value. But neither of these will be thematic: the problem of justification will.

A familiar enough way to justify ethical judgments is to cite or demonstrate their rationality. Husserl uses such an appeal in both his formal and his material or content ethics. But first a preliminary word on this division.

The acknowledged source for the idea of a formal ethics is Kant. Though Husserl finds Kant's formalism to be inadequate in a number of key respects, he does see the need, as Kant did, to uncover and formulate a set of rules, laws, and principles which will hold across all contexts where value – here ethical value – is potentially present. In contrast with such purely formal a priori rules, a material or content ethic, though still governed by a priori relationships, would speak more specifically and concretely to the particularities of experience. Though we may determine, for example, from a rigorous phenomenological examination that in form all judgments of value are founded ones, that they are carried by and dependent on intellectual judgments, such a priori and formal truths are not instructive on what particular values are the most important ones for a human life. The latter would be the content of the so-called material ethic. One additional note to place the modality of further discussion. As is Husserl's want throughout his phenomenology, so too in his ethics: the structures delineated, the values identified, and the intentional relationships described are all claimed to be a priori, necessary, essential, and given to Husserl, qua phenomenologist, by self-evidence which is at least adequate if not always apodictic.

This note of mine is not merely an editorial notice for it points at the root difficulty of anyone who wants to *argue* with a phenomenologist. As Husserl insisted in his writings on ethics, as well as frequently in his published works, and as others with varying frustration have reiterated, phenomenological descriptions are not matters about which one argues. If you do not see it the way it is described, then the appropriate response is not debate but redescription. To address this issue head on would be quite a different paper, but I want to acknowledge this contention and nonetheless pursue a critical debate. My warrant for doing so is this: though the regions of human experience of value may be all exactly and precisely structured as Husserl says they are, *nonetheless* the additional achievements he claims these structures accomplish could be quite thoroughly mistaken. That is, though it may be that, as he intimates, the whole of the region of human preferring and willing is intentionally related to a necessary and universal hierarchy of timeless objective values – even though all that may be true – it is *not* thereby proven that such an intricate network could thereby provide an adequate ground by itself to validate my side of a disagreement with you on what percentage of our annual salary should be given to the United Way. Justification, as I construe it, must involve the giving of reasons and that can not be accomplished by description, not even a description that is apodictically certain, exactly accurate, one which excludes everything inessential and which includes nothing but the a priori necessary structures of a situation. In a phrase, we have projects of two different categories.

Husserl determines that values, as value objectivities (ideal objects), are involved in all ethical judgments. Through a phenomenological analysis of acts of preferential feeling, he determines that the intentional structure of feeling, that is, emotions, necessarily involves reference to a value. This value is carried by or founded on some desired real or imaginary (wished for) object or state of affairs. Values are not given on their own; rather, they are co-given with some desideratum. The noetic act is (at least) two part – a judgment that A is an x accompanied by the founded feeling that Ax is desired; the noematic reference is equally two part: that A is an Ax and Ax is valuable. This (here oversimplified) scheme, even if in its basics accurate, will not, however, provide us with any adequate basis for anything more than descriptive claims. At most, such a structure might tell us how a value is present in some situation. It cannot instruct us on the relative worth of this value in relation to other values nor could it provide evidence to settle controversies over whether a putative value really is a value. These two questions are central to any discussion of justification.

We can find an implied means of addressing the first issue, the problem of relative worth, in Husserl's idea of a formal ethic. This aspect of his ethics involves the development of a logic of values: a hierarchical scheme showing how given *types* of ethical statements are related to other types. The model for this project comes from formal logic. In idea at least, the formal ethic should show us the rank ordering of the purely general (formal) claims that can occur in ethics – and thus, to eye our earlier issue, in principle to give us a guide as to which values are the more valuable, that is, to decide the question of relative worth.

Unfortunately, what we see of the formal ethics is less helpful than it might be on this question of relative merit. Husserl, on a number of occasions, favorably cites the revelatory parallelism between formal logic and formal ethics and gives at least a few examples of the kinds of formal (axiomatic) truths he finds in formal ethics. For instance (and I am here quoting Ms. FI 24, p. 286) the law of excluded fourth:

> If M is any content (and always within any one axiological region), only one of three cases is true: either M is the content of a positive value in itself, or a negative or it is in itself value free.

This, of course, is a variation on the logical law of excluded middle, but for three not two values (Ms. FI 24, p. 276):

> Analogous to the law of contradiction in logic, which is its highest law, is this law of axiology: something which in some perspective is a value cannot in that same manner be a nonvalue.

In a similar vein, Husserl formulates a number of other laws which illustrate transitivity,[1] symmetry,[2] identity (for example, "If A is a value, then it is not not a value" [Ms. FI 24, p. 283]), and similar elementary logical relations for values. This enterprise, in my view, is not terribly helpful in ranking values for the laws here cited, as well as those I've omitted, appear to be little more than slightly unusual versions of standard logical laws.

I believe that the apparent vacuity of these formal ethical laws is explainable by a misconception on Husserl's part. Formalization is most profitable, that is, inferentially rich, in fields whose import is not dependent on their content. That is, formalization is most plausible and successful in areas that can be adequately defined extensionally. To take the extreme case, our most successful project in formalization is in mathematics: one which is so unlikely that it is queer even to think about it would be formalizing poetry or, say, begging or apologizing or making excuses. It is not, I think, very controversial to say that judgments or claims are ethical precisely because of their content.[3] The consequences for Husserl's ethics of this mistaken assumption about a parallelism to logic are manifest in the formal ethical laws Husserl does develop. They are either obviously, or with minimal decoding, patterns of logical inference examplified with ethical or value related statements. This, however, is just formal logic with uncommon examples. To show that ethical assertions must obey logical rules is to demonstrate something about assertions and not ethics. Thus, to return to my theme sentence about Husserl's use of rationality in ethical justification, whatever rationality there may be to the patterns of this formal ethic it is a rationality that is a consequence of the implicit formal logic and not the ethics found there. Husserl's answer to the first of the two questions on justification I raised is, I would say, inadequate. The question of how can we justify the ranking of one value or kind of value higher than another receives little or no answer from Husserl's formal ethic.

The second problem of justification previously raised, the problem of a controversy over putative value, is implicitly addressed by Husserl's conception of a material/content ethic. A material ethic consists of the ordered set of specific ethical values, values whose hierarchical arrangement is revealed as a priori in specific acts of evaluative feeling. This view is opposed, by Husserl, to Kant's notion that there could only be a formal a priori and it claims that Kant refused to see how acts of feeling are cognitive and reveal a priori values.

Husserl once again refers to a parallelism to logic to get a general rationale for his material ethics. Even as in logic one can find both laws and particular patterns of interference, so too there would be two parts to ethics. Thus there would be a material ethics correlative with the formal one and the former would exhibit what we might expect to be the more instructive portion of ethics. Unfortunately, Husserl is even more purely programmatic on this. We can determine what he thought it should be but we learn little of what it actually is since he did not undertake the detailed analyses which would tell us of the particulars.

For purposes of the topic of this paper this omission, though regrettable, is not destructive since even from the sketchy outline of what a material ethic would be, I believe we can see it would do little to settle controversies over putative value.

The material ethic, when completed, would show the rank order of values revealed in acts of preferential feeling. But the notorious variability of feelings and, additionally, the contentious quality of the evaluations of such preferences indicate the immediate need for a solution to the problem of justifying a judgment that rests on such preferential feeling. That is, in a controversy over whether or not A really is valuable, or in a dispute over whether A is preferable to B, we need dependable independent means to settle the disagreements. Husserl's suggestion is that the rationality of a judgment is its justification. But even ignoring the very sticky issue of what rationality means, this is no solution.

The appeal to rationality must face a troublesome dilemma. If rationality is intended to be a sufficient justification for an ethical judgment, then, to be sure, we will need a full explication of the troublesome concept of rationality. But even if we had it, it is thoroughly opaque how any general understanding of rationality could inform one that in situation S, A really is valuable; or even more problematically, how such a general concept could resolve a particular dispute on what is the more valuable in a specific situation. The general scheme that Husserl appears to have in mind would be a kind of casuistry unprecedented in its detail. In fact, one might venture the project is, in principle, unworkable since it is impossible to imagine the details of virtually any and, for sure, not all future situations. But any question of whether A is valuable and any question of whether A is more valuable than B would always arise in some specific situation.

In addition, and still on the claim that rationality would provide a sufficient justification, if we think of particular cases of disputes they typically are not conflicts between a rational and a nonrational judgment. If I believe that this month the amount of the family budget allocated for charity should go to the Cystic Fibrosis Foundation and my wife believes it should go to the United Jewish Appeal, it would only be rhetorical for me to tell her she's being irrational. To be sure, there can be cases where we would call some judgments irrational, but charitably, those are hardly the typical cases. My point here is that even if, somehow, rationality could play a justificatory role, it wouldn't help us resolve the kind of cases that are typical disputes, the kind for which we most need some adequate scheme of justification.

The other side of the dilemma of using rationality for justification can be more quickly sketched. If rationality is not a sufficient justification, but still a justification, then either it is a necessary or a contingent condition for a justified judgment. However, in either case to be rational is not sufficient and, hence, being rational cannot of itself serve to settle disputes about putative values.

The problem of using rationality as a justification in ethics, whether done by Husserl or others, is rooted in a more basic problem. It is completely unclear how either rational or irrational have anything determining to do with what is specifically ethical, for what noncircular proof could ever justify the claimed supportive (justificatory) relationship of rational to ethical? This is not the problem of an unjustified first principle (that is, an assumed sense for rationality) – although that, too, is a pertinent difficulty – but rather the problem of what might serve as evidence to support the claim that the relationship between these two terms is one of justification. One cannot appeal to ordinary experience and ordinary language for support since they recognize that rational acts can be unethical and irrational acts can be ethical.[4] One cannot define or stipulate that to be rational means to be justified, for as seen, such a solution is unhelpful because, minimally it is too general and vacuous. Nor would it seem that there could be any other noncircular way of specifying that those ethical judgments that are rational are justified.

The source of both the difficulty and the illusion that there is no difficulty lies in the fact that ethical judgments are judgments. Rationality is an intelligible comment on ethical judgments insofar as they are judgments but not insofar as they are ethical. If there is any justification possible for ethical judgments, it must be found elsewhere than in rationality.

Notes

1. Ms. FI 24, p. 269: "If W is a value and if, accordingly, if A then W, then A is also a value" *or* Ms. FI 21, p. 118: where A, B, C are three values in the same region of value, for example, values of beauty, then: "If A is greater than B and B greater than C, then A is greater than C."

2. For two values A and B from the same region of value: "If A = B, then B = A" (Ms. FI 21, p. 5).

3. This does not contradict even Kantian formalism: Kant's universalizability principle, for example, is there to let us test an ethical claim to see if it's legitimate; the universal quality is not what makes it be ethical — for any number of things can be universalized that are not even remotely related to ethics — for example, time, number, logical relations, and so on.

4. As an example of an unethical, rational activity, note the methodical deliberateness of the Holocaust. As an example of a nonrational ethical act, note the willing sacrifice of a life to save that of a stranger.

Part VI.
Continental Philosophies
in the University

19. The Liberal Tradition and the Structure of Phenomenology

Edward Goodwin Ballard

About a year ago, in an unguarded moment, I read a paper at a philosophical colloquium suggesting that a way of transforming many of the dangers inherent in modern large-scale technology was by way of a renewed practice of the liberal arts.[1] But I expressed a suspicion that this remedy would sound like old hat to many philosophers. Sure enough, one of my critics rose to the bait and described my prescription of the liberal arts as a moth-eaten remedy.[2] But, I cannot help but wonder: if a good and needed thing is moth-eaten, why not refurbish it? I suspect one reason lies in a widespread loss of the tradition of the liberal arts. These arts have come to be associated in a vague way with literature, fine arts, and "the humanities." Hence to those philosophers who aspire above all else to be confused in the public mind with scientists or perhaps with mathematicians, a turn to the liberal arts would be embarrassing to say the least. And even to philosophers who do not desire to be confused with scientists and mathematicians, espousal of the liberal arts could suggest a return to an outworn and dry medieval curriculum which is said to be anything but liberating.

The liberal arts, however, are not the special prerogative of the humanities nor of medieval professors and pursuit of them does not turn a scientist into a literary man, nor a philosopher into a pedant. They may be understood – and properly understood, I should like to maintain – as arts, ways of doing things, ways of producing a product, specifically an intellectual product. They compose the craft of the mind and are practiced successfully whenever anyone succeeds in an intellectual endeavor, whether in science, technology, the humanities, or in an art more narrowly understood. Often it is said that the very recondite use of mind in the hard sciences and the highly specialized (i.e., mathematical) language in which its results are stated renders these

258

sciences inaccessible to the unspecialized person. This view is dangerously false. The unit of the mind's opertion, whether instanced in the field of the sciences or the field of the humanities, is certainly suggested by the fact that complex mathematical statements can always be expressed in English intelligible to any well disciplined person.[3] Also phenomenological philosophers have come to a similar view of the unity of mind by discovering one and the same source for logicomathematical thought and for the everyday and other uses of mind.[4] The contrary belief is dangerous in that it encourages the two cultures (or many cultures) view of our society, furthers it by building it into the curricula of our schools, and even defends it by incorporating it into a metaphysic (I allude to the metaphysics of primary and secondary qualities which, oddly enough, is still widely credited, mostly by non-philosophers). The consequence is that our left hands know not what our right hands are doing; that is, the scientific and technological parts of our society, and the humanistically oriented parts, are deprived of the assistance and guidance which each might provide for the other.

To do anything more than to suggest here, however, that the sciences as well as the arts are equally the product of the liberal disciplines is too large a demand for the present essay. But by no means irrelevant to this larger task is the more modest one of showing that phenomenology is the product of and may be structured by the liberal arts. In order to accomplish this task in the present paper I want first to describe the liberal arts in a language and a contest which once were quite familar but have since more or less fallen out of our culture. Then I would like to point briefly to an exemplary use of these arts in a classic and relatively familiar writing, Plato's PHAEDRUS. Finally I would like to outline the way these arts have in fact been utilized by a phenomenologist; for this latter purpose I choose as my main text a book which is both indisputably phenomenological and familiar to philosophers in the European tradition: Edmund Husserl's IDEAS, Book I.[5] The way will then be open to show briefly, if not in detail, that the liberal arts, operating in this philosophical context, offer a key not only to understanding the structure of phenomenology but also to forming a phenomenologically coherent and founded doctrine of values and ends and hence that they could play an essential part in the criticism, organization, and direction of the modern technological means.

1. The Arts of Liberation

Part of the difficulty in understanding the time honored phrase "liberal arts" arises from an ambiguity. Sometimes the phrase refers in a narrow sense to the arts of using language. Also the phrase may refer in a broad sense to three dimensions or to three general characteristics to be found in the practice of any art (*techné*). (In addition, the phrase is widely used in an ill-defined sense more or less equivalent to the title "the humanities"; I shall ignore this characteristically modern usage so far as possible.)

In an important and general sense, any art or technique may be said to be liberating.[6] The key to a grasp of this broad sense of 'liberal', no one will be surprised to hear, is Aristotle's causal analysis of art (PHYSICS II, 3–9) with, however, one modification: the efficient or moving cause is to be closely conjoined with the formal cause. This close conjunction is quite reasonable, for after all the moving or operative cause must be intimately related at every step to the form which is to be introduced into the material; otherwise the operative cause would contribute only accidentally to producing the final product.

Bearing this modification in mind, observe first that any art, e.g. any mechanical art, liberates certain characteristics of the material it works on, as the carpenter or cabinet maker brings out useful or beautiful properties inherent in the wood but not accessible to anyone without the artisan's labor; second, the artisan by continued practice of his art acquires skill or, as it might be said, he liberates his own powers to work or to incorporate skillfully the form of house or table in the appropriately chosen wood; third and finally, it may be said that art itself is liberating, for the arts are dependent upon each other in complex ways. For instance, unless one art produces its product, another, perhaps many others, are inhibited. Unless the woodcutter produces logs for the sawmill, the sawyer as well as the carpenter, cabinetmaker, and cartwright will perforce be idle. The product of the woodcutter, therefore, liberates these and other and dependent arts from inactivity or ineffectiveness. That is, the exercise of an art is often indispensible to the liberation or efficient functioning of a group of interdependent arts.

When we turn from this general understanding of the ways in which any art is liberating to the narrower and intellectual sense of "liberal arts," we shall find that the notion of liberation is still further enriched. In comparison with these new freedoms, the mechanic arts are usually recognized to be merely servile.

Consider the agronomist in comparison with the farmer. Both deal with the same thing, earth and her increase, but in different ways. The farmer deals with the earth itself, the rain, the seed, the seasons; the agronomist with knowledge about these matters, a knowledge mediated through symbols. He is freed from the backbreaking toil of the farmer; instead he works with language about the farmer's toil and the earth. Agronomy is an application of the liberal arts narrowly so called; it is an application of the arts of using language to the task of producing resolutions to problems encountered in the practice of farming.

In general, the arts using the tools of language endow men with a new dimension of freedom in that they liberate them from the physical labor associated with the mechanical arts; they are the "liberal arts" *par excellence*. Their superiority was traditionally said to arise from the fact that the human being is essentially the living being using *logos*, language, or the animal using *ratio*, reason, or ratios. Hence practice in these arts was practice in the most specifically human function. These arts bring us into an understanding and control of our humanity and render possible some modest direction of our own destinies.

Still these linguistic arts pursue the same three kinds of liberation – kinds which I called material, operative, and productive – which the mechanical arts seek, only these three factors are, *mutatis mutandum*, exercised in a linguistic context and hence are altered in appearance, but it is important to see that this alteration is not so profound as a casual glance might suggest.In an earlier age the three functions of language, its three possible forms of liberation, were described by observing that language may be used in three ways. It may be used to refer to itself or to refer to other things; and other things were said to be of two general kinds, either particulars or universals. These three functions of language point to three arts: (1) language used reflexively to refer to itself deals with the material of speech. Thus employed, it organizes language and renders it more intelligible and efficient in referring to its appropriate objects; in this usage it is commonly called grammar. (2) It may be used operatively to refer to particular things; but one does not just refer to particular things arbitrarily, but to particulars in a context. Or as it might be said, particular things are not just there, ready-made, as if on a stage happily waiting to be referred to by modern English speakers. Rather things are the particulars which appear to us only in the contexts within which we have learned to see them. Later I want to note that analogies are the means by which we have been persuaded to see particular things as in fact we do perceive them. In other words, analogies or prevailing types of analogies (paradigms they are sometimes called) give a structure to contexts. The art of discovering and effectively utilizing paradigms and analogies has since ancient times been called rhetoric. (2) Finally, language is used "productively" to discover and refer to universals, concepts, and laws, the laws in virtue of which analogies hold; this product has in the tradition been considered to be the final and greatest achievement of the liberal arts. As thus used it is called logic or dialectic.

Arts or techniques of language of these three primary kinds (material, operative, and productive) are the arts of the trivium: grammar, rhetoric, and logic. The quadrivial arts (arithmetic, geometry, music, astronomy) do not differ in principle, and they offer the same kinds of freedom. This point is important; it represents an insight into the unity of the mind's operation, lost by Renaissance philosophers, but recaptured by phenomenology. Of course, there are differences as well as similarities in the mind's operation as it turns from field to field. One important difference between the arts of using natural language and the not dissimilar arts of using the language of quantity can be expressed as two different ways of using the verb to be. Once it was said that all thought proceeded by noting the samenesses and differences among things, whether these "things" be particulars or universals. The trivial arts, using natural language on common human matters, do not need to define their sense of sameness with much exactitude. The Aristotelian doctrine of the predicaments specified the several senses of the trivial "is" adequately for ordinary usage.[7] On the other hand the artificial languages of the quadrivial arts need a sense of sameness which is quantitatively exact. Thus the "is" of mathematical statements means "equal to" or perhaps "measurably or demonstrably the same as." This meaning is illustrated in the ratios and proportions of mathematical and geometrical analogies (See Euclid V for the general doctrine).

In addition, there are two basic senses of the quadrivial "equal to." That is, there are two kinds of quantity: discrete and continuous quantity. Hence there are two quadrivial grammars: arithmetic and geometry. A good illustration of the rhetoric of mathematics, its use in manipulating quantified particulars, is numbering and mensuration. The most dramatic application of numbers to things was accomplished in ancient times by the Pythagoreans in their studies of music, specifically in expressing the harmonies of the lyre in simple arithmetical ratios. Hence mathematical rhetoric came (perhaps regrettably) to be called music. Similarly the movement to the universal was most successfully accomplished by ancient mathematicians in astronomy, hence mathematical dialectic received the name of astronomy. The quadrivium, then, arithmetic, geometry, music, and astronomy, consists of the three arts of the trivium developed in the contexts of the two languages of quantity, arithmetic and geometry; consequently, the quadrivial arts are said to be four rather than three in number.[8]

Retaining grasp upon the similar nature and structure of these two complementary groups of the intellectual arts is crucially important,

Failure of this grasp is responsible for the inadvertently comic character of much of modern intellectual life.[9] In particular, it is responsible for the supposed division between the two cultures, the scientific and the humanistic.

Together the trivium and the quadrivium constitute the arts of using language, whether natural or artificial. That is, they are the arts of achieving such material, operative, and productive liberation as the human mind is capable. They define the craft of the mind in whatever context that mind happens to labor, whether scientific, technological, legal, literary, or philosophic. Lumping the liberal arts vaguely together with the humanities and opposing them to the sciences is productive only of disaster (the comic disaster), for it introduces destructive and meaningless distinctions and conceals the primary ground of unity of the intellect's operation, not to mention the unity of the operation of a university. Perhaps, as it is sometimes said, the most successful practitioners of the liberal arts in modern times are to be found among the scientists; however, scientists, owing to their high degree of specialization, are often unaware of the tradition of the arts which they practice and of their kinship with these arts as they are used in the humanities. And humanists, for whatever reason, often seem oddly to fail to recognize their own brothers in arms.

I want now very briefly to indicate how these three arts are used, two of them (rhetoric and dialectic) referred to by name, in one of the earlier and most notable writings in this tradition: Plato's PHAEDRUS. My purpose in introducing these remarks on the PHAEDRUS is only to illustrate the nature and structure of the liberal arts and the way in which analogy functions in them by pointing out their usage in a classically perfect instance. My remarks are not intended to clarify any doctrine of Plato's, much less to demonstrate any influence of Plato's upon Husserl. But if the illustration is effective, it will contribute to rendering evident the liberal arts structure and function of phenomenology.

2. The Art of Liberating Phaedrus

The relevant part of the PHAEDRUS of Plato opens with a speech by Lysis. The author of this speech is innocent of grammar, so as one might expect the speech is without discernable structure, disjointed, and sloppy. Socrates, after taking due note of Lysis's grammarless abomination, delivers his own first speech; it is clearly organized, pointed, and well disciplined by the grammatical art. Later in the dialogue, he abstracts this structure, a bit of the grammar of speeches, and points out that an effective speech can properly begin with a general definition of the topic, and then proceed to divide that which is thus defined into its subordinate kinds until the speaker reaches in all its articulated relations the *eidos* which he wishes his hearer to see (PHAEDR. 256D–266B). Thus he renders persuasive the point and his evaluation of it which he offers for his audience's critical consideration and acceptance. His own speech all too effectively utilized this structure; I say "too effectively," for it was persuasive, but persuasive of error; it argued that self-concealment and manipulation were appropriate ways of approaching and relating to another person, a view acceptable to Phaedrus but hardly a genuinely Socratic conviction.

If, then, rhetoric is the art of persuasion, this art can be misused. It can be used in the service of an inappropriate end, e.g. the persuasion or the manipulation of others to conform to one's own desires. Rhetoric, therefore, is only a relatively free art; it depends upon another art, dialectic, which can discern the appropriate end, that for which persuasion is properly to be used. The dialectical art, Socrates claimed, can discern the end or value which the rhetorical art is to serve. Without this discernment the rhetorical end will be determined by custom, the uncriticized interests, or the mere preference of the speaker. Then the rhetoric will be sophistical.

Genuinely philosophical rhetoric is quite another thing. Socrates' second and great speech is a powerful illustration of philosphical rhetoric, one which builds up a succession of figures relating to and truly (if figuratively) depicting the nature of the human soul, until finally it becomes evident that the thread relating these figures is the best insight into the human soul, and the good for the soul, which dialectic has achieved. Here the productive and illuminating goal of the dialectic is reached; it effects "a divine release of the soul from the yoke of custom and convention" (PHAEDR. 265B) and works a change, evidently, in the young Phaedrus, endowing him with a more human freedom. Later in the dialogue this insight is discussed under the extraordinary figure of the word (*logos*) not so much written or even spoken, as living and speaking – "the intelligent word graven in the soul of the learner," as Jowett translates it (PHAEDR. 276A). This *logos* is the origin of the spoken or written word; this is the *logos* as *zōon*, the word which is the living, acting being of the speaker. The discussion culminating in these remarks about the living *logos* is a classic instance of a dialectical movement to the universal, a universal whose presence is not precisely expressed but is signaled by its placing the whole previous discussion in a new and illuminating perspective. This is logic, not in the modern grammatical sense, but in the sense of the *logos* operating in that most human of all human operations, the actual production of intellectual "seeing," an unveiling, a disclosure, in this instance a disclosure of the self or psyche. Here the dialectician (Socrates) used speeches the rhetorician (Socrates) produced in order to free Phaedrus (and himself) from the bonds of ignorance and prejudice. Here the effective element is the analogy drawn on the one hand between reason, the erotic soul, and pursuit of the good, and on the other hand a charioteer, his horses, and the race he seeks to win. This analogy is the operative element which is used to generate insight into the direction of the soul's growth into its maturity and actually excites the soul to engage in this movement. The reader will recall the powerful figure of the chariot of the soul striving to follow in the path of the gods where the prize to be won is lasting life in beauty and harmony.

Thus the rhetorician operates with language the grammarian has studied and set into usable order. Rhetoric proceeds by making analogies. If it is to be persuasive, it accepts as its initial analogy a belief which the audience already entertains, as Socrates seemingly accepted Phaedrus' uncritical faith in Lysias' opinions. Then it shows that this belief is somewhat like another (Socrates' first speech) which is closer to that which the speaker desires to move the audience. And this latter is rather like another (Socrates's second and great speech) which is still closer to the end point, and so on by such steps until the audience has been insensibly moved to just the position where the speaker aimed. The PHAEDRUS is a beautiful illustration of this movement as tending toward liberating Phaedrus from the yoke of Sophistical custom and convention. The essential element in rhetoric, however, is not merely that it should move or excite some audience upon some occasion. Rather its essential element lies in its technique of manipulating particulars into analogies which may be fruitfully subject to the needs of a philosophical dialectic whose end is insight into truth and into the good of those to whom it is addressed.

In sum, the content of rhetoric is analogies (words having meaning in and because of analogical structures) which are in turn subject to an adequate apprehension of value. Since this point is essential to understanding the nature of the liberal arts, I pause to illustrate it in several other contexts.

Consider first an illustration taken from Keats' sonnet "On First Looking into Chapman's Homer;" the poet writes,

> Then felt I like some watcher of the skies
> When a new planet swims into his ken.

The full-blown analogy is the following: Pope's familiar translation of Homer is to Chapman's translation as the astronomer's familiar night sky is to that sky at the moment when the astronomer discovers a new planet, a new world. Now in order further to illustrate the view that the content of the liberal arts can be fruitfully regarded as analogies, I cite another (a quadrivial) kind of analogy. I say this table is seven feet long. Here the full analogy or proportion is this: the number 1 is to the number 7 as a unit length of the table is to its total length. And now consider a still more elaborate quadrivial analogy drawn from the science of physics: the law expressing the force (F) of gravity:

$$F = 1/[g(m_1 \cdot m_2)]$$

(where g is the gravational constant and $m_1 \cdot m_2$ is the product of two measured masses.) This law can be written thus:

$$2F = g(m \cdot m),$$

and this later transformation is a mathematical analogy or expression as a proportion:

$$2{:}g = m_1 \cdot m_2{:}F.$$

Whether modern physicists are in the habit of using this latter formulation in their thinking and writing is irrelevant to my point: that the liberal arts, the linguistic arts, can be understood as the arts of formulating and using analogies, whether the context be a myth of the soul's life, the discovery of poetic values, the measurement of distance, or a law relating masses and gravitational force.

In all these illustrations the skill of the rhetorician (and that of his audience) is required to make a translation. In one instance the translation moved from the language of driving chariots to that of the soul's growth; in another it moved from the ordinary language of literary criticism to the language of astronomical-poetic discovery. In the illustration drawn from mensuration, it moved from the exact language of number to the relatively precise language of equal lengths. In the final instance, it moved from the language of numbers to that of certain measured magnitudes (force and mass). The rhetorician is skilled in seeing similar meanings in different languages and different contexts or in devising several languages for expressing the same meaning. Rhetoric might be called the art of translation, the art of exhibiting or seeing the same invariant in different embodiments.

In all instances like those I have cited, let it be noted, a value dimension is involved. In the PHAEDRUS this dimention is explicitly recognized and elaborated. In Keats' sonnet it seems to be accepted without question that poetic discovery is an element in the intrinsic good for man. In the instance of measuring the table length, the measurement presumably subserves some further use value, such as making another table. Finally in expressing the law of gravity, the good achieved is something we all accept as unquestionably desirable: the physicist's insight into the unity and order of the cosmos. At this point, however, we recall that such insights as Newton's are susceptible of all kinds of practical and technological elaborations whose good, through usually unquestioned, loudly cries for investigation and judgment by some rational standard, an examination which dialectic was once wont to provide.[10]

Logic or dialectic is a movement beyond the analogies which the rhetorician has devised to the universal or law in virtue of which the several members of an analogy are indeed analogous. And it moves toward an apprehension of the extrinsic or intrinsic good which that discovery can subserve. Alternatively, we might say the several ratios in a proportion all express the same invariant. And precisely in consequence of re-expressing the invariant in the several ratios, the mind is able to grasp and use the law they embody. Thus the fall of an apple can be said to be analogous to the motion of the moon around the earth because both embody or instantiate the same law of gravity. And similarly the young Phaedrus seems to catch a glimpse of some such law or universal which may properly direct the life of the soul; accordingly he seems to turn away from the sophistical use of rhetoric to a love of wisdom and of the speech which aspires to truth about order and harmony in the soul.

If the content of rhetoric is analogies and if the art of the rhetorician consists in finding or making analogies appropriate to the purpose which the artist has in hand, then the content of dialectic consists in the universals or laws extracted from or discovered in a series of particular analogies. This movement from particular analogies to their law (*eidos*) is the production of what has generally been called insight and is marked by a reordering or reevaluation of the relevant particulars, or where the insight concerns human life (and what discovery does not eventually concern human life?) by a reformation or reidentification of the personality of the protagonist or a redirection of his energies toward his greater good. Sometimes this production is called an experience of illumination; Longinus spoke of it as "transport"; scientists describe it as discovery.

Thus in sum, grammar makes or sets in order the language in which analogies may be expressed. Rhetoric uses this language for the expression of analogies, perhaps in an order productive of persuasion. Dialectic elicits from these analogies the law or universal which they embody. If the dialectic becomes philosophical, it moves further to measure this discovery by an apprehension of the good for man.

It is easy to see that the persuasive power of rhetoric renders it a powerful and dangerous instrument, one which constantly calls for moral and philosophical direction, so it will be used in a manner pleasing to the gods, or at least good for men; Socrates' prayer at the end of the PHAEDRUS alludes to both of these kinds of evaluation. In our own time the success of many scientists working within their specialties has provided means for rhetorical and technological application (e.g., the hydrogen bomb). These means now call loudly for the kind of value dialectic and intelligent direction which Socrates knew so well how to provide. Today, though, Socrates cannot be heard; that is to say, insight into the good for man is more or less unavailable to us, for in this era of enormous expansion of the quadrivial arts unbalanced by the humanistic insights available to trivially disciplined artists, the prevalent metaphysics of primary (measurable) qualities largely relegates value, the good (and other non-quantifiable qualities), to the sphere of the unreal, the "subjective." And there is assumed to be no persuasive or binding insight into subjectivity apprehended value.[11] Here we are back again with the two relatively unrelated cultures. Though we make use of the sciences and technology, we cannot provide this or any other use with a rational defense so long as the prevalent metaphysics holds sway. We can no longer take very seriously Socrates' recommendation to Phaedrus, that he strive to follow in the procession of the gods and to banquet with them upon true being.

Phenomenology, however, reexamines these matters and rethinks experience in such a way that the human good is brought once more upon the stage.

3. The Liberal Arts Functioning in Phenomenology

One of the more prominent developments in contempory philosophy lies precisely in phenomenologist's genial practice of the liberal arts in the direction not only of securing a sounder and more concrete basis upon which to philosophize and to scientize, but also toward achieving the insight into values and ends which may direct the power derived from success in the sciences and technology. I want to illustrate this point and, more generally, to display the liberal arts structure of Husserlian phenomenology. This structure will be developed in three steps corresponding to the three liberating arts.

In IDEAS Husserl moves through two phases in order to accomplish the grammatical task, the task of providing phenomenology with a language capable of distinguishing and communicating the various translations and transformations necessary to reach an understanding of its subject matter. The first step is contained in Chapter 1 of IDEAS. Here meanings of important terms are set forth, usually as distinctions between pairs of terms. The reader will recall the distinctions between fact and essence, essential insight and individual intuition, generalization and formalization, region and category, and the like. I do not linger over these familiar lexical matters.

The language thus specified, however, is not all that is needful for carrying out the grammatical part of the program enjoined by the phrase *"zurück zu den Sachen Selbst"* – back to experience – which animated Husserl. For as this philosopher came more and more clearly to recognize, one's use of language at any time in history is dominated and directed by certain pervasive analogies and metaphors (paradigms, Thomas Kuhn calls them)[12] which pervade an epoch, direct and limit its perception, and structure its experience. Husserl referred to these pervasive and mostly unconsciously employed analogies as presuppositions. One such dominating presupposition which determines our experience in advance of that experience is the machine analogy inherited from Renaissance thinkers and experimenters. According to this analogy, objects are all like each other in that all are organizations of spontaneous analogizing of my experienced body to the other's similarly behaving body, a basis which conditions empathy and other such experiences (we have already allueded to this account). The he describes personalities of a "higher order," or intersubjective and intercommunicating groups of those who have learned to constitute their experience in similar ways.[17]

Husserl concludes that the character of our experience and especially its regularities owe in principle their character and regularity to our transcendental intersubjectivity, specifically to its common noetico-noematic structures operating or bestowing meaning in definite, regular, and common ways (cf. CRISIS, pp. 369ff.). Especially should it be observed this common objective world includes all that we experience, the ideals we pursue, the values we achieve, the culture we institute, as well as the nature we study and the technology to which we subject both nature and ourselves. Just this enlarged grasp of the objective, as including the whole of culture[18] renders available a basis for the criticism of our technological culture and for guiding it toward the human good.

Husserl's peroration to consciousness as the wonder of wonders, would seem to be one expression of the end to which his practice of the art of dialectic leads. Transcendental consciousness, the constituting and bestowal of meanings which form our world and which bring objects to presence before us in different kinds and relations, in linguistically structured ways, is the expression of a living *logos*, the living speaking word which is in, perhaps *is*, the human soul. This perception marks the high point of Plato's PHAEDRUS as well as of Husserl's phenomenology. As we noted earlier, the practice of the *epoché* frees the philosopher from a narrow and partial metaphysical view of reality. Now in addition, we see that a philosophical understanding developed on the basis of concrete experience reveals a positive freedom. It reveals the meaning-giving power of consciousness, a power of consciousness, a power which can either operate as custom dictates and without forethought, or it can be wielded with critical awareness and responsible self-direction, effecting a release of the soul from submission to the popular obvious. Paul Ricoeur takes particular notice of this recognition. We owe Husserl, he says, an understanding of a new possible freedom of our creative and meaning-giving powers.[19]

Assuming now that I have demonstrated that the liberal arts may be mapped over on Husserl's philosophy (at least on a significant portion of it), what of moment has been achieved? I think we have accomplished two disiderata.

The first is to have given one more reason to believe that Husserl, so often called the least historical of philosophers, nevertheless philosophized strictly and recognizably in accord with Western methods and aims, so deeply was he imbued with the whole of the tradition. He ably represents the great liberating arts ideal, although he eschews much of its terminology, in that he moves quite clearly through the three stages of liberating treatment of his topic. First he develops a clarified and purified grasp of his language, and of the (phenomenal) field wherein he is to employ his language. This is the grammatical stage. Then he elaborates his basic analogy – the neotico-noematic structure of consciousness – demonstrates its operative presence in many contexts, and persuasively exhibits its ramifications in contexts where it is not simply or obviously applicable; here is the rhetorical stage. Finally we observed that Husserl moves by way of the dialectic art to the law or universal whose presence illuminates and unifies particulars and finally unifies all that has preceded (cf. CRISIS #49). This final law or universal is, I believe, the productive power of meaning-giving whose effect is the ordered world of objects and values we all inhabit; this is a power of sense-bestowal, of meaning actualization, whose primary and paradigmatic form is discovered in that *lebendige Gegenwart,* our own living, creative, and integrating presence. This is our active and productive consciousness, the wonder of wonders. Such is Husserl's version of that living *logos* which is human being.

A second virtue of this treatment of Husserl's philosophy is to have emphasized that in developing his views, Husserl reinstates values and experiences of value essentially on a par with what is generally accepted as objective experience. Objective criticism of culture, of our ends and values, then becomes possible. That is to say, Husserl, by his superior skill and unprejudiced practice of the liberal arts reached a more complete grasp of experience than past and contempory Enlightenment philosophers, and thus he was enabled to reintegrage experience of good and evil, of the desirable and the undesirable, back into the real world.

In this respect and for purposes of this paper, I am suggesting that as Phaedrus was related to Socrates, so are we of the modern world related to Husserl. Judgement of a culture, in particular of our scientific and technological culture, is appropriately entered again on the philosophic agenda. This latter is just the item Husserl treated in CRISIS. By this route he returns to a primary responsibility of philosophy, a responsibility first recognized and genially discharged by Socrates and Plato and illustrated in the PHAEDRUS, but in modern times ignored, owing to the prevailing failure to discover an adequate basis for value judgments. With Husserl's practice of the liberal arts in the study of phenomena, though, we are freed from this value-ignorance, and philosophy is once more enabled to become the "functionary of humanity."[20] Although Husserl does not press his philosophy toward such a view of the human end as that expressed in (say) St. Thomas' philosophical theology, still the notion of Reason, Reason as a highest value, seems to occupy a similar position at the apex of his philosophy. The human being is essentially meaning-bestowing, and in actualizing meanings which are in accord with this Reason, he is realizing the full human possibility and achieving the final human freedom.

Notes

1. Edward G. Gallard, "Man or Technology: Which is to Rule?" in *Phenomenology and the Understanding of Human Destiny,* edited by Stephen Skousgaard (Washington, D.C.: The Center for Advanced Research in Phenomenology and The University Press of America, 1981), 3–19.

2. David Schenck, "Thinking Technology" *Science Technology Society Newsletter 28*, (February 1982), 14.

3. For one very interesting restatement of some theories and conclusions of physics in plain English, see H.R. Pagels, *The Cosmic Code: Quantum Physics as the Language of Nature* (New York: Simon and Schuster, 1982).

4. Cf. Edmund Husserl, *Formal and Transcendental Logic*, translated by Dorion Cairns (The Hague: Martinus Nijhoff, 1978).

5. Edmund Husserl, *Ideas Pertaining to a Pure Phenomenology and to a Phenomenological Philosophy: First Book, General Information to Pure Phenomenology*, translated by Fred Kersten (The Hague/Boston/London: Martinus Nijhoff, 1982), hereafter cited as IDEAS.

6. Roman writers (e.g. Seneca) used 'liberal' to refer to those studies appropriate to one born free. The Greek and the Medieval traditions, however, use the term to refer to a freedom which is to be attained through study and practice. There is a good article on the liberal arts in *The New Catholic Encyclopedia* (New York: McGraw Hill Book Co., 1967). See also Scott Buchanan, *The Doctrine of Signatures* (London: Kegan Paul, 1938), chapt. 1 & 2; and Mark van Doren, *Liberal Education* (Boston: Beacon Press, 1943).

7. Cf. Porphry, *The Isogoge*.

8. It remained, of course, for Descartes to show that these two grammars are isomorphic, i.e. possess the same meaning.

9. Johnathan Swift perceived this inadvertent comedy more clearly than most writers and derides it in his account of Laputa. Scott Buchanan touches upon many aspects of this comedy in his *Poetry and Mathematics* (Chicago: University of Chicago Press, 1929; Midway Reprint, 1975).

10. I attempt an examination of this kind in my *Man and Technology* (Pittsburgh, Duquesne University Press, 1978).

11. For Husserl's views on the metaphysical reification of measurable and mechanical properties to which I allude, see his *Crisis of European Sciences and Transcendental Phenomenology*, translated by David Carr (Evanston, Ill.: Northwestern University Press, 1970), part II; hereafter cited as CRISIS.

12. *The Structure of Scientific Revolutions* (Chicago: University of Chicago Press, 1970), esp. 112–17 and 192.

13. For Husserl's account of this mathematization, see *CRISIS ## 9–13*.

14. The originality and centrality in Husserl's philosophy of this doctrine of intentionality is emphasized by Aron Gurwitsch; cf. his *Studies in Phenomenology and Psychology* (Evanston: Northwestern University Press, 1966), Study 7, "On the Intentionality of Consciousness." Indeed, Gurwitsch finds the ensuing concept of consciousness to bhe the most adequate of the three con-

cepts of consciousness produced in the modern world; cf. op. cit., Study 9, "The Kantian and the Husserlian Conceptions of Consciousnes," especially pp. 159ff. of this excellent essay.

15. Edmund Husserl, *Cartesian Meditations: An Introduction to Phenomenology*, translated by Dorion Cairns (The Hague: Martinus Nijhoff, 1960), Meditation V, esp. pp. 110ff.

16. The relations between *Ideas I* and *Cartesian Meditations* as touching this point, are analyzed and evaluated by Professor K.M. Haney in an unpublished dissertation, *Husserl's Philosophy of Intersubjectivity* (Tulane University, 1982).

17. Note that intersubjectivity for Husserl does not play the part which intersubjective verification plays for an experimental science. it does not strengthen a conviction or tend to confirm a hypothesis through repetition of particular predicted experiences. Rather its function is transcendental and is the condition of any objective experience. It is a necessary component in the constitution of a genuine or common world. Recognition that one constitutes one's world as other do — however varied the detail — is the source of the assurance that one lives in a human world.

18. See *Cartesian Meditations*, 132–34. See also Gurwitsch, Study 18, "The Last Work of Edmund Husserl," esp. 399–402.

19. See his *Husserl: A Study of His Phenomenology*, translated by Edward G. Ballard and Lester E. Embree (Evanston, Ill.: Northwestern University Press, 1967), 18–20. Also see CRISIS, 151.

20. *Crisis*, 71. See also Gurwitsch, 399–402.

20. Habermas on the University: *Bildung* in the Age of Technology

A. Anthony Smith

Jürgen Habermas is considered the leading contemporary representative of the school of thought referred to as "critical theory," often termed the "Frankfurt School." Habermas was born on June 18, 1929. Within four years from this date the early members of the Frankfurt School — Max Horkheimer, Theodore Adorno, and Herbert Marcuse, among others — were forced to flee from fascism. Their organization, the *Institute für Sozialforschung*, transferred its headquarters from Frankfurt (where it had been affiliated with the University of Frankfurt) to New York. After the war Marcuse remained in the United States, where he became the most important theoretical influence on the new left of the sixties. Horkheimer and Adorno returned to the University of Frankfurt in 1949. Habermas was profoundly influenced by them during both his studies at the University of Marburg and his teaching of philosophy at the University of Heidelburg between 1961 and 1964. Finally, in 1964, Habermas himself moved to the University of Frankfurt to teach philosophy and sociology. Here he worked closely with Adorno until the latter's death in 1969. Habermas has recently returned to teaching at the University of Frankfurt, after leaving in 1971 to direct the Max Planck Institute in Starnberg.[1]

Critical theory is an approach to the analysis of society which is not content simply to collect and correlate data in a supposedly "value free" manner. Instead, the theorist is called on to evaluate this data and to judge it according to the standard of whether or not it counts as a furthering of human emancipation.[2] For the most part the early members of the Frankfurt School subjected political and asethetic phenomena to this sort of critique. While Habermas has continued these investigations in his own work, he has also expanded the range of critical theory by discussing topics his mentors had not considered. Among these topics is the role of the university in modern society. This is the topic of the present paper.

Habermas' views on the university emerged in the course of an attempt to come to grips with both the historical transformation the university had undergone in the twentieth century, and the beliefs of other contemporary German theorists of education. First we shall examine the move from early capitalism to contemporary capitalism in terms of the effects this transition had on the university. Then two responses made by German philosophers of education in the post-World War II period to the new role of the university will be presented. One will be dismissed as anachronistic. The other will be shown to be inadequate. Then Habermas' own response will be discussed. This response seeks to retain the classical German notion of *Bildung* in today's scientific-technical university.

I. The Changing Function of the University

Early capitalist society introduced what we may term the *principle of liberalism*. In Western Europe the monarchy had actively fostered the development of capitalism through granting charters, protecting trade routes, and so on. The monarchy, however, also threatened capitalist interests by remaining tied to the old feudal nobility and by intervening in economic activity at the monarch's whim. The principle of liberalism was developed by the rising bourgeoise in order to protect itself from arbitrary interference by the monarch. This principle strictly deliminated a sphere of economic activity apart from the political realm. It asserted that decision making in the former must be left to private individuals. This would, it was thought, lead to individual initiative and thereby to economic progress. The political realm was also to be transformed, as more and more administration passed from the king's favorites to trained state officials.

The principle of liberalism was not only applied to economic activity and the state. If early capitalism was to stabilize itself other institutions would have to function in a manner consistent with the functioning of economic and political institutions. And so the principle of liberalism was applied to the university as well. As a result, the university had two defining characteristics in the period of early capitalism. First, the relationship between the university and the other spheres of society was fixed by what Habermas terms the "quarantine model" of the university. Just as the liberal principle delimited a realm of economic activity separate from the state, so too the university was conceived as possessing an institutional autonomy that must be preserved at all costs from external interference: "In the period of early liberalism, of the self-sufficient entrepreneur, the university with its claim to autonomy and with the institutional form of a self-administered body tied itself to the laws of its time."[3]

The second impact of the principle of liberalism on the university concerned its educational ideal. If liberalism asserted that economic decisions were to be made by autonomous individuals, and that officials of the state were to act in a responsible manner, then it must be the task of the university to produce autonomous and responsible individuals. This is the sociological framework for the development of the classical German humanist notion of *Bildung*, self-formation. This notion is central in the works of German philosophers of the period of early capitalism, and was the central concept of the philosophy of education worked out by thinkers such as Schleiermacher and Humboldt. On this view the mission of the university was to provide a solid grounding in the traditional faculties. In this study philosophy was looked on as the centerpiece, integrating the content of the other faculties into one coherent view. An individual having undergone training in this *Universitas litterarum* would possess the moral and aesthetic sensibility and wide ranging learning required for enlightened autonomy. The concept of *Bildung* theory thus was directly connected to *praxis*. The theoretical knowledge one acquired in the university served to orient one's practical activity.

It is important to note that training in the techniques of production was *not* part of the role of the university. Scientists in the universities engaged in what is called "natural philosophy," the goal of which was the discovery of ultimate metaphysical truths regarding the universe. These men had no concern whatsoever for the practical application of their theories. Conversely, the practical men in the shop had little use for theory. They regarded traditional lore and the lessons of experience as sufficient in their search for profit. These techniques of production were rules of thumb passed from generation to generation without formal instruction.

Around the turn of the twentieth century all this changed. The centuries long split of science and the useful arts was overcome. Science became a direct means of capital accumulation through the application of discoveries in physics and chemistry to the processes of commodity production. David Noble describes this transformation as follows:

Modern science-based industry – that is industrial enterprise in which ongoing scientific investigation and the systematic application of scientific knowledge to the process of commodity production have become routine parts of the operation – emerged very late in the nineteenth century. It was the product of significant advances in chemistry and physics and also of the growing willingness of the capitalist to embark upon the costly, time-consuming, and uncertain path of research and development. This willingness reflected both the intensifying demand to outproduce competitors at home and abroad and the unprecedented accumulation of sufficient surplus capital – the product of traditional manufactures, financial speculation, and industrial consolidation – with which to underwrite a revolution in social production.[4]

This transition to science-based industries required both the employment and training of scientific personnel and the operation of large-scale industrial research and development. For example, in the United States, research and development expenditures rose from under $100 million in 1928 to $5 billion in 1953 to 1954, $12 billion in 1959, $14 billion in 1965 and $20.17 billion in 1970.[5] The figures for Germany are analogous. There was, in short, a tremendous demand for scientific-technical education. State administration also became rationalized during this period, which created a further demand for scientific-technical research and personnel.

In response to this demand the university itself was transformed.[6] Its new role was to provide the needed scientific-technical research and expertise.

As a result of this new function both of the characteristics which defined the university in the age of early capitalism changed. While certain features of the old university remained (self-government by the faculty, for example), by and large the quarantine model of the university broke down. The university, now funded to a large degree by contracts and grants from corporations and state agencies, became connected with the social life-world in a most direct fashion.[7] This breakdown of the quarantine model was closely connected to a shift in educational ideals away from those advocated in the classical German university. No longer was the goal of producing persons capable of discovering and applying technically employable knowledge. No longer was the ideal the well-rounded humanist of the *Universitas litterarum*. Instead the ideal became the specialist, one who concentrated on a particular area and was able to produce causal knowledge of the regularities of that object realm. With this philosophy lost its place of priority among the faculties. As specialization increased, philosophy's claim to offer a synthetic perspective uniting all knowledge into a theory capable of providing practical orientation appeared more and more implausible.

II. Two Responses to the Contemporary University

Different perspectives on this new role of the university have emerged among German philosophers of education in the last decades. Before presenting Habermas' evaluation, two other positions must be mentioned.

The first response to this new function of the university can be termed *"neoromantic."* This perspective is characterized by a longing for the old ideal of the university and an attempt to make that ideal alive today. Karl Jaspers was very influential in this direction, as was the neothomistic movement in vogue in German universities during the immediate post-World War II period.[8] Both camps called for a return to the *Universitas Litterarum* with philosophy once again holding its position of priority, uniting all the other disciplines in a world view. Creating this world view, Jaspers said, would require an exercise of *Geist*, spirit. Once created, those educated within it would possess a theoretical system capable of orienting their practical activity, thereby keeping the classical notion of *Bildung* alive in the twentieth century.

Despite initial popularity in postwar Germany, the neoromantic view of the university confronted one ineluctable fact. No matter how much spiritual energy was exerted there remained "that which spirit worked against in vain, in which an objective contradiction – produced by the social life context and not to be removed without removing the context – obviously was fixed and continued."[9] Increased specialization provides one example of something produced by the social life context and not to be removed by mere spiritual renewal. Faced with such specialization the attempts of Jasper's *Geist* to work out a synthetic perspective could result only in a diletantish digest that would itself count as a betrayal of the *Bildung* ideal.[10]

A second perspective on the role of the university in modern society has increasingly held sway among German thinkers. This can be termed the "technocratic" perspective. This position insists that the increased specialization required to master a particular scientific area, and the direct bond between the university and the needs of industry and government, have made the classical-humanist ideals totally outdated. This stance was taken by thinkers such as Schelsky.[11] He saw the contemporary university as so totally integrated into today's technological society that any return to older ideals was out of the question.

This position on the university was grounded in a general social theory, a key characteristic of which eliminates "the political" as a valid category. According to this view, society has increased in complexity to such an extent that it has become a self-regulating system. Technical experts, it is true, must manage this system in order for it to maintain an equilibrium. But the question of the ends of social action does not arise according to this perspective. *All* industrial societies, no matter what their ideologies might be, must fulfill the same technical impera- tives. If the question of ends no longer has any relevance given the com- plexity of contemporary society, then it follows that the university ought to abandon once and for all the ideal of *Bildung*. Rather than training students to select ends, to orient their practical activity, the university must instead provide what is needed by the society: technical specialists who possess the expertise required to attain the end already given, the maintenance of the system in an equilibrium state.

If there is one idea that has remained constant throughout Haber- mas' writings it is that the social theory, just described, is fundamen- tally in error. It is, of course, true that in contemporary society technical expertise plays a greater role than ever before. But this is not to assert that the question of ends is now irrelevant. Ends must be selected as before. To assert that a given end is technically necessitated is simply to mask the actual situation. For the direction in which technology develops, the pace at which it develops, the manner in which it is employed, and so on involve political decisions which technology in itself does not necessitate: "The scientifically solved problems of technical manipulation are transformed into life problems, for the scien- tific control of natural and social processes does not absolve humans from action. Now as before conflicts must be decided, interests pierced through, interpretations found . . . only these practical questions are today largely determined through the system of our technical achievements."[12] To mask this reality is to mask the exercise of power which occurs when these decisions are made outside of any public con- trol: "The direction of technical progress can be very much influenced by government research policy; however until today it is still depen- dent to a high degree upon private economic interests, interests which as such are not made objects of discussion of a science oriented to the general interest and beyond that of a formed (gebildeten) political public sufficiently knowledgeable of the practical consequences (of technical development)."[13]

III. Habermas' Proposal

The previous account leaves Habermas in the position where the neoromantic view of the university is seen as correct in insisting that contemporary industrial society has no way made irrelevant the need for a theoretical training that would orient practical activity. But its appeal to philosophy as a discipline capable of providing a synthetic theory with practical implications is most questionable. Conversely, the conservative technocratic view wrongly rejects the very notion of education as *Bildung*. Yet it correctly insists on the necessity for specialization and technical training. Is there any way of combining the strengths of both positions while avoiding their weaknesses?

Habermas thinks so. He begins by agreeing with the technocratic view that specialization is a feature of contemporary society that is not about to disappear. The problem, he asserts, is that this specialization is not carried far enough. The implementation of technical knowledge involves practical consequences for the social life-world, and the study of one's speciality should be pushed until the student is forced to reflect on these social consequences. *This* sort of theoretical reflection can lead to the orientation of practical activity. It is thus a form of *Bildung*, a form which does not retreat back to the nineteenth century ideal of the person of letters but which is instead compatible with the degree of specialization demanded in the age of technology. "Reflection on the foundation (of the specialized sciences) forces one to a critique of the relations between science and society. And once again this critique must be bourne by the single sciences themselves."[14]

Habermas mentions some measures for structuring the course of university study so as to encourage this sort of reflection among those in the sciences.[15] But this is nothing more than the first stage. For if university researchers are to connect their activities with the social life-world then they cannot simply reflect on the social consequences of their research in isolation from this life-world: *Bildung* is ultimately a social process, not something that individuals go through alone. The interpretation of the social consequences of research made by those within the university must be mediated with the interpretations of the public at large:

> A double function of teaching corresponds to research: first the transmission of formal and empirical knowledge for training in job techniques and in the research process itself, but then also that re-translation of scientific results in the horizon of the life-world. This would permit the informational content of technical recommendations to be brought into discussions on the practically necessary, the general interest. Today

we no longer can leave that to the contingent decisions of individuals or to the pluralism of opinion makers. It is a matter not only of continuing to give a practically effective level of knowledge to the administrative apparatus of technically operating persons, but of also incorporating it back into the language possession of the communicating society. *That* is today the task of an academic *Bildung* which now as before must be taken over by a science capable of self-reflection. If our universities decline to undertake *Bildung* in this sense . . . the enlightenment of a politically mature public also cannot be expected.[16]

Habermas envisions a model in which public discussions unite planners from government and industry, scientific-technical experts from universities and research labs, and representatives of public interest groups to determine policy through a dialectic of will and skill. Those with the requisite technical expertise would inform the community of the range of possibilites allowed by the present level of scientific-technical knowledge. The public sphere would be engaged in ongoing discussions (following rules to ensure that the discussions are as free from coercion as possible) to select which of these technical possibilities best satisfies generalizable social needs. And government and production units would have the task of planning the most efficient means of carrying out these public mandates.[17] This would ensure the satisfaction of universalizable interests, the common good.

The university's tasks in this model include (a) the scientific-technical training needed by scientists and engineers in order to fix what is technically possible; (b) the training of government and busines officials in the management techniques necessary for production to work in an efficient manner; (c) the training in self-reflection required if scientists and engineers are to consider the social implications of various technologies in an adequate fashion; and (d) the transmission of scientific-technical knowledge to the public sphere, so that choice among the various possibilities will be as informed as possible. In short, the university must combine the transmission of technical knowledge with *Bildung*.

I would like to conclude with a consideration of some objections that could be made against Habermas' proposal.

First, it could be objected that public discourse on university research would lead to an illicit politicization of scientific activity, thereby threatening the autonomy of the university. This objection is based on what was the quarantine model of the relationship between the university and society. This model is not applicable when modern society is as permeated by science and technology stemming from the university as it is today. When this is recognized it becomes apparent that the attempt to quarantine scientific research from public input does not so much preserve the universitiy's autonomy as block off conscious reflection on the links between that research and the social life-world. The true issue is not whether scientific research should or should not be politicized, but whether the practical consequences of scientific research will be made explicit: whether scientists are to be conscious of their responsibility for the foreseeable direct and indirect social implications of their research. If one accepts the view that the university's ideals demand that these last questions be answered in the affirmative, then a forum within which different sectors of the public have the opportunity to articulate how a specific research proposal affects their concerns would provide an aid in making these social consequences of research explicit and in helping individual scientists reflect on their social responsibilities. Indeed, Habermas, going even further, argues precisely that the *lack* of such institutionalized public discourse is what most threatens the autonomy of the university. For without regular public scrutiny the danger is ever present that private interests will be able to dictate the direction university research takes.

> Discussion over the goals of the courses of study, over criteria for the selection of research projects, over the social context of scientific qualifications and the information begotten in the research process can first place the groups immediately participating in teaching and research in the position of reflecting upon avoidable and unavoidable social dependencies.[18]

Second, it could be objected that any attempt to institutionalize public input interferes with the academic freedom of the individual researchers in the university. This raises profound questions regarding the notion of democracy. In a democracy, cerain decisions are left to the private individual and his/her conscience. Should I become a member of this church or that? Should I marry this woman or not? No one has a right to infringe on these sorts of decisions.

But in a democracy not all decisions are categoriezed as private matters. The decisions made by state officials, for example, are categorized as public. And in a democracy decisions within which public power is exercised are *not* left to the dictates of one's private conscience. They are instead subject to public control. Democracy could even be defined as that system which *restricts* the freedom of those who exercise public power, as the freedom of a democratically elected president is restricted in comparison with an absolute monarch.

Now it follows from this that the attempt to institutionalize public input into decisions regarding university research would count as an infringement of freedom *only* if such decisions were private in scope, like the choice of a religion or the choice of a marrriage partner. But, as has been argued in this paper, in a scientific civilization such as our own this is not the case. Scientific research conducted in universities regularly has ramifications far beyond the intimate sphere of the researcher's private life, ramifications which may extend throughout the very fabric of society. Given this public nature of scientific research it follows that public input into decisions regarding that research should be looked on not as restrictions on freedom but as furthering the process of democratization.

A third objection remains. It is most difficult to change a central institution in isolation from other institutions to which it is structurally related. To bring the university to a new notion of *Bildung*, as has been described, requires a democratization of the university which is not likely to occur without a general democratization of society as a whole. One cannot question the right of private corporations to dictate the direction of university research without simultaneously questioning their right to determine which sections of the economy will be invested in, which geographical areas will be developed, whether investment will be productive or speculative, and so forth. *All* exercises of public power must be subject to public control, if the university is to be transformed. We have reached the limits of a critical theory perspective on the university. We now must begin a critical theory perspective on society.

Notes

1. For an account of the history of the Frankfurt School see Martin Jay's *The Dialectical Imagination: A History of the Frankfurt School and the Institute for Social Research, 1923–1950* (Boston: Little, Brown and Company, 1973).

2. See Max Horkheimer and Theodor Adorno, *The Dialectic of Enlightenment* (New York: Herder & Herder, 1972), for an example of this approach.

3. "Das chronisch Leiden der Hochschulreform," in *Politische Schriften* (Frankfurt: Suhrkamp, 1981), 19. All translations are my own.

4. David Noble, *America By Design: Science, Technolgy and the Rise of Corporate Capitalism* (New York: Alfred A. Knopf, 1977), 5. Noble describes how this process occurred first in Germany and only later came to characterize the United States.

5. Ernest Mandel, *Late Capitalism* (London: Verso, 1975), 257.

6. Of course, the mere fact that a certain type of change would be functional for a social system is no guarantee that such a change takes place. The

struggle to bring about this change must first be successful. Noble describes this struggle as follows: "In the early nineteenth century the colleges were firmly in the hands of the classicists and the clerics, and there was considerable academic disdain for the study of experimental science and even more for the teaching of the useful arts. Technical education . . . developed in struggle with the classical colleges, both inside and outside of them. One form of this development was the gradual growth of technological studies within the classical colleges, resulting from the reorientation of natural philosophy toward the empirical, experimental, scientific search for truth and from the pressures of some scientists and powerful industrialists for practical instruction; the other was the rise of technical colleges and institutes outside of the traditional colleges in response to the demands of internal, improvement projects like canal-building, railroads, manufactures, and, eventually, science-based industry" (Noble, *America by Design*, 20). Here, too, this occurred in Germany prior to the United States.

7. "In the industrially developed lands the maintenance of the social system has become ever more dependent upon the vocational qualifications and scientific information produced in the universities. . . . In the measure that individual scholarship gives way to organized research and science becomes the foremost productive force, the universities (which today demand considerable investment) become integrated – partly spontaneously and partly according to plan – in a growth oriented, state interventionist social system" ("Demokratisieruy der Hochschule – Politisierung der Wissenschaft?" in *Politische Schriften*, 189-90).

8. For a discussion of these two perspectives see "Das chronische Leiden).

9. Ibid, 17.

10. "All attempts on the part of academic philosophy to interpret the knowledge of relativity theory, atomic theory, organic chemistry, virus research, morphorlogy, animal psychology, etc. into traditional categories – even attempts which take seriously the undermining of the classical framework and do not resort to a conventional interpretation – have reached for the time being hardly more than the speculations of philosophizing special scientists, speculations not free from naivete" "Das chronische Leiden," 36.

11. Habermas discusses Schelsky's view of the educational system in "Konservativer Geist – und die modernistischen Folgen," in *Politische Schriften*, 41-57.

12. "Vom sozialen Wandel adademischer *Bildung*," in *Politische Schriften*, 108-9.

13. Ibid., 115.

14. "Das chronische Leiden, 37.

15. For example, Habermas argues against imposing a fixed length of study.

16. "Vom sozialen Wandel, 116-17.

17. See Habermas' "The Scientization of Politics and Public Opinion," in *Toward a Rational Society* (Boston: Beacon Press, 1970).

18. "Für ein neues Konzept der Hochschulverfassung," in *Politische Schriften*, 175.

21. Epistemology and Academic Freedom

David L. Thompson

The Classical Theory of Academic Freedom

Academic freedom as a practical problem may be said to have
started with the death of Socrates. Mediaeval universities fought for
and obtained very high levels of institutional autonomy, higher than
that of present-day universities.[1] As a theoretical issue, however,
academic freedom, as we understand it today, was developed in the
modern period and was justified on the basis of Enlightenment concepts of knowledge and human nature. I wish to show that with the
emergence of post-Enlightenment theories of knowledge in the twentieth century, this classical justification for academic freedom is in
severe difficulties.

The classical theory of academic freedom justifies the right of professors to teach and conduct research without interference by appeal
of a theory of knowledge. Implicitly or explicitly, traditional defences
of academic freedom presuppose a specific role for the individual: the
freedom of the individual to discover and justify a search for knowledge,
a role which is assigned to the individual by, what I shall call, following Searle, Enlightenment epistemology.[2] Some theories, those I would
call "intrinsic values" theories, assume that the knowing activity of an
individual is a value in itself. Other theories, such as consequentialist
theories, consider knowledge of value because of its pragmatic use in
achieving other human goods and claim that academic freedom is the
best way for society to gain such knowledge. Some authors argue that
it would be unfair to give professors the task of reaching knowledge
while denying to them the academic freedom that is an essential means
to this end.[3]

286

All of these arguments, whether consequentialist or based on the intrinsic value of truth, presuppose two basic premises: first that "knowledge is most likely to be advanced through free inquiry" as Searle puts it;[4] second, that the autonomy of the institution is auxilliary to the freedom of the individual researcher or teacher. In nearly all of the arguments defending academic freedom, these two premises are themselves left unjustified and are simply taken for granted within what Searle calls "contemporary ideology and methodology."[5] While I agree with Searle that the classical approach to academic freedom comes from the Enlightenment, I am unhappy with the phrase "contemporary," since I will maintain that this ideology has been recently superceded and that herein lies the cause of the current crisis in academic freedom.

The Enlightenment Concept of Knowledge

First I will show how the two presuppositions discussed in the previous section are related to the Enlightenment concept of knowledge. The Cartesian tradition will be taken as epitomizing the modern or Enlightenment approach and I will present it as I think it needs to be interpreted in the light of epistemological development since that time. I do not wish to imply that Descartes himself would have put things the same way.

From the Cartesian point of view, knowledge is always an activity of the individual mind. The order of the world itself, the symbols written in a book or recorded on magnetic tape, are not themselves knowledge until they are grasped by a self-conscious subject. We may speak metaphorically of the knowledge of a corporation, a nation, or an historical period, but strictly speaking this must be cashed out as the actual or potential consciousness of individual subjects.

Even within the subject, information which is nonintuitive, that is, information which does not have the explicit acquiesence of the conscious mind, is not truly knowledge, it is not scientific. The ideas which Descartes finds in his mind, which have been put there by his upbringing, but which have never been brought to the clear light of reason for judgment, are excluded from the realm of knowledge.[6] Descartes' first rule of (scientific) method was "to accept nothing as true which I did not clearly recognise to be so: . . . to accept . . . nothing more than what was presented to my mind so clearly and distinctly that I could have no occasion to doubt it."[7] When something is grasped in pure rational intuition it is knowledge, otherwise it is not.

The claim that knowledge is ultimately intuitive implies that it is

noncreative. Intuition constates ideas as they already are, independently of the act of apprehension. It is the nature of a concept to exist
independently of human will, intellect, or knowledge, and not to be
created or produced by the activity of the human mind. If the Cartesian position allows for any process of creating meanings, it is God who
does the creating, and so the process is beyond the reach of the
sociohistorical forces.[8] It is this transcendent warranty that guarantees
the universality and objectivity of science.

It is above all in opposition to a theory of knowledge based on
authority that the intuitive theory is posited. Intuition is intrinsically
free from any extraneous influence, so free that Descartes claims that
it is as absolute as the freedom of God,

> for the faculty of will consists alone in our having the power of choosing
> to do a thing or choosing not to do it, that is, to affirm or deny . . . it,
> or, rather it consists alone in the fact that in order to affirm or deny . . .
> those things placed before us by the understanding, we act so that we
> are unconscious that any outside force constrains us in doing so.[9]

In other words, I cannot be forced to know what I see to be false;
epistemic freedom is assured by the very nature of the mind and is
inalienable from it.

The impartiality of science depends on this freedom of intuition
from all nonrational influences. The personal and social involvements
of the subject, his existential choices, the linguistic, social, historical
or cultural environment, his moral or aesthetic maturity, his commit-
ment to destroy the world or to eradicate cancer, are all factors which
neither reduce nor enhance the truth of the knowledge he discovers.
The freedom of the rational subject is his ability to surmount his situation and grasp the universal concept.

From this perspective, academic freedom would have to be
understood as the institutional correlate of the intuitive subject's
epistemic freedom. The scholar's mind itself, of course, is in no need
of such protection; its freedom to recognize truth could never be taken
from it, as the Stoics long ago pointed out, but his opportunities to teach
students, to communicate with his colleagues, and to have access to
research faciltiies must be assured, if his truth is to advance and not
remain solipsistic. Since the locus of truth is the individual subject, the
function of academic freedom is to shield the individual's external
expressions of knowledge from the influence of social forces in a manner analogous to the way in which Descartes' method of doubt protects
the intuition of the inner mind. It is quite proper, then, for the university to be an ivory tower, protected by the moat of academic freedom

from the forces of political power, commercial interests, or public opinion. To be the arbitor of truth, pure science, and pure knowledge (and what other kind is there?), the uninvolved intellect of the individual academic must be preserved from corruption by the grace of academic freedom.

The claim that "knowledge is most likely to be advanced through free inquiry," when traced to its origins in Enlightenment "ideology," can then be seen to be no mere utilitarian proposal, but a requirement based on an essential link between freedom and knowledge which depends only on the concepts involved. If knowledge is not free, it is not knowledge, at least as the Cartesians understood the concept. Similarly, the supposition that academic freedom is essentially an individual freedom is related to the essentially individual nature of that intuition without which knowledge would not be knowledge, at least in the Enlightenment sense.

Contemporary Epistemology

During the last one hundred years or so these Enlightenment concepts of knowledge and of individual intuition have come under attack on a number of fronts. Theories developed by the human sciences, on the one hand, and most recent theories of epistemology, on the other, although radically differing from each other in the majority of their theses, maintain in common the subordination of individual thought to epistemic influence beyond the control of the thinker. The foundations of knowledge have been recentred outside of consciousness, so that the classical sovereignty of the subject is replaced by an activity conditioned by factors of which the individual is unaware. This change in epistemic world view undermines the classical justification for academic freedom, as I will try to show.

The human sciences, each in their own specific way, take as part of their vocation the explanation of thought by something which is other than thought. The work of such diverse thinkers as Darwin, Freud, Kuhn, Watson, Mannheim, Worff, or Margaret Mead, embeds human intellectual activities into processes such as evolution, culture, language, history, or desire.

In philosophy, similar tendencies are to be found: practically every contemporary theory of epistemology, with the possible exceptions of Logical Empiricism and the early Husserl, reject the Enlightenment reliance on individual intuition. We will look at the theory of Michel Foucault as a typical example of a post-Enlightenment epistemology.

For Foucault, the problem of science is the problem of discourse. Knowledge is a series of statements, a discursive practice, and he sets out to discover the regularities of such practice. Linguistics can exhibit regularities in our language on one level, but on a level that leaves discourse open, since it cannot tell us why, of the infinity of possible statements which are all linguistically permissible, these particular ones actually are generated. Why, for example, could one speak of organisms in the nineteenth century while one could not have done so in the sixteenth?

Foucault rejects two interrelated approaches to the problem. First, he is opposed to diachronic treatments which present intellectual history as a continuity of influences, an accumulation of discoveries that inspire later thinkers to even greater heights. Secondly, he doubts the explanatory appeal to individual subjects.[10]

> I should like to know whether the subjects responsible for scientific discourse are not determined in their situation, their function, their perceptive capacity, and their practical possibilities by conditions that dominate and even overwhelm them. . . . I tried to explore scientific discourse not from the point of view of the individuals who are speaking, . . . but from the point of view of the rules that come into play in the very existence of such discourse.[11]

His own project is to investigate the conditions of possiblity which permit what is said to be said.

> What I would like to do, however, is to reveal a *positive unconscious* of knowledge: a level that eludes the consciousness of the scientist and yet is part of the scientific discourse. . . . It is these rules of formation, which were never formulated in their own right, but are to be found only in widely differing theories, concepts, and objects of study, that I have tried to reveal, by isolating . . . a level that I have called . . . archeological.[12]

> In the analysis proposed here, the rules of formation operate not only in the minds or consciouness of individuals, but in the discourse itself; they operate therefore, according to a sort of uniform anonymity, on all individuals who undertake to speak in this discursive field. . . . The pre-conceptual field allows the emergence of the discursive regularities and constraints that have made possible the heterogeneous multiplicity of concepts, and, beyond these the profusion of the themes, beliefs, and representations with which one usually deals when one is writing the history of ideas.[13]

A discursive field covers a number of sciences in a given historical period and is separated from earlier and later fields by a discontinuity or rupture. Within each field, the rules of formation govern the permissible concepts, objects, methods, modes of communication and expression, and so on, of the specific sciences. For example, Foucault has investigated the dependence of the concept of madness, of who is to be defined as mad, of psychiatric methodology, of the organization of confinement, and of the authority of the physician on the preconceptual practice of various historical periods. The sciences of living things, of capital and wealth, of grammar and language, of clinical medicine, of peneology, and of sexuality, almost invariably human sciences, have each been studied by Foucault's "archeology." "It seems to me," he says "that the historical analysis of scientific discourse should, in the last resort, be subject, not to a theory of the knowing subject, but rather to a theory of discursive practice."[14]

From Foucault's point of view, then, the individual subject is more like an instrument than an autonomous, free instigator of scientific discourse. An individual may say something, but what he says and the basis on which he can say it, is controlled by an order external to him. What is more, who can say something, and even his unity and identity as a scientific subject, are subordinated to the rules of formation, the episteme.

> The analysis of statements operates therefore without reference to a cogito. It does not pose the question of the speaking subject, who reveals or who conceals himself in what he says, who, in speaking, exercises his sovereign freedom, or who, without realizing it, subjects himself to constraints of which he is only dimly aware. . . . [C]ertain intersections [of the configuration of an anonymous field] indicate the unique place of a speaking subject and may be given the name of author.[15]

In summary, then, we can say that Foucault's theory is an attempt to construct an epistemology of the discourse which is science without reliance on individual intuition.

Foucault is not alone among contemporary philosophers in insisting on the secondary role of individual intuition. What Foucault does for the human sciences in the rationalist and phenomenological traditions, Thomas Kuhn does for the physical sciences from within the Anglo-Saxon empiricist tradition. Marxist epistemology takes as its leitmotif the dependence of ideology on the infrastructure of technology and production relationships. Wittgenstein also is led to affirm the dependence of truth on a kind of human agreement, a form of life, which itself is taken for granted. In Heidegger, too, the clear intellectual knowledge of the cogito is a "founded mode of being," founded on the mode of being-in-the-world, which, at least in Heidegger's later work, is nonindividualistic. Even Husserl, who is surely the closest of all twentieth century philosophers to the cartesian position, finishes his life with the much less classical claim that transcendental subjectivity is ultimately an intersubjectivity.

Meaning and Truth

All of these approaches, in one way or another, distinguish what I call two levels of knowledge: the level of truth and the level of meaning. Facts, propositions, and, maybe, observations, as entities that can be true or false, are on the first level, that of truth; the concepts on which these entities are based is the level of meaning. The fact that the mass of a specific volume of water is one gram is an issue of truth (or falsity); that we are conceptualizing the world in terms of "mass" and "volume," instead of, say, beauty and purpose, however, is on the level of meaning. The level of meaning is presupposed by those concepts and entities which we observe or about which we assert truths. The Kantian distinction between empirical and transcendental, the difference in Husserl between the constituted and the process of constituting, and the Wittgensteinian separation of opinion from form of life, all reflect this discovery of a new leveling analyzing knowledge, although I do not wish to maintain that the three positions are in any other way similar.[16]

Individual intuition is on the level of truth. Whether we understand intuition in either the rationalist mode, as the grasping of innate ideas, or, in the Lockean, empiricist manner, as sensory experience, it has the common sense of apprehending that which is given. The questions to be asked on this level are about either the truth or falsity of particular beliefs, statements or observations of facts, or else about the criteria by which we can be certain of such things in general.

The origin of the given itself is not to be found in intuition but must be referred to some extraneous agency, to God for the rationalists, to the external world for Locke.[17] On this level the questions concern how the meanings are themselves generated, and in accordance with what principles. Hume already traces them to the rules of human nature rather than to a divine source, and Kant, facing the implications of this position, refers them to a transcendental categorization whose validity is based on the absolute universality of necessary conditions for intelligibility or for experience. Twentieth century desacralization has challenged these external warranties and has searched for the genesis of meaning in some preintellectual realm of human activity, history, or culture; it therefore poses immediately and acutely the contemporary quandaries of relativism. The question, however, is no longer the relativity of truth, the sceptic's problem that what is true for one might be false for another, nor is the issue the search for a criterion for certainty; contemporary relativity is relativity on the level of meanings, of discursive formations, paradigms, forms of life. There are many theories which attempt to render comprehensible these changing structures of meaning; few, if any, however, trace them to individual creativity, and, with the possible exception of existentialism, none appeal to the freedom of the researcher for their explanation.

The classical theory of academic freedom was founded on Enlightenment epistemology's concern with the level of truth; it concerned the right of the individual to search for truth through his or her own intuition and to publically express and teach the conclusions. It is not at all as obvious that academic freedom in the individual sense is relevant to knowledge as it is analyzed by contemporary theories on the genesis of meaning.

Notes

1. The faculty elected their own deans and other administrative officers, the university could strike against the local community, or it could even pull up its roots and move to a more hospitable environment when that became necessary. See Richard Hofstadter and Walter P. Metzger, *The Development of Academic Freedom in the United States* (New York: Columbia University Press, 1955), 3–11.

2. The classical theory of academic freedom . . . is that professors should have the right to teach, conduct research, and publish their research without interference. . . . The justification for these rights derives from a theory of what the university is. . . . They are special rights that derive from particular institutional structures. . . . [T]he university is an institution designed for the advancement and dissemination of knowledge. . . . To derive the rights of academic freedom, we need also a theory about how knowledge can be attained and validated; we need an epistemology, a theory of knowledge. And not just any theory will do; for example, if you think that knowledge is best obtained by looking up a sacred text, you will not be able to derive the classical theory of academic freedom. . . . [A]n important part of this theory is that knowledge is most likely

to be advanced through free inquiry, . . . The university may be an essentially mediaeval institution, but its contemporary ideology and methodology come not from the mediaeval period but from the Enlightenment.

This is from John R. Searle's "Two Concepts of Academic Freedom," in *The Concept of Academic Freedom*, edited by Edmund L. Pincoffs (Austin and London: University of Texas Press, 1972), 87–88. Compare the following statement by Bissel:

> The concept of academic freedom may be summarized as follows: the teacher in a university has a special competence by reason of his long period of systematic study and his mastery of the scientific method. He is thus in a position to expound what is known and to add to the store of knowledge. He has the individual's right to express his own ideas, and, in addition, a social obligation to advance knowledge. Interference with this right is not only a violation of individual freedom, but a threat to social progress. This concept derives from the scientific method (Claude Bissel, *The Strength of the University*, [Toronto: University of Toronto Press, 1968], 217).

3. These arguments are presented in one or more of the papers collected in Pincoffs, *Concept of Academic Freedom*.

4. Searle, "Two Concepts," 88.

5. Ibid.

6. Descartes, *Discourse on Method*, Parts I and II, and *Principles*, 1, in Elizabeth S. Haldane and G.R.T. Ross, *The Philosophical Works of Descartes*, vol. 1 (Cambridge: Cambridge University Press, 1911, 1975).

7. Descartes, *Discourse on Method*, 92.

8. In fact, Descartes may have maintained that ideas are eternal, uncreated by God. For a detailed discussion of this point, see Emile Brehier, "The Creation of the Eternal Truths in Descartes' System," in *Descartes*, edited by Willis Doney (New York: Anchor Doubleday, 1967).

9. Descartes, *Meditations*, Meditation #4, 175.

10. Which amounts to the same thing. See Michel Foucault, *Archeology of Knowledge* (London: Tavistock Publications, 1972), 12.

11. Michel Foucault, *The Order of Things* (London: Tavistock Publications, 1970), xiv.

12. Foucault, *The Order of Things*, xi.

13. Foucault, *Archeology of Knowledge*, 63.

14. Foucault, *Archeology of Knowledge*, xiv.

15. Foucault, *Archeology of Knowledge*, 122; see also pp. 50–55 for a full discussion of this point.

16. Heidegger's essay, "The Essence of Truth," is particularly inspiring on the issue, once allowances are made for the change in vocabulary, for it is precisely "meaning," in my way of using the term, to which the word "truth" in the title refers. Martin Heidegger, "On the Essence of Truth," in *Existence and Being*, edited by Werner Brock (Chicago: Henry Regnery, 1949), 292–324.

17. See Frederick Broadie, *An Approach to Descartes' Meditations* (London: The Athlone Press, 1970), 166–75, for an interesting discussion of the necessary role of God in assuring the stability of ideas for Descartes.

Index

297